A SHORT GUIDE FOR MEN ABOUT TOWN

Edwardian Florin. Photograph by courtesy of Chard (1964) Ltd.

This book is dedicated to True Britannia and to the action and the Spirit of the Phoenix.

If the red slayer think he slays,
Or if the slain think he is slain,
They know not well the subtle ways
I keep, and pass, and turn again.

From 'Brahma' by Ralph Waldo Emerson

A SHORT GUIDE FOR MEN ABOUT TOWN

A Short Miscellany, Including Some Unusual Titbits and Tips on Grooming, Accessories and Fine Living

by

NICHOLAS STOREY

REMEMBER WHEN

First published in Great Britain in 2011 by
Remember When
an imprint of
Pen & Sword Books Ltd
47 Church Street
Barnsley
South Yorkshire
S70 2AS

ISBN 978 1 8446 811 50

A CIP catalogue record for this book is available from the British Library.

Typeset in 11/13pt Baskerville by
Mac Style, Beverley, East Yorkshire

Printed and bound in the UK by
by the MPG Books Group

Pen & Sword Books Ltd incorporates the imprints of Pen & Sword Aviation, Pen & Sword Maritime, Pen & Sword Military, Wharncliffe Local History, Pen and Sword Select, Pen and Sword Military Classics and Leo Cooper.

For a complete list of Pen & Sword titles please contact
PEN & SWORD BOOKS LIMITED
47 Church Street, Barnsley, South Yorkshire, S70 2AS, England
E-mail: enquiries@pen-and-sword.co.uk
Website: www.pen-and-sword.co.uk

Contents

Acknowledgements and Permissions

I am immensely grateful for the generous help and advice on the draft chapters of this book from experts in the fields that I have covered. In chapter order, as follows:

For reading and advising on Chapter 2 (Colognes and Scents), except the notes on individual colognes (for which I take responsibility), I thank John Bodenham, Chairman and family member of J Floris, as well as for use of the illustration that appears in plate 6.

In relation to Chapter 3 (Dressing Accessories), I thank David Hober of Sam Hober for discussing the production (by spinning and weaving) of spider silk; Angus Cundey, Chairman and Joint Managing Director of Henry Poole, for the firm's file on the origin of the dinner jacket/tuxedo; the writer James Sherwood in relation to these records, and Lord Dupplin for information about his ancestor's role in the origination and adoption of the dinner jacket; as well as Oriole Cullen, of the costume department of the Victoria & Albert Museum, and 'Sator' founder of www.cutterandtailor.com, for several useful references (and 'Sator' for plate 12, the original by JP Thornton). For reading and advising on that part of this chapter dealing with the firm of Charles Frodsham & Co, I thank Richard Stenning of Charles Frodsham & Co as well as for the illustration in plate 15. I thank Amaya Cerdeirina, of Penfriend, for reading and advising on writing instruments; I thank Bluemantle Pursuivant of HM College of Arms for reading and advising on the granting and bearing of arms in England, Wales, Northern Ireland and the British Commonwealth; and I thank Mr BG Hamilton in respect of the granting and bearing of Feudal Baronial arms in Scotland. I also thank Richard Edgecliffe-Johnson, Chairman of WS Foster & Son and Henry Maxwell, for reading and advising on the rest of the chapter as well as for the illustration in plate 7.

For reading and advising on drinks in Chapter 4, I thank Alessandro Palazzi, Bar Manager of Dukes Hotel, St James's; for reading and advising on sweets I thank Pat Stewart of Maynards Sweets; for reading and advising on tea and coffee I thank Dr Andrea Tanner, Archivist, of Fortnum & Mason.

For reading and advising on Chapter 5 (Matching Food and Drink) and for the photograph in plate 24, I thank Laurence Mann, gourmet, devoted oenophile and, despite the consequential extra weight, an ardent and accomplished bicyclist.

For reading and advising on Chapter 6 in relation to tobacco pipes and for the chart in plate 20, I thank Mr Moty Ezrati, Managing Director of the James Upshall Pipe Company. I thank Simon Chase of Hunters & Frankau for reading and advising on that part of the chapter dealing with cigars and for the illustrations in plates 22 and 23 respectively; I thank Christopher J Snowden, author of the acclaimed *Velvet Glove, Iron Fist: A History of Anti-Smoking* for reading and advising on those parts in this chapter dealing with a short history of tobacco and on cigarettes; and I thank Dave Atkin, mill manager and snuff blender, Carol Walker and Mr JR Archdale (family member and owner) of Wilsons of Sharrow for reading and advising on snuff and for the illustrations in plates 27 and 28. I also thank Anne Bradley, Archivist of the Bristol Records Office, for locating the records of Fribourg & Treyer.

For certain information about the Oriental Club in Chapter 7, I thank Maggie Cook of the club.

I also thank, for looking over and commenting on the draft, Michael Alden, founder of the website the London Lounge (whose comments on my first book of this kind inspired this one) and I thank friends on the London Lounge for their knowledge freely shared. Also for reading over the draft and their helpful comments I thank Dr Marcelo de Araujo of Laranjeiras, Rio de Janeiro, Dr Julian Critchlow and Chikashi Miyamoto.

This book would not have been the same without this generous help and advice but, for any remaining errors, I alone am responsible. Moreover, no one who has rendered help and advice should, necessarily, be taken to agree with any of the opinions (political or otherwise) that I voice.

For kind permission to use other illustrations, in plate order, I thank the following:

John Chard of Chard (1964) Ltd for the picture of Britannia standing on the Florin in the dedication, deriving from the original engraving of GW De Saulles, Engraver to the Royal Mint.

Barry Klein and Paul Chessell of Taylor of Old Bond Street for the illustrations that appear in plates 1 to 5 inclusive.

Luke Eyres for the illustration in plate 8.

Kenneth Lim for the illustrations in plates 9 and 10, taken by arrangement with Mr Rowley and with the kind permission of Sarah Webster of Budd shirtmakers.

Janet Taylor of hatter James Lock & Co for the illustration in plate 11.

Rowland Lowe-MacKenzie, formerly of Turnbull & Asser, for the image of the smoking jacket on the cover and the illustration in plate 14.

J Delage for the illustration in plate 16.

James Smith & Sons for the illustration in plate 17.

Liz Johnson for the illustration in plate 18.

David Nathan-Maister of oxygenee.com for the illustration in plate 19.

C Paul Taylor for the illustration in plate 21.

Dmitry Alexandrov of RomanovRussia.com for the illustration in plate 25.

Sophie Wootton of Bentley & Skinner (Bond Street Jewellers) Ltd for the illustrations in plates 26 and 33.

Nikki Share and Jill James, Marketing Director of Genting UK on behalf of Crockford's Club, for the illustration in plate 29.

My father, for help with the illustrations in plate 13 (original photograph by Lallie Charles), plate 30 (the cartoon originally from Pierce Egan in *Life in London: Or, the Day and Night Scenes of Jerry Hawthorne and his Elegant Friend Corinthian Tom*) and plate 31 (Brummell at Almack's, the cartoon originally by Grego).

Kieran McCarthy of Wartski, London, for the illustration in plate 32. This illustration, as well as those in plates 11 and 30, have also been used on the cover of this book, and I extent my thanks to those who allowed their use.

I thank my daughter, Gyvania, for her thoughts on factors relevant in making choices of scent as well as for use of her expression 'scents of security' in relation to the trigger effect of fragrances.

I thank as well Andy Gilchrist, 'Sator', and friends and colleagues on their internet sites (separately listed).

I acknowledge the usefulness of information to be found on the internet sites of some of the firms that I cover. I also thank Lisa Hooson, Commissioning Editor, Jill Morris, Copy Editor, Helen Vodden, in production, and the whole team at Remember When.

Finally, there is no directory of firms' addresses and contact details as this too quickly dates. Most of the firms have websites under their own names and those that do not are in the telephone directories.

Nicholas Storey,
Estado do Rio de Janeiro,
Brasil

Introduction

Let us drink and be merry, dance, joke and rejoice,
With claret and sherry, theorbo and voice!
The changeable world to our joy is unjust,
All treasure's uncertain,
Then down with your dust!
In frolics dispose your pounds, shillings and pence,
For we shall be nothing a hundred years hence.

From *Coronemus nos Rosis antequam marcescant*
[Let us crown ourselves with roses before they wither]
by Thomas Jordan (1612–1685)

Characters such as James Bond are enduringly popular as fictional heroes because they combine intellectual and physical vigour with a taste for luxury and a yearning for dangerous adventure. This all inspires many of us, so far as we are able, to seek the things that they might have and experience the things that they might experience. This book is about some of the smaller personal possessions and some of the acquired tastes that are within the grasp of successful men. But this is not a book for those who can have absolutely everything (and would wish to have much of it, including their mobile telephones and even taps plastered in gold plate and diamonds). Such people (with the sole exception of Ian Fleming with his gold-plated typewriter) generally lose the yearning to possess anything at all.

This is partly a book of particular things, which I believe to be amongst the best of their kinds. They are often (but not exclusively) British things, or things that Britain has made famous, because I happen to believe that they often truly are amongst the very the best. Also, I harbour a hope that this very fact demonstrates that the real heart and spirit of True Britannia still beats beneath the yoke of the apparent spirit of the age: all the over-regulation ('Don't do that, George!'), suggesting that our politicians are so ignorant that they have never heard of John Stuart Mill and his treatise *On Liberty*; the architectural and environmental vandalism (demonstrated by the loss of some beautiful trees and several great buildings to the developers and those responsible for the so-called 'regeneration' of our old towns); the dumbing-down of many things to the very lowest common denominator (plainly seen in the open sewer of much television and the mass-production of all the highly priced rubbish bearing 'designer labels'); and all the general flummery which, lately and by insidious encroachment, has taken a firm grip and even threatens the spirit of individualism and adventure that marks out the British people, who have gone out (and still go out) all over the world.

I make certain remarks here and there against the elephantine and unproductive organization known as the EU. I mean them. If ever an organization proliferated over-regulation and the reduction of the UK (as a member state) increasingly to a police state, this is it; moreover, a police state with fewer and fewer actual policemen in evidence on the streets to deal with the real criminals and far too many 'jobsworths' employed to read through our e-mails and regulate myriad other details of our personal lives. Honoré de Balzac put the general point rather well: 'Bureaucracy is a giant mechanism, operated by pygmies.' However, I mean no inferences to be drawn against the other individual member states themselves or their good citizens.

I hope for the re-emergence of the spirit of True Britannia; hence the dedication, in effect, to her spirit of resilience and renewal, fairly recently exemplified by the news that the great (international and originally American) Sulka is going to be back in business, online, from London, with every good wish, I am sure, from all who know the name.

Therefore, this book is also my own small further tribute (in addition to my book *History of Men's Fashion: What the Well-Dressed Man is Wearing*) to the best of, largely, British craftsmanship and discernment. Many of the products of that craftsmanship are available internationally, through telephone and online ordering.

However, especially since many of the things described are easily available by delivery anywhere, I have avoided the narrow-mindedness that might have had me ignore truly fine products from all the many countries in which they are made.

This book is also written in a spirit of vehement rebellion against another aspect of the *Zeitgeist*: nearly the whole western world now exists in a secular environment under the martial rule of health and body fascists (and the regulators who step in time to their death-in-life funeral march). All these Tin Hitlers commend to us especial care in how we live: 'Give up smoking or you could die' is the mantra on the cover of a health leaflet that I have seen, but, excuse me, has someone found the elixir for eternal life on earth (itself conditional on clean living) and not told the rest of us the fine detail? Or is a pharmaceutical company about to start retailing this elixir to the same people that will become the first space tourists? I do not recommend a life of vicious self-indulgence and dissipation but, surely, there does need to be a mid-point between this and a craven abstinence from any pleasure that could even lightly erode the skin.

Increasingly afraid of dying, more and more people are becoming too afraid to live: they don't smoke or drink (neither did Adolf Hitler – remember him?), enjoy dangerous sports, ever eat too much or even just sit in the sun. Everything pleasurable is proscribed by the threat of an early death, so they sit all their lives, meekly and soberly, in the germ-free, smokeless shade just waiting for a later death instead.

If you are with me on my general point, you will enjoy this book. If you are not, put this book back on the shelf.

This is not a primer in etiquette, nor is it intended to be exhaustive in any sense, although I hope that some parts of it present a detailed summary of useful information about enjoyment in the areas covered. It is also a book of titbits and ideas intended to provoke thought and lead to a desire for an expansion of experience beyond the merely commonplace. If this desire is pharmaceutically assisted, so much the better, as long as the components are restricted to those to be found in alcohol and tobacco. There are some sections on these substances too.

This book has been written in a spirit of fun and this should be borne in mind at all times. It had its beginning around forty years ago in the forked boughs of a Holm Oak tree (*Quercus ilex*), one of those puzzles of nature, an evergreen broadleaf, in Trethosa Park.

Finally, many of the firms mentioned in the text have internet sites on which there are viewing and ordering facilities, aimed especially at those who live overseas.

CHAPTER 1

Grooming and Care

Give me a look, give me a face
That makes simplicity a grace …

From '*Simplex Munditiis*' by Ben Jonson

In relation to each day's grooming, the maxim 'live each day as though it were your last' has a good application. If you start by treating each day (and the preparation for it) as equally important as every other day, you begin each day as well as you possibly can.

Some Introductory Notes On Grooming Accessories

DR Harris is an old and famous chemist near the top of St James's Street, London. One of their most enduring products is their morning tonic, which may be bought in tablet form or consumed by the glass on the premises (a most satisfying experience, guaranteed to blast the cobwebs away and put the spring back in one's step). They also stock and re-bristle hairbrushes, stock combs and toothbrushes as well as various brands of soap, shaving soap and toothpastes. The best brushes, especially hair brushes, are hardwood or *faux*-ivory backed in a military pattern, that is to say with deep, oval, concave backs and white bristle. However, I understand that they have been having difficulty in obtaining these larger brushes recently.

Taylor of Old Bond Street ('Taylor's') is actually now in Jermyn Street and, besides being barbers, also stock all the usual requisites: especially fine are their own-brand shaving soaps and creams (a particular favourite of mine is the almond-scented variety) and shaving brushes as well as (sea) sponges (the soft skeletons of simple sea creatures *Spongia* and *Hippospongia*); loofahs (which are the fibrous skeletons of a gourd of the family *Cucurbitaceae*); pumice stone (which is solidified volcanic lava); bath salts (including Epsom salts, sodium chloride, phosphates, magnesium sulphate and scents and essences) as well as bath and nail brushes. Floris bath oils cannot be beaten; a fact not overlooked by Ian Fleming's Dr No, as there was Floris lime bath oil in the 'mink-lined prison'.

Hair

Long after men generally ceased to go to the barber each day for a shave they continued to have their hair trimmed once a fortnight at one of the better establishments, most eminently Taylor's, Truefitt & Hill, Geo F Trumper ('Trumper's'), the Waldorf Hotel, Claridge's, or one of the many City of London establishments. Everyone knows the look of the modern classic haircut, which has remained constant since the beginning of the twentieth century. The best secret of a good haircut is that it doesn't look as though it has just been done. Sideburns should be no more than about one square inch, unless a full set of beard is worn. Mutton chops and Piccadilly weepers, those immensely long whiskers often worn with a handlebar moustache (and always with a shaven chin), have gone the way of opera cloaks and all flesh, but in Victorian times men especially prided themselves on these enormous whiskers, the longer and more luxuriant the better.

Taylor's supplies a mild daily shampoo, but shampooing hair with stronger preparations should not be undertaken more than a couple of times a week and many of the shops already mentioned have large ranges: Taylor's Luxury Shampoo with Rosemary is especially fine. For itchy scalps, wood tar shampoos, such as Polytar shampoo, are very effective. Of course there is the 'prince of shampoos', Pinaud Elixir Shampoo with Quinine, as used by James Bond in *On Her Majesty's Secret Service*. This is still just about available.

Taylor's still have the military-backed brushes mentioned above. There are also fine brushes, of all kinds, produced by Kent (established in 1777).

Combs come in a variety of materials from horn to plastic and a range of fineness of teeth. Many shops stock good combs, as do famous barbers such as Truefitt & Hill and Trumper's. There are also shoe horns, carved out of real horn, in various lengths.

Hair Preparations

After drying, Pinaud's Bay Rum, Eau de Portugal or Eau de Quinine stimulate the scalp with a good combing and brushing. Some people have been known regularly to stand on their heads to stimulate the scalp and the potency drug Viagra was, apparently, a byproduct of hair renewal research.

Brilliantine is a hair pomade or pomatum invented by Edouard Pinaud in 1900, containing petroleum jelly, beeswax and scents. Yardley makes a version of this, scented with English lavender. Brilliantine is the stuff responsible for the glossy hair of early Hollywood matinée idols.

Macassar oil is another hair oil that used to be popular (and is still available), prompting the house-proud to invest in 'antimacassar' chair protectors. In fact the oil is a mixture of scented oil from the Ylang Ylang tree (*Cananga odorata*) and coconut oil, for which 'macassar' was an early trade name.

Grooming Kits

There are several makers of finely made small, boxed, steel grooming kits, including blunt-ended safety scissors, tweezers, nail files, nail clippers, razor, travelling shaving brush and penknife. Orange sticks are especially effective at removing dirt from fingernails. There is a fine example of a boxed kit by Taylor's in plate 2.

Shaving

Razors

There used to be a time when anybody who was anybody would have had a cased, seven-day set of open razors. They are, amazingly, still available from makers such as Dovo and, apart from them, excellent open razors are still to be found, old and new, for example, those made by Acca Kappa, Dorko, (Fried.) Schick, Joseph Rodgers & Sons of Sheffield, Mappin & Webb (established in 1774), Merkur, Thomas Rudd, Truefitt & Hill, Wacker and Wilkinson. The company of Joseph Rodgers & Sons held a registered trademark from 1682 and was the holder of many royal warrants around the world, as well as supplying General Ulysses S Grant. It was, probably, the greatest cutler of all time and anything made by it, including seven-day sets of razors, table cutlery, pocket knives and corkscrews, is certainly worth having.

However, if you invest in vintage razors, make sure that they are not damaged and *never* use a damaged blade. You will find that the older razors sometimes have marvellous workmanship in the way of Damascus work on the blades (etching over layers of different steels) and rare materials in the handles, such as ivory, tortoiseshell and rare hardwoods. Although no one in their right mind would buy new ivory or tortoiseshell, I am sure that there is no real reason against owning pre-ban ivory or tortoiseshell, or old items made of currently protected woods, for that matter.

In the course of research for this book I have been repeatedly astonished not so much at how many skills are still plied, from bespoke gun-making to razor-making, but that they are still plied by so many, demonstrating that there is still a significant call for top-rated men's goods.

A man's beard can grow up to about 15 centimetres a year and the average man spends around 3,000 thousand hours of his life shaving. This is a custom known even amongst the ancients, such as the Mesopotamians and Egyptians, followed by the Greeks and Romans. At the earliest times, sharpened shells and flint were the most razor-like instruments for the purpose of shaving. Times moved on to metal straight razors, just like very sharp knives – the Roman *novacila* is an example. The Romans also used to pluck body hair.

In 1770, Jean-Jacques Perret wrote a treatise on the art of shaving, proposing safety razors along the way. By the early nineteenth century, the carefully clipped cleanliness of Beau Brummell and his *coterie* played a part in leading the refinement of Sheffield steel open razors. Solingen, in Germany, also developed a fine steel industry, which is still there. Both of these places are famous for the production of stainless steel or Inox, which is steel made with a high chromium content that resists staining and corrosion. Harry Brearley of Sheffield devised an early type in 1912 for use in gun barrels and the use spread, especially to surgical instruments, razors and cutlery. However, the resistant properties of chromium steels had been recognized from the early nineteenth century.

By 1847 William Henson had developed the first of the modern type of safety razor and, before the century ended, specialized shaving soaps had come into use. Kampfe Brothers took out a patent on a safety razor in the USA and in 1895 King Camp Gillette invented the modern safety blade. Firms such as Wilkinson Sword also took up manufacturing safety blades. This firm, originally a sword-maker (established by Henry Nock, the famous gunsmith, in 1772), later branched out into garden tools and even motorbikes. They recently ceased to make swords, but this side of the business was bought by a German company that continues the production, using Wilkinson patterns and even the sword forge for naval, military and ceremonial swords around the world presumably in some recognition of the famous advertising slogan: 'Wilkinson Sword: the name on the world's finest blades.'

Shaving skills

Given that there is at least one book on shaving skills and that nothing like shaving can wholly be learned from a book, I suggest that, if you wish to embark on open razor shaving, you take lessons from one of the great barbers mentioned in this chapter. Certainly, do not just have a stab at it uninformed and on your own. Moreover, essential kit to maintain an open razor includes a leather strop with a hanging hook at the top and a bar handle at the bottom (to give it tension, by stretching it). The strop is used to sharpen the razor before use and, sometimes, even mid-shave. You will also need to hone the razor on a whetstone from time to time. The most widely used stones are Belgian yellow Coticule waterstone or Belgian blue waterstone. The yellow is finer and more expensive. The density and smoothness of such materials is measured in units of 'grit' and the greater the grit number the finer the stone. The very best can go up to a grit rating of 12,000. A stone-holder is useful and a razor stand is too. As with the actual use of the razor, ask your barber to demonstrate stropping and honing and practise them.

Safety razors

There are fine safety razors, such as Gillette Mach 3, advertised as 'The best a man can get'.

Dry shaving

I am sure that there is nothing to beat a proper wet shave with a good razor but there are dry electric shavers for sale that might be a convenient alternative on long-haul flights. Some good makes are Braun, Gillette, Philips and Remington, and they all have large ranges.

Shaving brushes

Badger bristle is the universally acknowledged best material and it comes in various grades, silver-tipped and white being at the top of the range. Horn handles are the best material at the current time. Plainly, also, the thicker the head of bristle the better the brush. The market leaders are Acca Kappa, Vulfix, Rooney, Semogue, Kent, Plisson High Mountain Badger and Simpsons. Taylor's, Trumper's and Truefitt & Hill also sell brushes from these manufacturers under their own branding. It is very important to remember not to press too hard on the soap or the face when lathering up and to rinse the brush thoroughly after use and not to dry it in a towel but to shake the water out and let it dry, preferably upside-down on a stand, in a dry and sunny spot. If you start rubbing the bristles with a cloth you will break them and damage the brush.

Shaving mugs

These very often come in sturdy glazed stoneware. You place the rounded tablet of shaving soap on the top and fill the mug with hot water, wetting the brush in the spout of the mug and then lathering up from the soap tablet.

The principal British purveyors are Crabtree & Evelyn, Trumper's, Taylor's, Truefitt & Hill and Penhaligon.

Shaving soaps and bowls

There is a good range of scented tablet shaving soaps available from the suppliers mentioned under mugs. The main scents are almond, rose, lime, lavender and sandalwood. For those who do not have or do not use a mug there are some shaving soaps that are supplied in handy hardwood bowls. Besides these, there is Boellis 1924 Panama shaving soap, which is a very good product.

Shaving creams

An alternative to tablets of shaving soap is shaving cream and, besides those sold by the shops already mentioned, an excellent type is produced by Santa Maria Novella, which also produces the Santa Maria Novella *Crema Pre-Dopo Barba* (pre-shave).

Alum sticks and powder

Potassium alum (a potassium sulphate of aluminium) is a naturally occurring mineral that is made into sticks, blocks or powder and is a strong astringent and coagulant to deal with slips and minor cuts when shaving. It is generally available in chemists.

Brushes

For shoe brushes, the shoe-makers sell good brushes, and for clothes brushes there are antique shops where some fine examples can be found. Stores such as John Lewis are suppliers of Kent brushes.

Mouth and Teeth

Dental care is not just for appearance's sake: the state of the teeth can affect general health, not least because the organic matter that we consume gets trapped between them and, well, it rots, creating nesting sites for bacteria, which cause dental decay and halitosis (bad breath), not to mention ulcers, bleeding gums, general soreness, blunting of the palate and consequential digestive disorders.

Evidence of types of toothbrushes, dating from 3500 BC, has been found in ancient Babylonia and chewing sticks made of aromatic woods have been found, dating from ancient times, in China too. Walnut bark, whole and powdered, is still an acknowledged (and very effective) teeth-whitening agent and supplies can be readily found in Asian shops and supermarkets. The Chinese were amongst the first to have brushes bristled with boar bristle.

In 1780 William Addis made the first boar- and horsehair-bristled toothbrushes in England and these were set in bone heads and handles. In 1937 nylon bristles appeared and as early as 1939 the electric toothbrush was invented, although not mass-marketed until the 1960s.

There are many types of toothbrushes available on the market today. There are some of those available from certain traditional suppliers in central London, such as Harris, Floris and Taylor's. The modern approach to dental care is to have a check-up every six months but sceptics might suggest that, apart from giving a general clean, some dentists are tempted to advise unnecessary treatment. I once told a dentist that I came to him because I was in pain and that it was my general policy to visit a dentist only on such occasions. He simply said that there was something to be recommended in such an approach. Since I take reasonable care of my teeth, I have, thankfully, not been back to a dentist since 1991. One might ask, what is reasonable care here? My own views are these: I try to brush my teeth after each meal and floss them once in a while; it is certainly necessary to brush the teeth morning and evening. Remember that it is not just your teeth that need the care, your tongue does too, and there are spatula-like tongue scrapers available to remove the white detritus of over-indulgence, but use these with care. J Floris makes superb mouth washes.

Tooth powder, paste and brushes

The ancient Egyptians devised a tooth powder, using such ingredients as ash from animal hooves and myrrh. The Greeks and the Romans also had receipts for tooth powder and by AD 1000 the Persians were advising avoidance of abrasive ingredients. Despite this, in eighteenth-century England abrasive dentifrice (including even brick dust) was used, which also included bicarbonate of soda, and, by the end of the century, borax too. Glycerine found its place in the early nineteenth century, followed by strontium. A dentist called Peabody added soap in 1824 and John Harris added chalk in the 1850s. In 1873 toothpaste was being produced in jars but it was 1892 before Dr Sheffield of Connecticut thought of the modern toothpaste tube. His idea became Colgate. After the Second World War fluoride compounds began to be added to the mix to help to fight decay. By the 1980s in England there was actual legislation to permit the addition of these compounds to household drinking water. Tooth powders, such as Eucryl, are still produced too and there is even one for dedicated smokers.

Exercise and the Joints

Juvenal undoubtedly got it right: *mens sana in corpore sano*, a healthy mind in a healthy body. Moreover, there is no point in trying to *look* your best if you are a mental and physical wreck. So far as the body is concerned, any gentle exercise is helpful: walking, swimming, tennis, golf, squash (of both kinds), team sports, weight training, sit-ups and press-ups, all in moderation, can help to keep the blood flowing and the muscles toned, but don't overdo it. I know of one fellow, obsessed with fitness, who kept going to the gym even when he had mild influenza and the result was a damaged heart valve: so much for super-fitness. Moreover, too much exercise of the joints will damage them and lead to much later pain and the possible onset of osteoarthritis while one's more sedentary contemporaries are still able (sometimes rather smugly) to move about unimpeded by the searing pain of this condition, often in the hips, shoulders, knees, wrists and even in the fingers and toes. Other complications can include multiple hernias from excessive weight training. One useful and fairly gentle exercise, not much spoken of outside golfing circles, to strengthen the hands and forearms, is to hold your hands up high and then, fast and repeatedly, to clench and unclench your hands until you can no longer do it, but you really have to will yourself to the end and push yourself further each time. You will find that this strengthens the hands and forearms to a remarkable degree so that you will be able, in due course, to give virtually *anyone* a run for their money at Indian arm wrestling.

CHAPTER 2

Scents and Colognes

The wandering airs they faint
On the dark, the silent stream;
The champak odours pine
Like sweet thoughts in a dream …

From 'The Indian Serenade' by PB Shelley

A Little History

Many ancient civilizations have used the scents derived from flowers, fruits, roots, leaves, wood tars and resins, animals and minerals (even petrified animal excretions and fossils) to create pleasant aromas, including the Greeks, Mesopotamians, Egyptians, Romans, Persians, Arabs and Indians. The Egyptians used to blend aromatic substances into bees' wax and put this on their heads; as the wax melted from the heat from their heads, the scents were released. Many ancient peoples burned aromatic substances to create perfume – and, indeed, the word 'perfume' derives from the Latin *per fumum* (meaning 'through smoke'). In the middle ages, perfume production found its way further into Europe, initially into Hungary and France. France famously remains a world leader in scent production.

Most men's scents come as eau de toilette, eau de cologne, aftershave or balm, but it is worth understanding something of the categorization of all scents, in terms of strengths and types as well as a little of the jargon and components, before proceeding to specific products. A further benefit of this is that, if you are buying scent for a woman, you will have some understanding of what that is all about. Moreover, makers such as Clive Christian and Ormonde Jayne notably carry stronger fragrances (even eau de parfum) for men.

Some say that the modern generic term 'Cologne' derives from the first manufacture of this type of fragrance, at Cologne, in the early eighteenth century by an Italian called Farina. A type is now branded '4711' (and made by Maurer & Wirtz), after the house number of a manufacturer of the product, dating from 1792. In German, eau de cologne is called 'Kölnisch Wasser'. Santa

Maria Novella claim that what is now branded as their Acqua di Colonia dates from its formulation as a scent for Catherine de Medici.

Strengths of Scents

Perfume oil or **pure perfume** is the strongest and is carried as fifteen to thirty per cent of perfume oil in an oil base. **Soie de parfum** is fifteen to eighteen per cent perfume oil in an oil base. **Eau de parfum** (EDP) is eight to fifteen per cent perfume oil in (generally) alcohol. This contains the strongest concentration of scent commonly available in the retail market and is, typically, a scent for women. Sometimes this is labelled *millésime*. **Eau de toilette** (EDT) is four to ten per cent perfume oil in alcohol. **Eau de cologne** (EDC) is two to five per cent perfume oil in alcohol. **Aftershave** is around three per cent perfume oil in alcohol and balm is a similar strength, but omits the alcohol and substitutes creams.

'Notes'

The science of perfumery is, because of the tiny amounts of the ingredients used, arguably much more exact than the science of wine, although the jargon used in *that* is bad enough. It is, perhaps, no coincidence that the production of both perfume and wine can bring profound satisfaction to the human mind and they both depend entirely on a perfect expression of chemical science and art. You might hear perfumers and the *cognoscenti* talking about 'top notes', 'middle' or 'heart notes' and 'base notes' and, blinded by science, wonder what they mean. It is straightforward in principle: 'top notes' are the most voluble, first scents to strike the senses in a perfume, as it 'develops' on and evaporates off the skin. Many good scents (especially complex scents) take many minutes to 'develop' after application. Of course, all applied scents continue to change until they fade away. The 'middle' or the 'heart notes' are the centre of the fragrance, making it essentially, say, an oriental, a citrus, leather, chypre or woody scent (these terms are explained later). The 'base' notes derive from the fixatives used, such as oakmoss, patchouli, various wood essences, musk, tonka beans, ambergris and vanilla, and these reinforce the heart notes. There are also some modern, 'linear' scents that don't have these 'notes', or layers, but just comprise a single fragrance.

Triggers

So far as individuals are concerned, it is well known that scents trigger memories of places, people, seasons and events, stir our feelings and conjure up atmospheres: the aromas of rain on fresh asphalt; new-mown hay; cut grass; warm horse leather; English spring mornings and

> Daffodils that come before the swallow dares,
> and take the winds of March with beauty …

English autumn leaves and garden bonfires; old colouring pencils in a pencil box; brown paper; excellent cigars; Turkish cigarettes; aromatic pipe tobacco; roasted coffee; ice cream; garden roses and jasmine; old tweed clothes; the smell of cordite from a first good shot in the crisp morning air; the summer sun on sea and sand; the smell of burning coal and wood fires ... These are all strong, clear, first memories from childhood and youth of things as important to us and as immutable as anything that we have or know. They are the strong smells of first experience and that is, maybe, why we like perfumes that bring these memories back to us, stir our feelings and conjure up these atmospheres: these are our scents of security.

Types

The major traditional categorizations of scents are into olfactive families or accords: the Amber Oriental family has an earthy, ambergris, spice and vanilla aroma and is warm, intense and heady; Citrus Hesperidia is fresh and contains, predominantly, citrus and fruit oils, especially bergamot, bitter orange and lime; Leather Tobacco scents include tobacco, honey and wood tars; Chypre (French for Cyprus) might comprise such ingredients as sage, lavender, oakmoss, patchouli, labdanum, bergamot, sandalwood, jasmine, rose and resins; and Woody Fougère (fern) includes sandalwood, cedar, patchouli, lavender, coumarin and oakmoss. There are sub-divisions of all these families but it is beyond the reach of this book to go into those. The main men's fragrances are Citrus Hesperidia, Leather Tobacco and Woody Fougère. We might note along the way that there are also more modern scents known as 'Green', including the scents of tomato leaves and cut grass. Recommended reading for more depth in this whole subject is the fascinating Royal Society of Chemistry's publication *The Chemistry of Fragrances*.

Major Components

There are many staple favourites in the perfumer's workshop–laboratory. Below are some of the traditional types. A few of these are now synthesized, owing to legal bans on the use of the natural product. Some vehicles render more than one aromatic product; for example, bitter orange renders neroli from the fruit and petitgrain from the leaves and twigs and different methods of extraction also result in different products.

Ambergris
This is an earthy, animal substance that used to be found, aged and used as a fixative. It is produced in the digestive tract of the sperm whale and expelled (at front and back) by that creature as a grey, waxy solid, found floating on the sea. Nowadays, a synthetic is mainly used and called 'Amber'.

Agarwood (*Aquilaria malaccensis, Lam.* or *Aquilaria agallocha*)
The Agarwood tree, from south-east Asia, can become infected with a mould (*Phialophora parasitica*) that produces, over hundreds of years, a most precious resinous substance called Oudh Oil in the heartwood. This is harvested and used in perfumery.

Anise (*Pimpinella anisum*)
Anise is a flowering plant of the east Mediterranean, commonly called aniseed and also much used as a flavouring, such as in pastis and crunchy, aniseed twist sweets.

Balsam (Peru) (*Myroxylon peruiferum*)
Balsam is a scented resin from this South American tree.

Bergamot
This is the oil from *Citrus aurantium bergamia* and is famously used to flavour and scent Earl Grey tea.

Birch
Birch oils are extracted from various species of tree in the family *Betulaceae betula.*

Cabbage rose (*Rosa centifolia*)
Easily recognized oils are extracted.

Camphor
Camphor is a strongly scented, waxy solid, obtained from the camphor laurel tree (*Cinnamomum camphora*), which grows in Asia.

Cascarilla (*Croton eluteria*)
This is the wild rosemary of the West Indies and renders volatile, aromatic oils. The bark is also used in the manufacture of Campari.

Castoreum
In scent, this is the dried and tinctured secretion from the castor sacs of the North American beaver *Castor canadensis* and the European beaver *Castor fiber.* The beavers use the scent to mark their territories.

Cedar (*Pinaceae cedrus*)
Within the genus, there are cedars of Turkey, Cyprus, Atlas, Deodar and, most famously, Lebanon: 'Now, therefore, command that cedars of Lebanon be cut for me ...' (1 Kings 5:6). Cedars render oils with the familiar scent. As well as having famously been used for building King Solomon's Temple, water-resistant and aromatic cedar wood is also used for cigar boxes and cigar tube linings, shoe trees, weather boarding, roof shingles and also for lining wardrobes, as the scent repels moths.

Champak (*Michelia champaca*)
This Asian tree, in the magnolia family, bears flowers that comprise a principal constituent of Jean Patou's famous women's Joy scent and, of course, there are the lines from Shelley's 'The Indian Serenade' that are at the head of this chapter.

Cinnamon (*Cinnamomum verum*)
A small tree in the laurel family, the scented oil is found in the bark, which is stripped and rolled or ground up and used in perfumes as well as in cooking and mulled wine.

Civet musk
Civet musk is an animal scent derived from the glands of the civet, which is an arboreal, carnivorous, cat-like creature in the sub-family *Viverridae.*

Copal
This is the resin from trees in the genus *Copaifera* but the word is, sometimes, generically applied to aromatic resins.

Coumarin
A chemical compound called benzopyrone, this is found in several plants, especially the tonka bean. It has culinary and medicinal uses too and the smell is said to remind some people of fresh hay and others of vanilla.

Frangipani
These are flowering trees in the genus *Plumeria*, indigenous to South America and southern India; the common name comes from the Marquis Frangipani (meaning 'breadbreakers' in Italian), who devised a scent, using many ingredients including this flower, in the reign of Louis XIII of France.

Frankincense
Along with myrrh, this was one of the gifts to the Christ Child and is an aromatic resin from a tree: in this case, of the genus *Boswellia*.

Gum benzoin
This is a balsamic resin from trees in the genus *Styrax* and is used in scents, incense and medicine.

Honeycomb
Honeycomb is very well known and is built by honey bees for storage of larvae and honey. The wax has many uses as furniture polish and even in scent manufacture.

Hyraceum
One of the stranger ingredients of perfume, Hyraceum is the petrified excretion of a small African mammal called the Cape Hyrax (*Procavia capensis*) and, apart from its use in its own right, it is a substitute for musk.

Jasmine
Shrubs of the genus *Jasminum* have flowers and scent that are well known.

Juniper
Berries, from the small trees and shrubs of the genus *Juniperus*, are most in use here. They also have culinary and medicinal uses, besides, famously, flavouring gin.

Labdanum
This is another resin, from the shrubs *Cistus ladaniferus* and *Cistus creticus*, which grow around the Mediterranean.

Lavender
These plants belong to the genus *Lavandula* and the oils from the flowers have many uses, including culinary and medicinal. The scent is very restful and

relaxing and the oil also has antiseptic properties and is another scent that repels moths.

Lemon verbena
Aloysia triphylla is a deciduous perennial shrub originally from South America but now also grown in Europe. The leaves exude a strong lemon scent, which happens to be one of my earliest memories.

Mignonette
This (*Reseda*) produces an oil.

Mimosa
From this, *Acacia farnesiana*, is derived an extract called 'cassie'.

Mint
Mint (*Mentha*) is very familiar to most people.

Musk
This is a fixative that comes from glands on the male musk deer (*Moschus moschiferus*). Synthetic musk (known as 'white musk') is much in use and, maybe unsurprisingly, lacks the animal earthiness of the real thing.

Myrrh
Myrrh is the dried resin from a tree (*Commiphora myrrha*) and some other trees. It has been valued since ancient times as incense, for embalming the dead, for use in anointing and in religious ceremonies and for flavouring food and wine (even early Egyptian toothpowder) as well as in perfumery.

Neroli
This is an oil from the blossom of the bitter orange (*Citrus aurantium amara*).

Oakmoss
Oakmoss is the very distinctive, furry lichen (*Evernia prunastri*) in a Guardi green colour that is hosted by oak trees and some pines and is used as a fixative in perfumery.

Orris root
Orris root, for example *Iris florentina*, is iris root from plants grown in Europe. A ton of the roots makes just five pounds of essential oil. It also has a use in herbal medicine.

Patchouli

Patchouli is a type of mint bush and the best of the genus is *Pogostemon cablin*. It has medicinal uses as well as a use in perfumery.

Petitgrain

This is an oil taken from the leaves and twigs of the bitter orange.

Root ginger

The root of the ginger plant, *Zingiber officinale*, is originally from Asia and, indeed, India remains the biggest producer.

Rose

Rosa damascena Mill. is the rose from which is distilled the famous attar of roses.

Rosemary

Rosmarinus officinalis is a woody herb found originally around the Mediterranean. It has culinary uses as well as its use in perfumery.

Rosewood

Rosewood is a dark, tropical hardwood of the genus *Dalbergia* and exudes a scent of roses that is extracted for use in scent. The wood is hard and has a beautiful grain that takes a high polish and so is much sought after for tables, furniture and even walking sticks and umbrella handles and shafts.

Safrole

Safrole is a sweet-smelling oil, extracted from the root bark of sassafras plants (*Sassafras albidum*).

Sage

Sage, *Salvia officinalis*, is a member of the mint family that grows readily in the Mediterranean area and the Balkans and is also known for its culinary uses.

Sandalwood oil

This is taken from the sandalwood tree, most famously the Indian variety (*Santalum album*).

Thyme

Thymus vulgaris is familiar as a gastronomic herb and even from the hedges of England's lanes.

Tobacco
This is a well-known product from plants in the genus *Nicotiana*.

Tonka bean
The tonka bean (*Dipteryx odorata*) is the bean from a tree that originated in the upper parts of South America. It is a rich source of coumarin and, as mentioned later in this book, this fruit can also play a useful part in keeping tobacco and snuff moist.

Tuberose
This (*Polianthes tuberosa*) produces a scent that finds a use in the middle notes of some perfumes.

Vanilla
Vanilla is very familiar from its culinary uses; it comes from the fermented pods of a particular orchid (*Vanilla planiflora*), famously grown in Madagascar, although it can be found in other places too.

Vetiver
Vetiver (*Chrysopogon zizanioides*) is a grass native to India but now grown in many tropical regions and the essential oil extracted from its roots is used as a fixative in perfumery.

Violet
Viola odorata renders the familiar scent that finds a use in perfumery. Violets also have culinary and medicinal uses.

Wormwood
Wormwood (*Artemisia absinthium*) is a woody, perennial plant that also famously renders the flavouring for making the alcoholic drink Absinthe, which is dealt with in Chapter 4 and used to be given many medicinal uses too.

Ylang Ylang
This is derived from the steam distillation of blossoms from the Asian Cananga tree. Extensively grown in the Philippines, this extract is famously present in Chanel No 5 and, as already mentioned, is used to scent coconut oil to make macassar oil.

Of course, there are others, but the above gives a good idea of the some of the great variety in the types of ingredients.

Methods of Extraction of Fragrances

There are several different methods of extracting fragrances. The methods might produce slightly different products from the same materials. First, there is distillation, either by steam or dry distillation; maceration of the material in solvents; expression (crushing) and *enfleurage* (a rare process by which the fragrance is absorbed into wax and then finally procured by the application of ethyl alcohol). Distillation and expression produce the important essential oils, such as attar of roses (produced by steam distillation of rose petals).

Uses

The above processes result in the production of primary scents, modifiers, blenders and fixatives, which are all essential to the making of most scents.

Choices

People have their own individual, natural smells, which can be affected by state of health, diet, consumption of alcohol, tobacco, medicine and even by our mood and, of course, there are powerful, but subliminal, natural pheromones that have a purpose in the chemistry of sexual attraction. All this should be borne in mind when choosing one's own bought scents. Besides this, there are different seasons, times of day and moods that call for different perfumes. The main purpose of scent enhancements, in a social context, is to send out signals of status, taste and personality and they are largely aimed as invisible indicators between men and women.

Storage

Keep scents in an airtight container, in a cool, dry, dark place, but not in an ordinary refrigerator and certainly not in a bathroom (with its variable temperature and humidity) and not in direct sunlight. All scents go off eventually and this will be marked by changes in colour and smell. Sometimes they can actually cause irritation or inflammation and allergic reactions, so try to avoid using scents that have passed their best.

Some Suppliers

Apart from the shops of the makers themselves, the great department stores in many countries carry large stocks of all sorts of ranges of fragrances. Les Senteurs in Belgravia can order and ship just about anything that you ask for.

Some Name Brands in Alphabetical Order

These are my suggestions for consideration. If you had several of these, you could hardly be said to be without scents. This list is plainly not comprehensive or exhaustive in any way and I do not make suggestions for different seasons or times of day, as these are largely matters of individual choice; although, generally, lighter fragrances are more suited to the summer and daytime than the heavier fragrances, which tend to complement colder seasons and the evening. Most suppliers have samples, so try them out and tell for yourself. Some indication is given below of the strengths and main 'notes' in the scents but I *generally* fight shy of trying to describe the comparative olfactory effect of the fragrances, as such likes and dislikes are instinctive and subjective. Some fragrances may also be offered in other strengths.

Acqua di Parma Colonia, EDC
This has sharp citrus top notes and settles to floral undertones.

Acqua di Parma Colonia Assoluta, EDC
This is a woodier version of the original.

Acqua di Parma Colonia Intensa, EDC
More complex than the two foregoing, it has citrus top notes, neroli and myrtle in the middle and cedar, leather, musk and smoky woods in the base.

Clive Christian No 1 for Men, EDP
Launched in 1872, it is still advertised as 'the most expensive perfume in the world', although I seem to recall that it has competition in the claim, from Jean Patou's Joy. The No 1 comes in a distinctive gold bottle. Amber and sandalwood notes predominate.

Clive Christian X for Men, EDP
This comprises smoked wood, orris, cardamom and ginger and comes in a black bottle.

Clive Christian 1872 for Men, EDP
Named for the year in which the firm was established; notes of clary sage predominate. It comes in a green bottle. There are 'travelling sets' combining miniatures of all three of these Clive Christian perfumes.

Creed Bois du Portugal, EDT
This is a warm, woody fragrance blending cedar, sandalwood, lavender and vetiver.

Creed Green Irish Tweed, EDT
Famously created especially for Cary Grant, this has citrus top notes and sandalwood and amber in the base.

Creed Neroli Sauvage, EDT
This is a strong, citrus scent, combining many citrus essences, including neroli, on a base of sandalwood and ambergris.

Creed Royal English Leather, EDT
In this, dating from 1780, the leather base scent is topped by tangerine notes.

Creed Original Vetiver, EDT
Creed says that it is a fresh and contemporary fragrance. It is certainly a complex green woody scent, blending vetiver, sandalwood, iris, musk, ambergris as well as mandarin, bergamot and ginger.

Creed Tabarôme, EDT
This comprises scents of sandalwood, patchouli, vetiver, green tea, citrus, tobacco and ginger, all adding up to an oriental scent. Unfortunately, this is being phased out but will remain as a millésime scent.

Czech & Speake Neroli
This comes in various strengths and products and combines, predominantly, neroli and the scents of the Ylang Ylang.

Czech & Speake No 88
This also comes in various strengths and products and is the house's signature scent. It has a fresh – even woody – top note of bergamot, suffused with geranium, rose and frangipani, over a base of sandalwood and vetiver.

Dunhill X-Centric, EDT
This is a modern fragrance with top notes of cypress, clary, citrus and green, middle notes of freesia and rose on a base of cedar, amber and musk.

Dunhill for Men, EDT
Their 1934 classic fragrance has top notes of lemon, clary and petitgrain, a middle including rose, jasmine, carnation and orris, and all backed up by a base of cedar, vetiver, tonka bean and leather.

Eau Sauvage (Christian Dior), EDT
This classic citrus cologne dates from 1966 – the middle of the Swinging Sixties. The 'Extreme' version is not an improvement.

Floris JF, EDT
This is a distinctive, aromatic, citrus floral scent (1992) from Floris, which was founded in Jermyn Street as a barber and smooth comb maker by Juan Famenias Floris, a Menorcan, in 1730. It still flourishes as a family firm, specializing in its famous scents and colognes. The first royal warrant came from George IV in 1820 and it has held sixteen in all. Famous past customers have included George 'Beau' Brummell, Ian Fleming, Florence Nightingale, Mary Shelley, Eva Peron (Evita) and Noël Coward. Floris fragrances are available at many outlets across the world.

Floris Limes, EDT
This is a highly refreshing classic, dating from the late eighteenth century, and blends citrus and petitgrain top notes with a heart of lime blossom, neroli and lily of the valley on a musk base. This is, probably, my overall favourite.

Floris No 89, EDT
This name derives from their shop number in Jermyn Street and was launched in 1951. Ian Fleming used it and so it is assumed to be one of James Bond's colognes of choice. It is a citrus–woody cologne, combining citrus top notes with a heart of geranium, rose and Ylang Ylang, on a base of cedar, musk, oakmoss, sandalwood and vetiver.

Floris Special 127, EDT
This name derives from the page number of the formula book on which the receipt is kept and dates from 1890 when it was formulated for Russian Grand Duke Orloff (originally called 'Orloff Special'). It is sophisticated enough in its dry, citrus–floral notes top and middle notes, on a base of musk and patchouli, to have appealed to such as Noël Coward and Eva Peron.

Floris Vetiver, EDT
This is a warm, woody cologne that dates from 1870, but you need to be quick as it is being phased out.

Fou d'Absinthe (L'Artisan Parfumeur), EDP
This unusual, hot, drunken scent dates from 2006 and has top notes of wormwood; middle notes are of ginger and pepper on a strong, pine base.

Freshman (Truefitt & Hill), EDC
Dating from 1815, this one has citrus and mint top notes, clary sage and geranium in the heart and precious woods, amber, moss and musk in the base.

Hermès Eau d'Orange Vert, EDC
A refreshing eau de cologne, dating from the late 1970s, it has citrus top notes with a fruit heart on a base of leathery, woody, oak moss and patchouli.

Isfarkand (Ormonde Jayne), EDP
After citrus top notes comes a peppery middle on a base of cedar, vetiver and moss.

Jicky (Guerlain), EDT
Dating from 1889 and, probably, made in honour of Guerlain's uncle, whose nickname was Jicky, this has top notes of lavender and citrus, a heart of iris and rose, over a base of vanilla, amber and musk.

Knize Ten, Aftershave
Dating from 1924, this has citrus, petitgrain and rosemary top notes, heart notes of geranium, cedar, rose, orris, carnation, cinnamon and sandalwood on a base of leather, musk, moss, amber, castoreum and vanilla.

Mouchoir de Monsieur (Guerlain) 1904, EDT
This is a sophisticated scent that begins with a musky, civet top note, breaking down to lavender and bergamot in the heart on a base of vanilla, tonka bean, musk, rose and iris.

Ormonde Man (Ormonde Jayne), EDP
This has top notes of juniper, bergamot, pepper, cardamom and coriander, a heart of Oudh and black hemlock and a base of vetiver, cedar, sandalwood and musk.

Penhaligon's English Fern, EDC
This composition, dating from 1911, might be described as young, vernal and woody-green. Penhaligon's flagship store is in Covent Garden. The original William Penhaligon was born in Penzance and set up in London in business in 1860, as a barber, next to the old Hammam Turkish baths in Piccadilly. By 1872 he had fused his first perfume – Hammam Bouquet – which is still one of their favourite colognes, with its musky, oriental smell, described by Penhaligon's as reminiscent of 'old books, powdered resins and ancient rooms'. In 1902 there came the Blenheim Bouquet, formulated for the Duke of Marlborough; this became a favourite of Marlborough family member Winston Churchill. Penhaligon has held several royal warrants and has stores also in Paris and New York.

Pinaud's Extract of Limes, EDT
This is a very good version of this extract that several others makers also provide.

Pinaud's Lilac Vegetal, Aftershave
This is a famous, bracing, lilac-scented aftershave.

Roger et Gallet's Extra-Vieille, EDC
Roger et Gallet took over Farina's formula in 1862 and this is what they make of it now. It has no heavy base but refreshing citrus and rustic top and middle notes predominate.

Santa Maria Novella Acqua di Colonia, EDC
As already mentioned, this is an old formulation, combining light citrus, floral and spice essences.

Spanish Leather (Truefitt & Hill), EDC
Dating from 1830, this is a musky, woody, spicy leather cologne.

Tabac Blond (Caron), EDC
Dating from 1919, this is another smoky, leather fragrance, with floral, amber and musk notes backed by vanilla and tobacco. It is also reckoned to be a 'unisex' scent.

Taylor's No 74, EDC
The name of this derives from their number in Jermyn Street and is a fairly strong, old-fashioned English cologne.

Taylor's Victorian Limes, EDC
This is another good example of this simple and refreshing product.

Trumper's Eucris, EDC
Dating from 1912, this has top notes of cumin seeds and citrus and oakmoss in the base; overall it is musky and peppery and few are indifferent to it but its detractors say that it evokes the smell of death. Maybe this is why Ian Fleming mentions the hair preparation version of this in *On Her Majesty's Secret Service*! Smiert spionam, indeed.

Trumper's Extract of West Indian Limes, EDC
A justly famous version of this extract.

Vetiver (Guerlain), EDT
Dating from 1961 and recently relaunched (but under the same formula), this has citrus and coriander top notes, vetiver and cedar in the heart and tobacco, nutmeg, pepper, tonka and capsicum in the base.

CHAPTER 3

Some Dressing Accessories

A sweet disorder in the dress
Kindles in clothes a wantonness

From 'Delight in Disorder' by Robert Herrick

Some Remarks on Dressing

Above everything, remember that we should dress to live and not live to dress. If you go riding on a wet day, you will (you *should*) end up spattered with mud. If you take your children on a summer picnic, you might do well to start out in a navy blue reefer jacket, white flannel trousers and co-respondent shoes – but it is a testament to a very fine day indeed if you end up with ice cream smeared over the knees of your trousers; the dog's footprints on the white buckskin of your shoes; your wife's lipstick on your face and a few strands of burnished gold from your daughter's head on your shoulder as you carry her, flushed, sun-kissed and sleepy, homeward bound.

The Dandy

The Dandy is the product of evolution and not of revolution or even (entirely) of education. Knowing full well the lines from Robert Herrick's words at the head of this chapter, the Dandy is never overdressed and is not going to be fretting about how to get to the head of the line for the loveliest girl in the room. He's going to be fretting (if at all and *never* perceptibly) over where the loveliest girl in the room is in the line-up for him.

Brummell (our constant hero as the epitome of the Man About Town) had many virtues and just as many vices, but he had the greatest gift of all, resulting in the fact that people *sought him out*. He even proudly declared that he 'could be standing in the pit at the opera and beckon to Lovain [Duke of Argyll] on one side, and to Villiers [Lord Jersey] on the other, *and see them come to me*'.

This gift we cannot much describe, beyond saying that it is a talent for conviviality. Moreover, if one is not interesting (and interested) in conversation generally – with men, with old people and with children (as much as with women) – and if horses and cats do not come up to you and if babies do not point at you excitedly over their parents' shoulders; if older children do not (somehow ineluctably) come up to you, involuntarily twisting their limbs and hair to overcome their shyness, you have not yet evolved to the state of the Dandy. These people (actually women just as much as men) hold the power of attraction for all these creatures are the True Dandies and, most of all, they don't *try* to be so or care that they are.

Small children are often shy, horses are normally docile chewers of the cud and cats just don't give a monkey's uncle (unless there's food in the offing), so, when they break their normal conventions of stand-offishness and (depending on town or country for the horses) come out of nowhere to go up to a particular person, then you know that you're in the presence of someone very special. And the quality of Dandyism, of panache, of charisma itself? You can see it and you can recognize it in action but you cannot exactly define it; it is largely inherent and can be neither wholly learned nor taught; certainly not bottled, canned or sold and bought; you cannot much burnish it or improve it; certainly not overlook it, hide it, embarrass it, nor can you greatly acquire it or (at all) dispose of it, or do anything much except to be glad if you have it, or admire it in others if you don't.

Accessories

Slippers

Bespoke slippers are a speciality of WS Foster & Son and Henry Maxwell, although the other makers that I mention in my book *History of Men's Fashion* also make them. They may be made in the customer's own choice of material, including leather, suede, silk velvet or needlepoint, and might incorporate any feature of a monogram, whether it be a coat of arms or just the crest or one's initials in gold, silver or coloured thread on the vamp (or front) of the slipper. WS Foster & Son and Henry Maxwell continue the famous traditions of Peal & Co, as well as their own.

The boot-maker Peal & Co was founded in Durham in 1565 and moved to Derby in 1765. They moved to Stepney Green, London in 1791 and, at this time, Samuel Peal was in charge. By 1886 they were in Oxford Street and then, ultimately, Wigmore Street. They exhibited at (amongst other exhibitions) the Great Exhibition of 1851 and the Festival of Britain a century later, in 1951, and numbered many of the great and good from around the world as their customers, from the Prince Aga Khan and the Duke of Windsor to Charlie

Chaplin, Douglas Fairbanks Sr (who swore by their slippers), Henry Ford II, Howard Heinz, Jehudi Menuhin, Faith and Gladys Rockefeller, Cary Grant, David Niven, Field Marshall Lord Allenbrooke, Theodore Roosevelt, Humphrey Bogart and Lauren Bacall, Laurence Olivier, Lord Mountbatten, President John F Kennedy, Steve McQueen, Mrs Walt Disney, Dean Martin and members of several European royal families, not to mention, in the words of a line from Cole Porter's song 'You're the Top', contributing (along with others) to 'the nimble tread of the feet of Fred Astaire'.

They took over Bartley & Sons in 1953, and Bartley's shop shingle of the fox and boot hangs outside the WS Foster & Son–Henry Maxwell shop to this day. In 1965, exactly 400 years after they were founded, the Peal family saw the writing on the wall and, still at the top, just closed their doors, with dignity. But that is not the end of their long story, because Terry Moore, of WS Foster and Henry Maxwell, had been apprenticed at Peal & Co and has kept (as well as his training) lasts and patterns from that old firm and through himself and his apprentices in a real sense he continues their 400-year-old tradition.

The American company of Brooks Brothers bought the trading name of Peal & Co and still sells shoes under the ghost of their name but the paper records of this great old firm, including their famous Feet Books (containing records and drawings of their customers' feet), are in the safe-keeping of the National Archives.

Dressing gowns and smoking jackets

Good readymade dressing gowns (Brandenburghs) are available at Budd, New & Lingwood, Turnbull & Asser, Charvet and, again, as I have already mentioned, A Sulka has been revived and will, presumably, once again make its superb dressing gowns and smoking jackets (even suits). A current good source of readymade smoking jackets is Turnbull & Asser. On the bespoke front, Joshua Byrne of Byrne & Burge was apprenticed to a coat-maker at Anderson & Sheppard and then to Arthur Catchpole of Henry Poole before he established a firm with his wife in 2007. His credentials speak for themselves and they have set up in a lovely building near Hanover Square, where there used to be so many firms.

One useful tip in relation to bespoke clothing is that Michael Alden's website of the London Lounge (listed at the end) has a 'Cloth Club' section, in which members may subscribe to limited edition projects for the recreation of (generally) heavier-weight cloths, which are becoming increasingly difficult to buy, in patterns deriving from illustrations that members find. Once enough members have committed to each project, the weavers are instructed to proceed.

Recent splendid examples have included a natural-coloured camel-hair cloth for polo coats and a blue 'windowpane' grey flannel for suiting. Once you have bespoken your cloths and had them made up, you can then tune into another section of the London Lounge, called Dress with Style, where Michael Alden gives informative and amusing video lessons on this topic.

Collars, braces, scarves, gloves, ties, cravats and smoking hats

Separate stiff collars (for formal occasions), braces, silk-backed and cashmere scarves for winter wear, evening gloves and scarves, ties, cravats and gloves and smoking hats count as accessories in my view. The shirt-makers (such as Turnbull & Asser, New & Lingwood and Budd) all supply collars and braces. New & Lingwood and Luke Eyres supply the best separate stiff collars. If you use braces, remember to get those with white leather buttonholes to avoid staining your clothes and in brightly coloured box-cloth for the daytime and in white or cream silk for the evening. Great selections of scarves and ties are to be found at Ede & Ravenscroft, New & Lingwood, Emma Willis and Turnbull & Asser. Michael Drake supplies several shops and also sells his own ties himself. Budd keeps a superb selection of ties and evening scarves and gloves as well as their famous Guards' Mess evening shirts; these comprise standard white material in the front, collar and cuffs but astonishing body-work, emblazoned with bright cartoons (such as the cat and mouse Tom and Jerry) that may be displayed to advantage once the commanding officer has retired from the table. Charvet in Paris and Marinella in Naples are famous old European firms; Marinella used to make just black ties for Aristotle Onassis, as he wore only these so that no one could guess his mood! There is also the excellent Sam Hober in Thailand.

Recently, a tapestry was woven from the golden-coloured silk of about one million golden orb weaving spiders (in the genus *Nephila*) and put on show in the American Museum of Natural History in New York. I have an ambition to find enough of this silk (in its abandoned web form) to take up the offer of David Hober of Sam Hober to have it spun and woven and then to make me a spider-silk tie, along the lines of those made for Roald Dahl's fictional Uncle Oswald. Whether I shall ever get enough silk is another matter, but it is a nice idea.

Old Hat in Fulham is renowned for its exclusive cravat designs. Gloves, in every kind of material, come from Pickett and Chester Jefferies. Bespoke gloves are also still obtainable and cost very little more than readymade gloves. There is also Dunhill for driving gloves. Smoking hats are still readily available from James Lock & Co.

Until it closed in around 2002, A Sulka of Old Bond Street always seemed to me one of the best places to get ties and scarves and they were also justly famous for their shirt-making. I mention something of their history and apparent demise in my book *History of Men's Fashion* but they are about to return through the website sulka.com, and news of progress is available by signing up on the site.

Some day ties and scarves come in the distinctive Paisley pattern. Paisley, in Scotland, was one of the first places to manufacture cloth in a replica, curled and colourful, teardrop pattern (called, in Urdu, phonetically, *ambi*), and first brought back, in the form of costly cashmere and silk scarves, from Kashmir to the British Isles by the English East India Company. The original patterns had been used in the east for thousands of years. Gradually, the patterns produced in Britain have developed into a flowery westernized version of the original geometric designs and have attracted the generic name 'Paisley pattern'.

There is also pashmina cloth, which, strictly, is a fine fabric made from just a type of cashmere wool. However, it is now often blended with a thirty-per-cent silk content. A real pashmina scarf or shawl (whether blended or not) can be tested true by passing it through a wedding ring. Cashmere and pashmina wools, from wild goats, used to be collected from thorn bushes as the animals shed their winter coats. Now the goats are farmed, and this has brought the price of the fabrics down.

The short history of the dinner jacket/tuxedo

Since I wrote *History of Men's Fashion*, I have kindly been given a copy of Henry Poole's complete file on the subject of the emergence of the dinner jacket/tuxedo, the results of the further researches into Henry Poole's records by James Sherwood, and also details of family lore by the current Lord Dupplin and feel that, although a dinner jacket is not strictly an accessory, it is sufficiently qualified for inclusion here, after mention of evening accessories.

There are several different versions covering the origins of the short evening coat, the dinner jacket, and its American cousin the tuxedo. Henry Poole's order book records that, in April 1865, Henry Poole had made a smoking jacket in blue (possibly midnight blue) silk with silk lining, collar and cuffs for the Prince of Wales (later Edward VII) to wear at informal soirées at Sandringham (where it was delivered).

Written records for the definitive, prototype dinner jacket of the kind worn outside the home seem to be elusive but the gaps are filled to some extent by family legend and the sources that I have mentioned.

According to the present Lord Dupplin, his predecessor, George Robert Hay (1849–1886), from 1866 Lord Dupplin, and nicknamed 'Duppy', was a contemporary and good friend of the Prince of Wales and, after one Season (although which is unclear), he was invited onboard the royal yacht. Lord Dupplin was a keen sportsman (owner, for a short period, of the successful, sometimes erratic, racehorse Petrarch, which won the St Leger in 1876 and then the Royal Ascot Gold Cup in 1877, a year after he was bought by Lord Lonsdale). This Lord Dupplin was much noted for his innovative sartorial style (including a scarlet neck tie). His orders, from Henry Poole for 1866, included 'a black angola lounging coat, lined silk' and 'a black cotton velvet dressing jacket lined silk, with quilted, silk collar, facings and cuffs' and his orders for 1870 included 'a shawl figured dressing jacket, lined silk, quilted'. Down to this year there is no explicit mention of a 'dress lounge' or 'dinner jacket' and the ledger with his orders after 1870 is missing.

However, according to his continuing family lore, for his royal yacht invitation Lord Dupplin consulted Henry Poole over what to wear and an early version of the modern dinner jacket resulted. Apparently, he was lightly ribbed over it – but the Prince of Wales adopted the style for informal events the next Season and so, naturally, it started to catch on. From the Prince's own order of a smoking suit, for intimate soirees in 1865, we can be sure that he was already inclined to comfortable, less formal clothes. The royal yacht invitation must have been before 1886, as this Lord Dupplin died, aged thirty-seven, in March 1886.

There might already have been a German version of this jacket and patrons of the casino at Monte Carlo sometimes wore a similar garment at around the same time, leading to its continental name of 'a Monte Carlo', sometimes a 'smoking', and, besides 'Tuxedo', it has sometimes been called 'a Cowes coat' by Americans. Originally, according to CW and P Cunnington, it was called a 'dress lounge' in England and the earliest examples incorporated a single-breasted style, with a silk-covered roll (or shawl) collar and lapels and two front buttons; by 1898 it was being called a 'dinner jacket' and, by 1899, the lapels were also being fashioned with 'pointed' (presumably, double-breasted [or peaked]) lapels; there was just one front button and the bottoms of the front parts were being cut square. Other features were either formed or silk gauntlet cuffs (the latter reprised for Sean Connery's dinner jacket in the 1962 film *Dr No*) and, as now, unflapped (jetted) side pockets. Step lapels appear as a further alternative in illustrations by the great pattern expert JP Thornton in the early teens of the twentieth century; although these have never really caught on in the long term and are considered by many to constitute the most informal type of dinner jacket (which, anyway, is a semi-formal type of dress). By the early teens of the twentieth century, the square-cut bottoms of the front parts had given way to rounded fronts. Then, as now, an inky blue vicuña cloth would be hard to better.

The early practice seems to have been to wear white ties and vests with these jackets and, even as late as 1911–1913, JP Thornton was illustrating dinner jackets worn with white ties, as shown in plate 12, where the three main styles of jacket (which he called 'semi-dress coat styles') are also shown. Oriole Cullen, of the costume department at the Victoria & Albert Museum, says that the move to black tie with a dinner jacket was a gradual process and it is difficult to put an exact date by which black tie became the norm, but it was sometime between 1910 and 1920. This is fairly clear from photographs from the 1920s. However, he also makes the point that some people wore a black tie from the early days of dinner jacket/tuxedos.

The *Tailor and Cutter* reported in September 1897 that 'the attempt which has been made for the past two or three seasons to introduce embroidered silk bows for evening wear, has not met with much success. They are hardly even being shown by the best tie houses. The small white plain cambric bow continues to be the correct thing for evening wear.' In 1898 the same journal complained about the increasing appearance of dinner jackets at events with ladies present (when, of course, only a full dress, swallow-tail evening coat was proper).

The *Tailor and Cutter* also reported that ties in primary colours were generally only demanded for the low-class trade and tartan neckties did not sell well. There is some mention too that black bow ties could be worn with evening dress but, after the First World War, it was customary to wear one only with a dinner jacket and not a dress coat.

It is indeed interesting to discover that a black tie had, sometimes, been worn with a dress coat and that this practice faded after the First World War. This fact lends some weight to the proposition that it was in this decade anyway that the general practice of wearing a white tie with a dress coat and a black tie with a dinner jacket became settled. There are certainly (albeit comparatively very few) pre-First World War photographs of men in dress coats and black ties and, of course (from Captain Jesse), we know that Beau Brummell (who was influential in the introduction of near-monochrome evening dress, including a superfine, white cambric cravat) was reluctantly reduced to a black silk neckerchief to save on his laundry bills. By far the greatest number of illustrations that I have seen, from Brummell's age to just before the First World War, show men wearing white evening ties.

Accordingly, wearing a white tie with a dinner jacket/tuxedo would now be unusual but would not constitute the post-First World War sartorial *faux pas* of wearing a black tie with a dress coat (unless a maître d', a servant, waiter, steward, porter or beadle). President Obama wore a white tie with a tuxedo to his inauguration ball and was not incorrect (because this is how it all began) but this combination is unusual in the twenty-first century.

Either a black or a white waistcoat also remains correct with a single-breasted dinner jacket/tuxedo, although, again, black is more usual now. A cummerbund is also (although deprecated by some) an option, with a soft-fronted shirt.

Prominent New Yorker Evander Berry Wall (himself a Henry Poole & Co customer) certainly possessed an adaptation of a blue silk smoking jacket that Henry Poole had made for Edward, Prince of Wales in 1865. The story goes that Wall was one of the first audacious souls to wear a dinner jacket in public – in fact, to a ball held in the United States Hotel in Saratoga in August 1886. The result of this outing was not auspicious as he was asked to leave by the manager; the expression of the ultimate social sanction for breach of a dress code, echoing Lady Jersey's exclusion of the Duke of Wellington from Almack's, nearly seventy years before, when he had pitched up (late) in pantaloons and not evening breeches. Interestingly, the dress code for the Caledonian Ball, held annually at Grosvenor House, specifically excludes dinner jackets.

In the London season of 1886 a prominent New York socialite named James Brown Potter and his beautiful Southern wife Cora (née Urquhart) were taken up by the Prince of Wales and invited to Sandringham. Potter learned that the Prince favoured a short evening jacket (presumably of the kind introduced to him by Lord Dupplin, who had died in March 1886) for informal evening wear and asked to have one made by Henry Poole. It is unlikely that Potter would have worn a smoking jacket (as we understand the term) outside his own home but he did order a short evening jacket. Henry Poole & Co have not yet found a record of the transaction in Potter's name (although he became a Henry Poole customer in 1883), but Angus Cundey, Chairman and Joint Managing Director of Henry Poole, thinks that this might be because the commission was paid for by the Prince.

Meanwhile, Pierre Lorillard IV, a tobacco millionaire, had started a club at Tuxedo Park in the hills outside New York. His youngest child N Griswold Lorillard's first Henry Poole commissions had been made in 1881 when he was aged seventeen and in the year that his father's horse, Iroquois, would win the Epsom Derby. None of his commissions appears to have comprised a dinner jacket, although one is tantalizingly described as a 'fancy dress coat with single-breasted facings', presumably meaning step (or notch) lapels.

When James Brown Potter returned to his home in Tuxedo Park, New York in the autumn of 1886 (with his new evening jacket) it seems, from an account of the subsequent undefended divorce proceedings (on the grounds of her wilful desertion, as reported in the *New York Times* on 5 June 1900), that Cora stayed in England to begin a career on the stage. Her husband sought to forbid it but she defied him. Her continuing connection with the Prince of Wales and his set is evidenced by her going to the extent of having a tattoo of the Prince of Wales's feathers emblazoned on her left upper arm, as shown in plate 13. After the divorce Cora insisted on keeping her married name as her stage name, even though, according to another report in the *New York Times*, on 3 January 1909, Potter had offered her $100,000 to abandon it to save his second wife's feelings.

From the photograph in plate 13, we may be quite sure that it was Cora Brown Potter's understandable fascination for the Prince of Wales that prompted the Prince's Sandringham invitation and started the transatlantic journey of the jacket that would become the American tuxedo. Moreover, from the evidence presented in the divorce proceedings, it appears that the breakdown in the Potters' marriage actually began in the very summer of 1886.

On James Brown Potter's return to New York, founder members of the club at Tuxedo Park, including Pierre Lorillard IV and Grenville Kane, began to adopt the evening jacket, brought back by Potter, for their informal dinners. Some club members even dared to sport the jacket out to stag (or bachelor) dinners at Delmonico's in New York where, according to Grenville Kane, talking in 1929 to Tuxedo Park resident J Earle Stevens Jr, people started saying 'Oh! That's what they wear for dinner up in Tuxedo!' Before he emigrated to England in 1888, William Waldorf Astor satisfied himself that the word 'tuxedo' derives from a phrase, in a native American Indian language, '*P'tauk-seet-tough*', meaning 'home of the bear'.

On 10 October 1886, N Griswold Lorillard and some friends attended the first Tuxedo Park Club Autumn Ball in a tailless dress coat (like a 'Spencer' or military mess jacket) as a prank. This was much shorter than the James Brown Potter dinner jackets that his elders had begun to adopt for informal occasions and a gossip sheet, called *Town Topics,* said that it made Griswold look like 'a royal footman'.

N Griswold Lorillard may not, then (although maintained by popular legend), really have introduced, at the age of twenty-two years, the dinner jacket/tuxedo (as we know it) to American society but the legend of his high-spirited prank, on 10 October 1886, has long survived his early death, aged twenty-five, in 1889 and played a real part in the long sunset of the swallow-tail coat. In any event, when entertainer Jack Buchanan popularized the double-breasted dinner jacket/tuxedo in the UK in the first quarter of the twentieth century (a style soon taken up by younger members of the royal family, starting with the then Prince of Wales in 1924, and remaining a favourite style in modern times), he was bringing back, from his tours in the USA, a descendant of the jacket that James Brown Potter had taken to America in 1886.

Moreover, although the Duke of Windsor had been noted, even in his youth, for his inky-blue dinner jackets, it was in fact his grandfather who had been amongst the first to wear a short blue evening jacket, and gave his *imprimatur* to the use in a wider social context of the dinner jacket/tuxedo, and the grandfather had been exactly half a century ahead of the grandson in his *penchant* for a married American woman.

Snuff and other handkerchiefs and socks

Most of the Jermyn Street shops sell colourful snuff handkerchiefs, as do snuff chandlers and tobacconists. In plate 14 are some from Turnbull & Asser. The shirt-makers in the gods' quad (described on page 13 of my *History of Men's Fashion*) also sell coloured silk handkerchiefs for country coat breast pockets and white linen and cambric handkerchiefs for those harmlessly determined to wear one of these in the breast pocket of a city suit or with formal wear. For socks, there are Pantherella and Bresciani.

Sunglasses

Here Cutler & Gross, Persol and Ray Ban top the list. Cutler & Gross and Persol sunglasses are also available with prescription lenses.

Watches

Our time is a very shadow that passeth away.

Wisdom of Solomon, 2:5

Besides the usual famous names, such as Breguet and Patek Philippe, there are some English watches too that certainly deserve attention. One of the most famous of the old makers of these is Charles Frodsham (which firm is still in business, for sales of vintage pieces, by appointment only). Charles was the son of William Frodsham and was born in 1810. Apprenticed for seven years to his father, he made marine chronometers for the Admiralty. Taking in other makers over time (including Vulliamy and William Johnson of Grimalde & Johnson) and, most famously, JR Arnold, the firm was known as Arnold & Frodsham between 1844 and 1857. Most of their best pieces, from 1850 onwards, are marked ADFmsz.

A Frodsham watch was tested at the Kew Observatory in 1906. It had a tourbillon escapement (a mechanism to counteract the effect of positional errors of the watch) and it scored record marks over every other English watch ever tested at the Observatory: 93.9 out of 100.

The firm of Charles Frodsham won many medals and diplomas in international exhibitions, held the royal warrant and became Keeper of the

Royal Clocks for 125 years. Charles was also a Fellow of the Royal Astronomical Society. The watches and indeed the clocks, chronometers and other instruments of this wonderful old firm are still sought after and prized. Some of the other instruments include time of flight instruments (for timing the flight of projectiles), speedometers, car clocks and camera timers. I asked for a photograph that the firm of Charles Frodsham feel really sums up their achievement and they came up with the image in plate 15.

Of course, Breguet is also still also very much in business and has an impressive former customer list: Queen Marie-Antoinette, Emperor Napoleon I, Prince Talleyrand, the Ottoman Sultan, Czar Alexander I and Marshal Ney, as well as Winston Churchill, Queen Victoria and Arthur Rubinstein. Abraham-Louis Breguet (1747–1823) was a Swiss inventor of escapements, including the tourbillon (already mentioned above) and gongs for repeating ('complicated') watches. These have a mechanism which, on depression of a lever, makes the watch ring out the hour and the quarter – some even the very minute of the hour – one different gong each for the hour, the quarter and the minute. From 1815, Breguet enjoyed the patronage of the French navy.

Since 1969, there has also been the firm of George Daniels, making wholly handmade watches and also strides in escapement development but these watches are, for obvious reasons, as rare as hen's teeth, although the maker insists that purchasers should *use* his watches and not just lock them up as investments.

Patek Philippe is another renowned Swiss firm, founded in 1839, which invented the keyless winding mechanism and made their first wristwatch in 1868. These, for men, were slow to catch on and regarded, at first, as 'not the thing', but now, of course, they most definitely are and pocket watches have generally become collectors' pieces.

Other current prestige makers include:

Audemars Piguet

Founded in Switzerland, in 1875, they started to specialize in chiming repeaters and made some very fine pieces, including one for the Imperial Count of Iran. They are now very well known for making ultra-thin time-pieces as well as the Royal Oak steel sports' watch. The top end of their current production is the range of chronographs called Tradition of Excellence.

Breitling

Founded in 1884 in Switzerland, they are famous for superb chronographs, have close links with aviation and, in 1962, an astronaut used a Breitling chronograph in the Aurora 7 space capsule.

Cartier

This firm is, first and foremost, famous for its art deco jewellery and jewellery in animal forms and the enormous diamond that Richard Burton bought for Elizabeth Taylor in 1969. They were founded in Paris in 1847 by Louis-François Cartier when he took over his apprentice-master's business. They were gradually taken up by crowned heads and aristocrats around the world, even before their first jewellery bracelet watch in 1888 and the neo-classical, platinum-set jewellery introduced in 1900. They opened a London shop in 1902 and had a warrant from Edward VII in 1904. In the same year Louis Cartier created a wristwatch with a leather strap for Brazilian aviation pioneer Alberto Santos-Dumont. In 1906 Cartier started to make art deco jewellery and the first Tonneau wristwatch as well as selling the Blue Hope Diamond to an American customer. In 1911 they devised the Santos de Cartier wristwatch and in 1919 the first iconic Tank wristwatch appeared. Since then they have continued to develop other watch styles, including the Tortue Chronograph and the Crash watch.

Girard-Perregaux

As a result of a merger in 1906 between this firm and a firm founded by Jean-François Bautte, they can trace their origins back to 1791, although Constant Girard founded his firm later than this (in 1852) and married Marie Perregaux, merging their names in the manufactory at La Chaux-de-Fonds. One of their most famous achievements was the building of a Tourbillon chronometer with three gold bridges in 1889. This won a gold medal in the Paris Universal Exhibition of that year. It had been as early as 1880 that the firm had been interested in wristwatches but it was not until 1930 that wristwatch sales started to outstrip pocket watches. 1940 saw the appearance of the Sea Hawk and in 1945 came the rectangular art deco model. This firm has notably straddled the manufacture of both mechanical watches and quartz and in 1966 introduced a high-frequency movement. 1993 saw a co-branding with Ferrari of a split-seconds chronograph and they continue to make advances in watch escapements. Interestingly, it was a complicated watch by this firm that Ian Fleming gave (as a rich man's badge) to the assassin 'Red' Grant in *From Russia With Love*, although he has him change it for an anonymous, battered silver watch as part of his disguise as British agent 'Old Man' Nash.

IWC (International Watch Company)

This is a Swiss company founded by an American called Florentine Ariosto Jones in 1868 and his aim was to produce for the American market. They are especially famed for diving and pilots' watches.

A Lange & Söhne

Ferdinand A Lange was born in Dresden in 1815 and apprenticed to Gutkaes' manufactory, eventually marrying a co-owner. In 1845 he decided to set up a manufactory in Glasshütte, to give employment to starving people in a depression. In this he succeeded magnificently and, when he died in 1875, the town erected a monument to him. The firm has gone under its present name since 1868. His sons took the business over and continued to thrive until the manufactory was lost in aerial bombardment in the Second World War. Before that, they had attracted the patronage of Kaiser Wilhelm II, who commissioned a presentation watch as a gift for the Ottoman Sultan.

After the War, owing to the communist occupation, even the company's land was expropriated and so began a forty-year hiatus in the firm's history. But on the reunification of Germany in 1989, Walter Lange, the founder's great-grandson, in an act worthy of his illustrious ancestor, returned to the town (from which he had escaped) and re-founded the company in 1990, 145 years to the day after the manufactory had first opened. It flourishes again, producing magnificent time-pieces such as the 1815 Moonphase. If we cannot find inspiration in this spirit, we may never find it at all.

Omega

This make had its beginnings when Louis Brandt founded an assembly workshop in La Chaux-de-Fonds in 1848 and also started to make precision watches himself. In 1885 he devised the futuristic Lépine calibre digital display of the hour and minute. The first Omega wristwatch dates from 1900 and the first Seamaster appeared in 1948, followed by the first Constellation automatic chronometer in 1952 and the Marine Chronometer in 1974. The firm continues to produce innovations in movements and enjoys endorsement in some modern James Bond films.

Rolex

The James Bond of the novels is described as wearing a heavy Rolex Oyster Perpetual with a 'metal' bracelet (presumably steel) and large luminous numerals in *On Her Majesty's Secret Service* (1963). Guiseppe Petacchi, the test pilot in *Thunderball* (1961), wears a gold version. The earliest portrayals in the Bond films has Bond wearing a steel Submariner version. Since then, the screen Bond has gone to Seiko and now (as mentioned above) Omega. Rolex was founded in London in 1905 by a German called Hans Wilsdorf, who became a naturalized Briton. In 1910, after specializing in the production of improvements in small movements for wristwatches, a Rolex wristwatch was awarded chronometer rating at the School of Horology in Switzerland. This was followed, in 1914, by a Class 'A' certificate, at the Kew Observatory, for a Rolex chronometer wristwatch. The Oyster series started with a patent granted on 29 July 1926. Initially the dust and water-proofing was intended to improve general efficiency but there was soon an advertising campaign, comprising a Rolex Oyster submerged in an aquarium in shop windows.

Their greatest advertisement, though, was probably secured on account of cross-Channel swimmer Mercedes Gleitze, who swam the Channel, in dreadful conditions, beginning at 2.55am on the morning of 7 October 1927 and ending at 6.10pm near St Margaret's Bay, Kent. Having reached land she was greatly celebrated, but owing to a hoax 'Channel swim' shortly after the truth of her feat was doubted and so she decided to make a repeat 'Vindication Swim' on 21 October following. Entering the water at 4.21am, in even worse conditions than before, she had to be taken (semi-comatose) out of the water just seven miles short of her goal, at 2.45pm. This time, she was wearing a Rolex Oyster around her neck, which was found, on examination, to be in perfect order. Her fortitude was much admired and a roistering advertising campaign followed. The fame of the Rolex Oyster watch was secured.

One defect that the early Oysters had was that the use of the winding mechanism caused the hermetic seal to be breached so, in 1931, they invented the 'perpetual' self-winding mechanism in the Rotor model. This charges the watch by movement of the human arm and so avoids breaching of the hermetic seal. Meanwhile, the Rolex Prince had appeared in 1928. During the Second World War the firm famously sent a Rolex watch, free of charge, to any British prisoner of war on receipt of just a simple written application.

Now, every Rolex watch is tested to be waterproof to at least 330 feet; the Submariner to a depth of 1,000 feet and the Sea Dweller to a depth of 4,000 feet.

TAG Heuer

The firm of Heuer was founded in 1860 in Saint-Imier, Switzerland, by Edouard Heuer. From an early stage this firm developed links with sporting events for which split-second timing is important and are involved in several events, including Formula 1 racing. The firm's first wrist chronograph was developed in 1914 and, in 1916, it produced a mechanical stop watch, called the Mikrograph, accurate to one one-hundredth of a second. They also developed early dashboard time-pieces. In 1969, it produced the first automatic chronograph. Tag acquired Heuer in 1985. The famous models include the Carrera, the Grand Carrera and the Monaco.

Ulysse Nardin
This firm was founded in 1846 in Le Locle, Switzerland, by Ulysse Nardin. Long famed for marine chronometers, since 1983 it has produced ranges of highly complicated watches.

Vacheron Constantin
Founded in 1755 by Jean-Marc Vacheron, it acquired its modern name in 1819. Well known for semi-skeleton watches (in which the movement is visible from outside the case), they started machine-making in 1839. Another landmark was one of the thinnest watches ever made (at 1.64 millimetres depth) in 1955 and, in 2005, they made the most complicated two-faced wristwatch in the world.

New watches are, obviously, available from the makers themselves and appointed outlets worldwide. Most firms have websites on which their extensive ranges may be viewed. Examples of businesses that deal in used and vintage watches of the best kinds are Armour Winston, Charles Frodsham and Pieces of Time.

Pocket watch chains, fobs and wristwatch straps

Watch chains come in a great variety, in every type of precious metal. The most familiar is probably the 'Albert' linked chain. Watch chains are seldom seen these days, stretched across a waistcoat, because both waistcoats and pocket watches are out of favour. Once, in the countryside, a leather strap might have been substituted for the chain. It is not especially unusual, even now, to see a watch chain threaded through the lapel buttonhole of a double-breasted coat, with the watch in the outer breast pocket.

Although some makers have made lighter evening chains, it used to be the fashion to wear an evening pocket watch on a plain black fob (in the form of a medallion) and ribbon, in the fob pocket on the right-hand side of the trouser waistband (hence the alternative name of 'fob watch'). Some makers, notably Patek Phillipe, are especially noted for elegant, thin evening wristwatches. Straps for wristwatches come in all variety, from metal bracelet, matching the metal of the watch, to leather, including exotic skins such as crocodile.

Writing instruments

> Beneath the rule of men entirely great,
> The pen is mightier than the sword.
>
> Edward Bulwer-Lytton

The earliest 'writing' instruments had, obviously, been stones on cave walls and from 3100 BC in Mesopotamia cuneiform writing was developed, using reeds on damp clay. The ancient Egyptian Rosetta Stone, which incorporates the same text in hieroglyphic and demotic Egyptian and in ancient Greek, was, later on, used to enhance an understanding of hieroglyphics.

A material from the pith of the aquatic papyrus sedge (*Cyperus papyrus*) that grows by the Nile was developed from 3000 BC. This became used in Egypt, Greece and Rome, in scrolls. From 1500 BC bamboo books started to be used in China and then wax, leaves and wood from the fifth century BC; palm leaves were in use in India and the Buddhists were using thin sheets of birchwood. The Romans in Britain used wood veneer. Double-sided pergamum and parchment came into use by the second century BC and, as well as vellum, became the standard material in Europe between the fourth and fifteenth centuries. Pergamum is made from goat or sheepskin and was invented by the ancient Greeks when the Egyptians banned the export of papyrus. Parchment and vellum are, similarly, made from fine animal skins.

Paper production was discovered in China in AD 105 but it did not reach Europe until the fifteenth century. Stones were used to write in the very earliest times, then from around 1500 BC and the development of the Greek, Hebrew, Byzantine and then Latin alphabets, a utensil called a stylus (the root of the word 'style') had come into use, at first on wax tablets. The Chinese invented India ink using soot, lamp oil, donkey gelatine and musk. Other civilizations used vegetable dyes as ink. The Romans eventually used a reed pen that even carried a reservoir.

From AD 400 there was a different ink developed, using iron salts, nutgalls and gum. Paper mills appeared in Britain in the fourteenth century and the quill pen has been around since AD 700, using (amongst others) goose, swan and crow feathers, preferably from the left wings (curving out for a right-handed scribe), and they were cut and trimmed with the 'penknife'. The Italian, running, or cursive hand was developed by a Venetian in the late fifteenth century.

Lewis Waterman took out a patent for a fountain pen in 1884 but it was not the first fountain pen as such – discounting the Roman reed pens, the oldest fountain pen had been invented by a Frenchman called M Brion in 1702. Peregrine Williamson had an American patent from 1809 and John Sheaffer had a British patent from 1819. John Jacob Parker had a patent for a self-filling pen in 1831. Waterman's great invention, though, was the air-hole in the nib and the internal grooves to moderate the flow of ink. There then followed further innovations in the different methods of filling, including the button, the lever and the click fillers. The ink cartridge was introduced in 1950. There are also 'dip' pens that carry no reservoir and are, sometimes, highly ornamented.

Famous makes of fountain pens include Conway Stewart, Caran d'Ache, Graf von Faber-Castell, Montblanc, Parker, Sheaffer and Waterman. For ranges of new and vintage pens (including the iconic Parker Duofolds and Parker 51s) and repairs to all types there is a business called Penfriend, with two shops in central London.

On fountain pen inks, try to use the inks produced by the makers of the pen that you are using. Also, remember that Parker inks contain a solvent that is not compatible with all other brands of fountain pen.

Graphite pencils have been around since 1564, after the discovery of graphite at Keswick, in England, and rubber erasers have been in the modern form since rubber was vulcanized by Charles Goodyear in 1839.

My favourite pencil is orange and triangular. On one side it reads The Cornish Mines Supplies Co Ltd and then Builders' Merchants, St Austell 2323 and then Penzance 3951, Plymouth 61149. It was given to me by a (seemingly) very old man called Fred, who worked on the site of the old St Austell Foundry, when I was around five years old and I still remember how pleased I was with this unexpected gift. It sits in a pencil box, which contains all sorts of things, including a button hook, an American silver dip pen, small bulldog clips, picture hooks, paper clips, a pebble from a Cornish beach, a key to my parents' house, other pencils from around the same time and more recent ones, including one advertising L'Hotel in São Paulo, a watch case, a horn suit button, a pair of nail clippers, two uncut Rowney pencils (also about forty-five years old), a bookmark, a plastic propelling pencil (promoting the singular merits of some no-doubt excellent banker), a book of matches from the Copacabana Palace Hotel, a PIA emergency sewing kit, and that dust that such collections always attract.

Yard-O-Led propelling pencils

Yard-O-Led silver propelling pencils (so named because they contain a cylindrical device for storing up to a yard of pencil leads) are great pencils to have and there is a big range of styles and sizes.

Pocket or penknives

A pocket knife is often a handy thing to have and, apart from the practical, multi-purpose Swiss Army knives with their multitude of attachments, there are fine makers such as Charles Bennica, Barry Davis and Jean-Pierre Martin. Also recall and look out for the older, fine pieces made by Joseph Rodgers & Sons, mentioned on page 14.

Remember, though, that the carrying of knives is discouraged by the authorities and, apart from having lawful authority or other reasonable excuse (such as a need for one's work, or national or religious costume), in the UK it is legal to carry a blade or a pointed instrument in a public place only if it is no more than three inches long and forms part of a *folding* pocket knife. This excludes lock knives and 'flick' knives, however long their blade or point.

Hip and hunting flasks

As mentioned, watch out for those made by Finnigans. Old hunting flasks are available from sportingcollection.com. Apart from that, the firms mentioned as dealing in luggage also often stock hip flasks.

Money-clips

A silver Morgan dollar makes a fine (although heavy) money-clip. Designed by engraver George T Morgan, following a great silver strike at the Comstock Lode in Nevada, the coin bears a classic image of Lady Liberty on the obverse and an eagle on the reverse. Minted between 1878 and 1904 and then also in 1921, this coin is much revered and collected. A fine gold coin as a money-clip is the Mexican 50 pesos, issued in 1921 to mark the centennial of Mexico's War of Independence. This comes in smaller and at much more outlay than a silver Morgan dollar. This coin bears El Ángel de la Independencia (deriving from the Greek goddess of Victory, Nike) holding a laurel crown in her raised right hand and a broken chain in her outstretched left hand on the obverse and an eagle, sitting on a cactus, devouring a snake on the reverse. These coins are all dated between 1921 and 1947. If you do decide to have a coin-mounted money-clip, remember that it is necessary to preserve the integrity of the coin and not to mount it in a manner that solders or pierces it.

Pins, links, rings and studs

Pins

So far as pins are concerned, you could do with a plain pearl stick pin for formal morning occasions and either a round pearl or a pear-drop shape is appropriate. Pearls have 'lustre' or iridescence and, obviously, the more reflection given off by the surface the better. There are natural (or 'Oriental') pearls and there are cultured pearls.

Natural pearls are the completely natural product of a pearl oyster or a mussel and result from the secretion of nacre over a natural irritant that finds its way through the oyster's lips. This hardens into a form of solid calcium carbonate. There are also saltwater and freshwater pearls. Saltwater pearls (from pearl oysters in the family *Pteriidae*) are the more prized and come from the Persian Gulf and the South Seas, as well as from Tahiti (Tahitian black pearls, especially the blue-green-black, being very famous).

Cultured pearls are the product of a process that was begun in the early twentieth century and popularized by a Japanese oyster farmer called Kokichi Mikimoto. In this, a piece of irritant is introduced into the oyster (it may be a piece of shaped mantle from another shell or a bead) and the nacre is provoked to grow around these substances. Usually the only way surely to tell a natural from a cultured pearl is to X-ray it (gemmologists have the equipment for this). Obviously, natural or 'Oriental' pearls are more prized than cultured pearls.

It is also good to have a couple of jewelled pins for less formal wear; maybe ruby, sapphire (both oxides of aluminium, called corundum) or diamond (a form of carbon). Of course, diamond is the hardest natural substance, followed by corundum and then topaz – the hardness of gems is rated according to Mohs scale.

Emerald (green beryl) and pinkish imperial topaz, although they can be spectacular, are not very masculine stones. Alexandrite (chrysoberyl) is an interesting pleochroic, semi-precious stone, which changes its colour according to the light.

Remember that jewels are generally judged by the 'four Cs' – clarity, colour, cut and carat – by reference to generally accepted standards (although 'grading' of coloured stones is not as universally uniform as the grading of diamonds). The specifics of coloured stone grading lie outside the bailiwick of this book. However, you need to look for stones that have good clarity and are not heavily included (marked inside) with extraneous material or shot through with fissures and flaws and that have a bright, clear colour, appropriate to the type of stone. A sapphire should be a rich royal blue and a ruby should be the colour of a glass of claret; the best emeralds are a rich, grassy green. The best sapphires came from Kashmir (nowadays Sri Lanka is a big producer, although more noted for the cornflower blue colour and padparadscha sapphires, which are of a peachy hue), Burmese sapphires can also prove very fine, the best rubies still come from Burma (Myanmar) and the best emeralds used to come from the Ural Mountains (nowadays they come from Colombia and Brazil).

You need stones that are thoughtfully cut and proportioned (in depth, width and length) to maximize the stone's potential but also evenly cut and, of course, all else being equal, bigger good stones command higher prices than smaller good ones. Stones are measured in carats (equivalent to one fifth of a gram) and each carat comprises one hundred sub-units called 'points'.

Heat treatment of sapphires, rubies and topaz to enhance the colour of the stones is common and reduces the value in comparison with stones that have not been heat-treated. Tanzanite is always heat-treated as part of its finishing. Tanzanite is also becoming scarce and for this reason probably represents a good investment. Emeralds are often subjected to another type of treatment, oiling, to obscure the fissures that commonly occur in them. Indeed, good emeralds that have not been treated attract a very considerable premium in the marketplace, especially if they are clean, because emeralds very often contain significant inclusions.

Diamonds are universally graded mainly according to the colour and the degree of inclusions (internal flaws). The best colour for a white diamond is 'D' and alphabetically this goes down the alphabet but you should not go beyond 'I' or you are entering decidedly yellow-stone territory. The degree of perfection of diamonds is determined according to recognized standards: 'internally flawless' speaks for itself; 'VVS' means 'very, very slightly included' and there are sub-categories of VVS1 and VVS2; 'VS' means 'very slightly included' (this has similar sub-categories); and 'SI' means 'slightly included'. Beyond that you should not go, as heavily 'included' stones seldom have any but industrial use.

Always insist on examining stones in natural light and use a 10x magnification jeweller's loupe (magnifying glass). These can often be bought in shops that sell mineral specimens or collectable stamps and coins. If you are spending a reasonable amount of money, insist on a certificate from a qualified gemmologist, who can verify the stone. If you are spending a great deal, insist on a certificate from a recognized laboratory.

Mounted stones are notoriously difficult to grade. As such many reputable laboratories will not offer certificates for mounted stones. Grading certificates are usually not issued by individual gemmologists but rather by gemmological laboratories. Two of the most highly regarded laboratories are the Gemological Institute of America and American Gem Society Laboratories, as well as the Gübelin Gemmological Laboratories in Lucerne (the last especially for coloured stones, apart from coloured diamonds). Grading certificates from reputable laboratories are technical documents and do not contain any information on value. Appraisals or valuations are done by appraisers (who may or may not be gemmologists). They normally charge a percentage on their own valuation of the stone. Certificates are also available as to any treatment that a stone has, or has not, received. Such treatment is often not fully apparent without the correct equipment. One readily accessible and excellent gemmologist and appraiser is Rosamond Clayton, in Hatton Garden, London.

Apart from these jewelled pins, just a plain gold bar stock safety pin is needed for hunting and, sometimes, these are used to secure an ordinary day tie to the shirt: pinned horizontally, about two thirds of the way down the tie, is usual.

Gold in jewellery comes generally as nine carat, fourteen carat, eighteen carat and twenty-two carat. Each 'carat' of gold represents the presence of one twenty-fourth part of pure gold. The alloy for gold, in carats of eighteen and above, consists of silver and copper. What determines the colour of the gold is the manipulation of the proportions of silver and copper. Rose, or pink, gold has a higher proportion of copper. Green gold has a higher proportion of silver. White gold used to have nickel until nickel was banned (by the EU) as an ingredient for anything that touches the skin directly. Some jewellers, such as Tiffany & Co, stayed away from white gold and preferred platinum because they considered white gold to be 'dirty'. Now, white gold is often achieved using a metal of the platinum family, such as palladium or rhodium.

Cufflinks

Cufflinks should be kept simple and good day links are plain or machined oval or oblong gold plaques, joined by a chain. These can be in yellow or white gold. Evening links might be just plain roundels, ovals or oblongs of mother of pearl or white gold for white tie or yellow gold for black tie; maybe including small, unobtrusive jewels but never anything too flashy. Deakin & Francis and Longmire are renowned for new ranges.

Rings

Men's rings are normally of two types: a plain wedding band (which is not, perhaps, very English) that may come in any kind of gold or other precious metal and a gold signet ring. A signet ring bears the coat of arms or just the crest to which the wearer is entitled (and any motto) in 'negative' (or reverse), in *intaglio* seal engraving, so that the emblem shows up, in relief, the right way around when applied to sealing wax. The engraving may be into a gold table on the ring or into a semi-precious stone (often cornelian, bloodstone, onyx, agate, lapis lazuli or sardonyx) set into it. Sometimes plain gold cufflinks are engraved with armorial devices too. One excellent engraver is Thomas Flack, with a worldwide reputation in this craft. Besides the deep seal engraving a lighter surface engraving can be worked in positive, so that the image appears the right way around on the metal plaque.

Arms, as heraldic devices, derive from the practice of armoured knights using symbols on their shields and their armour with crests mounted on their helms (armour helmets) as marks of identification in medieval tournaments. The Royal Heralds came to record and regulate the use of these devices, which became heritable. Today, in respect of England, Wales, Northern Ireland and the Commonwealth, the Heralds run HM College of Arms, under the Earl Marshal (who is one of the Great Officers of State), and take part in state ceremonials, such as the annual procession and service of the Knights Companion of the Garter, the State Opening of Parliament, state funerals and coronations. The Heralds used a common seal from 1420, received a first Royal Charter of incorporation, from Richard III, in 1484 and a further (their current) Charter from Queen Mary.

In Scotland, there is the Court of the Lord Lyon King of Arms, who is the holder of an ancient office. The first recorded appointment was by Robert the Bruce in 1318. The Lord Lyon is assisted by Officers of Arms. As in England, these are Heralds and Pursuivants and they also have ceremonial duties, including those at such events as the Ceremony of the Keys at Holyrood House, the Installation of the Governor of Edinburgh Castle and the Annual Service of the Order of the Thistle.

Very basically, a full achievement of a coat of arms comprises, firstly, 'the shield', the central part, on which appear the important emblems of the individual concerned in its divisions into 'the field', 'the ordinaries' and the 'common charges'. The helm, by its design and direction, denotes the rank (Gentleman, Esquire, Knight, Baronet, or Baron, Viscount, Earl, Marquis, Duke). 'The crest' is found on the helm; the 'wreath' or 'torse' between helm and crest; any 'coronet' (for Barons upwards) appears beneath the helm; and the 'mantling' is fancy design work around the sides of the shield. 'The supporters', normally animals or mythological creatures, are at the sides of the shield, such as the familiar lion and the unicorn in the Royal Arms; 'the compartment' is the mantling beneath the shield; and the 'motto' appears at the foot of it all, except in Scotland, where it is overall. A blazon of arms is a technical written description of the arms.

The right to bear arms (generally) passes only through the legitimate male heirs of the grantee, although legitimate daughters may also bear arms and 'quarter' (or combine) them with those of their husbands on marriage and, in default of a male heir, a female descendant becomes an heraldic heiress through whom arms become heritable. Women do not use crests as they have no helm, on which the crest (often a real or mythological creature or plant) appeared for the purposes of identification in tournaments and in battle, and the arms of women appear on cartouches (ovals) or lozenges and not shields, except when an heraldic heiress marries and then her arms appear discretely on an inescutcheon of pretence (a small shield) in the centre of her husband's shield. In addition to the arms and the crest, there are also badges and banners (subject to additional petition and grant when arms are granted). The badge may be worn by more than those entitled to bear the arms, for example, by grandchildren, through the female line, of an armigerous man. In Scotland there are clan crests, which members of the clan may use whether they are armigerous or not.

On behalf of the Crown, as *fons honorum* (the fount of honour), arms are still granted by Letters Patent (after vetting of the applicant and payment of a fee for the research and artwork involved) and regulated by the College of Arms, its Heralds and the Court of Chivalry, in respect of England, Wales, Northern Ireland and the Commonwealth and by the Court of the Lord Lyon in Scotland. So far as the first case is concerned, the granting of arms takes place after the presentation of a memorial (petition) to the Earl Marshal and upon the issue of a warrant by him to the Kings of Arms (the senior Heralds). In Scotland, the process is governed by the lodging of a petition to the Court of the Lord Lyon. Since 1592, in Scotland, it has been a criminal offence to display unauthorized arms.

The grant of arms recognizes the attainment of a sufficient 'eminence' to bear arms but it does not, in itself, create any rank or status.

Moreover, the purchase of transferable feudal titles does not, outside Scotland, confer any status either. This is because the Law of Property Act 1922 abolished the estates in land, called 'copyholds', held of the Lord of the Manor. The documents relating to this land are recorded in the Manorial Documents Register. The empty titles of Lords of Manors in England, Wales and Northern Ireland were not expressly abolished and holders of the titles (which remain transferable, by sale or inheritance) are entitled to describe themselves as (for example) John Doe, Lord of the Manor of Blankstead. However, they are not entitled to describe themselves as a 'Lord' by way of prefix to their own names, unless they are also peers or holders of courtesy titles. Occasionally, these feudal titles even bear encumbrances, such as an obligation to contribute to church repair or some service to the Sovereign, such as rendering a pair of white gloves, on certain occasions. According to the *Oxford Guide to Heraldry*: 'Lordship of this or that manor is no more a title than Landlord of the Dog and Duck.'

Scottish Feudal Baronies are a different case and, since legislation brought into force in 2004, these titles have been preserved as dignities but are no longer attached to any land and carry no rights or obligations. Scottish Feudal Barons are entitled to describe themselves as, for example, Richard Roe, Baron of Naeloch, or if he owns lands of Naeloch he might also have a territorial designation and be recognized as Richard Roe of Naeloch, Baron of Naeloch. The Lord Lyon has no jurisdiction over the dispositions of these Baronies, which are heritable and may be bought and sold by way of contract. Where a Barony is bought or inherited, other than by the natural heir on intestacy (to whom the existing arms would automatically pass), then subject to proof that the Barony exists and that the petitioner is the rightful holder of it and is a 'virtuous and well-deserving person', the Lord Lyon has stated that he will recognize the Barony and, in his discretion, grant arms appropriate to the status of Feudal Baron to the petitioner. However, the inclusion of Baronial additaments (certain armorial bearings) in the arms that had been associated with land-holding and feudal functions that are no longer relevant to the holding of the title has been (by legal cases decided or compromised) limited but the shield and the Baronial helm will be awarded. A petition including a prayer for recognition of a territorial jurisdiction will need to be backed by some appropriate land ownership. Moreover, the Lord Lyon is the sole arbiter of what constitutes a 'virtuous and well-deserving person' and a purchaser of a Scottish Feudal Barony has no absolute right to a grant of arms.

Shirt and collar studs

For shirt collar studs for stiff collars maybe just have the cheap and cheerful, easily replaced studs sold by the shirt shops or bought in sets of precious metals from antique and second-hand shops. The pointed 'bayonet' shirt collar stud is particularly efficient for securing the front of a stiff collar. Evening shirt studs for stiff-fronted evening shirts should match the links and be in the materials that I mention above for those or plain pearls for white tie.

Some suppliers

As well as at Wartski, London, and Bentley & Skinner, examples of all of these items of jewellery may be found antique or second-hand in places such as various big and small auctions in town and country, the shops of Camden Passage and of the London Silver Vaults and a great shop in Hatton Garden called Andrew R Ullmann (which presents a disorganized, but delightful, jumble of fine things), as well as other top-of-the-range West End shops, such as Asprey and Garrard (dating back to 1722 and formerly the Crown Jewellers). Indeed so far as antique and second-hand *objets d'art* are concerned, all these places are always worth a visit.

Others are SJ Phillips, Harvey & Gore and A Woodhouse (at the sign of the silver mousetrap). There are also several other shops in the Burlington Arcade selling good-quality antique and second-hand items, such as Armour Winston and Hancocks (founded in 1849 by Charles Frederick Hancock, and, on top of everything else, the only makers of the Victoria Cross).

Luggage

The recent history of luggage and its makers is bound up with the decline in servants, leading to a desire for smaller, portable items of luggage and also with developments in travel, such as the motor car and airplane, leading to a desire for lighter luggage too. Accordingly, vulcanized materials and light alloys have come to the forefront of mass-produced luggage-making. However, many people like to seek out vintage luggage in leather and wood construction; intact but, preferably, nicely patinated and, maybe, decorated with old destination labels.

Look out for the names of the famous makers, often found actually stamped on the leather, and be prepared to treat the leather carefully with saddle soap and the proprietary creams for leather preservation. Also watch out for protective canvas covers and best four-lever locks in silver, gunmetal or brass. Materials in the best cases range from cowhide (the best being Connolly leather) to Morocco (hand-tanned kid, to bring up the small, flecked bird's eye grain), shagreen (sharkskin, sometimes faked with ray-skin), crocodile and alligator on to white, rawhide (bleached leather) with linings of Morocco, cloth ticking, broadcloth silk, velvet and canvas. Fine dressing cases are fitted out with compartments and glass and crystal bottles, often with tops made of precious metals.

Some famous luggage makers' names to look out for include Asprey, EE Berry, Brachet, Thomas Brigg & Sons, Bramah & Co, J Chauret, Alfred Clark, Davis & Co, Drew & Sons, Ducas (Paris), Dupont, Alfred Dunhill, Ephtée (Bordeaux), Finnigans, R & S Gamage, Garrard, Globe-Trotter, Goldpfeil, Goyard, Hermès, Holland & Holland (guns and gun cases), Jabez Cliff & Co (saddlers and loriners and the oldest golf bag makers), F Lansdowne, Mappin & Webb, Norfolk Hide, James Purdey (guns and gun cases), Swaine Adeney and Louis Vuitton, the last still making the large matching sets of luggage for those with the time and space to make use of it all.

Apart from auctions and second-hand shops, for finding vintage luggage these businesses are amongst those that also deal in it: achome.co.uk and vintageluggage.net.

Bear in mind also that besides the makers mentioned above that are still in business there are also such firms as John Lobb, WS Foster & Son (with Henry Maxwell) and George Cleverley that make bespoke leather goods, apart from boots and shoes. Moreover, these businesses sometimes have uncollected luggage repairs and, after a suitable period, they sell these off, as well as uncollected bespoke shoes, boots and slippers.

Mary Upshire, contactable through fineshootingaccessories.com, trained at the renowned Finnigans, which boxed, packed and cased the men and women of the far-flung Empire, and she still turns out bespoke luggage as well as sporting accessories.

Finnigans was founded in 1875 by Benjamin Finnigan at 16 Market Street, Liverpool and had another shop in Salford besides the London shop at 18 New Bond Street. Finnigans also sold small items such as superb wallets and hip flasks, which are also certainly worth looking out for.

Apart from all of those, there are Papworth and also Pickett.

Wallets and notecases

Some fine examples of these can, sometimes, be picked up second hand, even in charity (thrift) shops. Other than that, there are shops such as Cartier, Ducas, Dunhill, Dupont and Pickett, all of which carry a regular stock. Firms such as WS Foster and Henry Maxwell will make up bespoke wallets to individual designs for very little more than best stock wallets available elsewhere.

Umbrellas and sticks

I dealt with ranges and suppliers of umbrellas and sticks in my book *History of Men's Fashion*. Briefly to summarize: for old and new umbrellas and sticks and canes, there are James Smith & Sons and Swaine Adeney Brigg; for umbrellas alone, there is also Fox Umbrellas; for collectable walking sticks and canes there is David German.

I also take this opportunity to make a correction to my earlier book, in which I said that Fox made John Steed's sword umbrellas for the 1960s–1970s television series *The Avengers*. In fact, both Fox and James Smith supplied ordinary umbrellas for the series, but only James Smith has retained records showing that they manufactured and supplied the sword umbrellas.

Buttonholes

I also covered buttonholes in my first book, but this chapter would be incomplete without some inclusion on the subject. For formal morning and full evening dress, the gardenia (*Gardenia jasminoides*) is just the thing. For a dark city suit or with a dinner jacket a crimson carnation is entirely suitable. Substitutes for the gardenia might be a white carnation or camellia. The Edwardians were very fond of orchids for nearly any time of day or night and red, white, orange and pink tea roses are also splendid flowers for day wear. Great suppliers of plants are Clifton Nurseries, McBean's Orchids and Peter Beales Roses.

CHAPTER 4

Some Fine Drinks and Sweets

O for a draught of vintage! that hath been
Cooled a long age in the deep-delved earth,
Tasting of Flora and the country green,
Dance, and Provencal song, and sunburnt mirth.

From 'Ode to a Nightingale', John Keats

The Essential Cocktail and Apéritif List

Before I turn to some receipts and history, I must just mention the wonderful book by David A Embury, *The Fine Art of Mixing Drinks*, which is a great read on this subject, most importantly for his division of cocktails into two basic types: sour and aromatic. However, do not expect any clear explanation anywhere that concludes precisely the *unrivalled* origin of the word 'cocktail', or the plain origination of the first such drink. Both are, though, probably much older than the nineteenth century – for example, Dr Johnson even mixed up gin and wine for James Boswell and called it 'a veritable cocktail of a drink'. Sazerac – originally a cognac and bitters cocktail – is, sometimes, said to be the first modern drink of this type (invented by Antoine Peychaud in the 1830s in Louisiana and, possibly, named after a brand of cognac, Sazerac-de-Forge et Fils) rather than the Martini, which itself probably started off as a far sweeter drink than its famous modern descendant, the Dry Martini. I do not specifically cover single-malt Scotch whiskies or even others – Irish and American (bourbon and rye) and even Finnish and Japanese – including the blends as there are so many of them and they are both so individual and plentiful that every man can make up his own mind easily enough what his tastes are here. The word 'whisky' derives from the Gaelic *uisge beatha*, meaning 'water of life'.

Occasionally, I mention 'alcohol by volume', and this just means what it says, expressed as a percentage. 'Alcoholic proof' or 'degrees of alcoholic proof' is a different measure of alcoholic content with an interesting history, although it has been replaced in the UK by the EU measurement of alcohol by volume. In the United States of America alcoholic proof is measured at 60°F and is the same as twice the percentage figure of the alcohol by volume. The old system in the UK, dating from the eighteenth century, was the Sikes system for measuring degrees of proof spirit. A 100°-proof spirit contained enough alcohol to enable gunpowder soaked in it to ignite. This was the test used to ensure that sailors' rum rations had not been diluted. Later on, hydrometers were used to make the proof spirit test, until 1980, when the UK bowed the knee to the EU and adopted the alcohol by volume measurement system.

Americano

This comprises equal measures of sweet vermouth, such as Martini Rosso, and bitters, usually Campari, served over ice with a splash of soda and a twist or slice of orange. It was originally formulated by Gaspare Campari in one of his cafés in Milan in the 1860s and named the Milano-Torino because of the names of the places making the ingredients. However, it was renamed in honour of American tourists, who favoured it. For my money, it does not hold a candle to the later refinement of it in the Negroni (see below).

Amontillado sherry

There are many good, nice and nutty amontillado sherries on the market, such as Amontillado del Puerto, Almacenista Obregon, Emilio Lustau and Berry's Amontillado Estilo Medium Dry, both available from Berry Bros & Rudd. Preferably, serve this at room temperature in either proper tulip-shaped sherry *copitas* or fluted schooners. If you happen to be having consommé as an *hors d'oeuvre*, bring it to the table with you. If you are being served by Spanish waiters and you pronounce the 'll' in the English fashion you will probably get something unexpected in your *tapas*, even though it was the British who kick-started the emergence of the fortified wines of Jerez, Oporto, Marsala and Madeira to help the wines ship better. This British influence is evidenced to this day by the names of some of the shippers.

Bellini

This was created by Giuseppe Cipriani, who opened Harry's Bar in Venice in 1931 and, although it is not clear when he created the drink, he named it after Venetian Renaissance painter Giovanni Bellini in 1948. It comprises Italian prosecco and a quarter of a skinned white peach. The peach should be hand pulped and sieved and then mixed with the prosecco. In some places now, a Bellini also includes a measure of crème de pêche and a dash of peach bitters as well as a peach ball. However, none of these is in the original receipt. Originally, it was a seasonal drink (from June to September) in Italy, during the period that white peaches were in season, but the availability of frozen peach purée means that it may be made all year round.

Black Velvet

Not just a cocktail, but a great drink with shellfish, especially oysters, lobster, langoustines or crab, and very easy to make: *gently* add half a jug of champagne to half a jug of stout and serve in a half-pint tankard or a deep champagne goblet. A good Californian cava or a prosecco might harmlessly be substituted for the champagne, although I am sure that James Bond and his creator Ian Fleming were not such skinflints when they enjoyed this at the original Scott's Restaurant (in Coventry Street, off Leicester Square, these days located in Mount Street, Mayfair).

Bloody Mary

This is my very favourite Christmas morning drink and I like mine extra strong. The basic combination of tomato juice and vodka was probably first served, under this name, in the King Cole Bar of the St Regis Hotel in Manhattan in 1939 by George Jessel. Fernand Petiot, who later worked there, told the *New Yorker* magazine for July 1964 that he had taken this combination up and improved it by adding the seasoning and other standard ingredients. Put a large measure of vodka (any reasonable brand) per person into a jug of cracked ice and add tomato juice, a good dollop of Worcester sauce and several drops of Tabasco or other good chilli sauce, maybe a spoon of horseradish sauce, grind in a good bit of black pepper and add celery salt just to taste. To this add the juice of several lemons or limes (limes for preference) and a good dash of amontillado sherry per person. Thoroughly mix this together (up and down as well as around) with a tablespoon and serve in long and generous highball glasses with a stick of celery in the glass and cashew nuts and pimiento-stuffed olives on the side. Hand-cut, homemade potato crisps, sprinkled with parmesan cheese, also go very well. The splendid addition of the amontillado sherry was taught to me, in around 1994, by John, the then landlord of the Seven Stars Inn in Carey Street, behind the Royal Courts of Justice in the Strand and one of the oldest surviving pubs in London. If it is Christmas morning and you are the host then better to remember, before you have a second one, that you have to carve the goose or turkey; before you have a third, remember that you have another meal to consume … Moreover, you could hardly do better than to start Boxing Day with this, as it is a first-rate hangover cure.

Bronx

There are other claimants but, according to his *New York Times* obituary, Bronx restaurateur Joseph S Sormani originated this variation on the Martini around the turn of the twentieth century. The modern receipt is: six parts gin, three parts sweet red vermouth, two parts dry vermouth and three parts orange juice, shaken over ice and served in a Martini glass.

Buck's Fizz

This is named after Captain Herbert Buckmaster, soldier, man about town and first husband of the early twentieth-century pinup and actress Gladys Cooper, who was supposed to have been so beautiful that people had been known to weep when they met her. He was the founder of Buck's Club in Clifford Street, Mayfair, which was meant to be a club aimed specifically at his generation who had been through the Great War and where, conveniently, he lived when in town. He was a pugnacious man but with such a passion for gardenias, with their gloriously scented, waxy, white blooms, that he bought his second wife, Nellie, a flower shop next to the club so that he would have a constant supply. According to the biography of Gladys Cooper by their grandson, Sheridan Morley, after Buck's divorce from Gladys their son had been the subject of a cartoon, complimentary to his boxing, in the evening paper, and both Buck and Gladys applied to the cartoonist to buy the original. The cartoonist approached Buck in some confusion as to what to do. Buck instantly provided the solution: 'The answer, my dear fellow, is very simple – I shall buy the picture and you shall send it round to Miss Cooper's dressing room.' I have heard two stories regarding the invention of Buck's Fizz. The first is that, in 1921, Buck challenged Pat MacGarry, the club's legendary first head barman, to find a use for a quantity of leftover champagne after a party and so was born this cocktail and summer tipple, which, besides champagne and freshly squeezed orange juice (in proportions depending on taste), is said to contain a secret ingredient, maybe Grenadine, but known for sure only to the club barmen. If this is true, then you can have a real Buck's Fizz only in the club. The second story is that he asked his barman to replicate a peach-and-champagne cocktail that he had enjoyed on a golfing holiday in France and the barman, short of peach juice, substituted orange juice instead. I prefer the first story as it has so much more panache.

Campari and soda

This is very simple – just pour your measure over ice and top it up with soda, but it could always do with a stir. Campari was devised as a type of bitters by Gaspare Campari in Italy in the mid-nineteenth century and the full ingredients remain a closely guarded secret. I have seen people drink it neat – but they have their own secret!

Champagne brut

This was famously invented, at Hautvillers in 1668, by a monk called Dom Perignon, who cut short the ageing of some wine during its fermentation period by bottling it. The people of Languedoc, apparently, claim that they had got there first. Still, a good plain champagne is hard to beat to get the party swinging and there are even some people, such as the playwright and novelist the late John Mortimer, who swear by starting the day with a glass.

This puts me in mind of an absolutely ideal champagne breakfast. I should start with a fresh tropical fruit salad comprising the following: sliced or diced fruits such as pineapple, papaya, orange, grapefruit, banana, passion fruit seeds, peaches, kiwi fruit and guava. That's for the first glass. For the second and third glasses, I should have some sliced and lard-fried Cornish hog's pudding, a couple of rashers of home-cured smoked, back bacon plus three of streaky, a couple of well-made sausages of any type from an increasingly large range (from venison to lamb), all with strong English mustard, halved, fried plum tomatoes, fried bread, two fried Rhode Island Red or Black Copper Maran eggs and fresh field mushrooms fried in butter. (The eggs should be fried in duck fat and all the rest in proper lard.) With this, a glass of chilled Badoit mineral water, a pot of Assam tea (taken with just a dash of milk), some slices of thick-cut toast and Frank Cooper's (or, better still, homemade) extra-thick-cut Oxford-style marmalade. After a brief pause, I should have a couple of cups of black Jamaican Blue Mountain coffee, which, just like Havana cigars in their own way, knocks the competition into a cocked hat. If that wouldn't set one up, heaven help us. Come to think of it, have a Havana cigar with the coffee – maybe a Cohiba Lanceros, and better make that a whole pot of coffee – as you sit back on your rattan-seated rocker, in your tropical veranda, and read the ex-pat pages of *The Daily Telegraph*.

There are several very good non-vintage brands of champagne on the market, of both white and rosé champagne. Examples, available from Berry Brothers & Rudd are: Veuve Clicquot ('The Widow') Yellow Label Brut; Charles Heidsieck Brut; Champagne Marguet Rosé Grand Cru; Billecart-Salmon Brut Rosé; Pol Roger Brut; Louis Roederer Brut Premier and Bollinger Special Cuvée Brut. Also check out selections at Justerini & Brooks and Waitrose as well as Oddbins (branches everywhere).

Nyetimber English sparkling wines have come a long way and there is Nyetimber Classic Cuvée made with sixty per cent pinot noir grapes as well as the première Cuvée Blanc de Blancs.

Of course, if you are pushing the boat out, there are great vintages to be had, although those before 1959 are certainly tiring and, of the older vintages, you'd be better off with a 1982 or 1983 or 1985. I always wanted to have a bottle of one of the immediate post-Second World War vintages that miraculously made it through (and are still available) but, alas, time has probably done its worst to most of them. Some other recommendations that should not disappoint are: 1998 Vintage Pol Roger Sir Winston Churchill; 1999 Vintage Dom Perignon; 2003 Vintage Gosset Celebris Rosé; 1995 Vintage Pol Roger Extra Dry; 1993 and 1995 Dom Perignon; 1988 Piper Heidsieck Rare Vintage; 2000 and 2002 Louis Roederer Cristal; 1998 Vintage Krug; 1981 and 1985 Vintage Krug Collection. Very small producer Diebolt-Vallois's Fleur de Passion 1995 has had an excellent press too. The 1996 vintage for champagne has been hailed by some as the best since 1928.

For a stag do, you will choose a white variety of brut champagne and, maybe, serve it in quarter-pint silver tankards. For mixed gatherings, champagne flutes or coupes are appropriate. Champagne coupes (dishes), so popular in former times, seem to have gone out of favour but, except for an argument that flutes retain the bubbles better, there is no logical reason for this that I can discern, and dishes are more likely to make the bubbles tickle the ladies' noses. An aeronautical engineer once told me that inverting a spoon in the neck of unused, opened champagne bottles before you put them in the 'fridge *does* actually retard the evaporation of the gas, although she did not expatiate on the scientific reason for this. But it does seem to work, to assist the morrow's Buck's Fizz. I insist on ignoring those who, in turn, insist in telling me that this is a myth.

But do remember never to over-chill champagne (or any drink for that matter), as over-chilling will both kill the flavour and dampen the effervescence. Fine champagne and still whites are best served at between eight to ten °C and lesser wines at maybe four to eight °C. Reds are generally best at between fourteen to eighteen °C and Port should be served at eighteen °C.

Champagne cocktail

This comprises a sugar cube, soaked in brandy, and a dash of Angostura bitters, all topped up with champagne.

Cuba Libre

Named after the battle cry of the Cuban Liberation Army meaning 'A Free Cuba' during the failed Ten Years' War (of Independence, 1868–1878), this most popular drink comprises simply two-to-one of cola and (usually white) rum over ice with a wedge of lime in a highball glass. Coca-Cola did not reach Cuba until 1900, and there is some evidence to suggest that the first drink combining 'rum and coke' took place in a bar in Cuba in August 1900. However, the cola drink had been around for some time in America as a chemist in Georgia, called John Pemberton, invented a non-alcoholic 'health drink' in 1885. This contained both cocaine and cola. Cocaine comes from the plant *Erythroxylum coca* and cola comes from the cola nut of the cola tree, *Sterculioideae cola*. Frank Mason Robinson thought of the name Coca-Cola, which became its brand name. Today no commercial cola drink contains cocaine and few even contain the bitter extract of the cola nut. Schweppes carbonated water long before Coca-Cola and had a patent in 1783. To prevent the corks drying out and the drinks going flat, they also designed rounded bottles that could not stand upright.

Daiquiri

This is also called a Caipirinha in Brazil and, maybe, derives from what became the Royal Naval grog: rum, lime juice and sugar (the lime juice warding off scurvy), a popular drink for a long time across the Caribbean and, as the Caipirinha, it is the national drink of Brazil, scotching the myth that it was invented by American mining engineers in a bar called Venus in Santiago, Cuba, in 1905. Papa Hemingway used to drink the Papa Doble in the Floridita Bar, Havana, involving a larger-than-usual measure of rum (use Cane 10 if you can get it). Try it with eight parts of white rum, a couple of measures of lime juice, the juice of half a grapefruit and six drops of maraschino, shaken over crushed ice and strained into a Martini or an Old Fashioned glass.

Dry Martini – gin or vodka

This is very simple in conception and may be the legitimate descendant of a sweeter gin-based drink devised by a bartender in Martinez, California for a celebrating gold prospector in the middle of the nineteenth century. Although the Dry Martini probably originated in New York it was famously made by Harry Craddock, head barman of the American Bar in the Savoy Hotel, too. Simply take your measures of gin or vodka for each person and a measure, to suit the taste, of dry vermouth; the less vermouth, the drier the Martini. The main brands here are Noilly Prat, Martini and Cinzano. Add these and crushed ice either to a mixing jug or to a shaker. I also add a dash of fresh lime juice, but this is not in the normal receipt. Then either stir or shake and strain to serve with a twist of lemon or lime rind in a Martini glass. The derivation of James Bond's prescription of 'shaken, not stirred' is described under Vesper Martini, below. Some people, such as the writer W Somerset Maugham, maintain that the Dry Martini actually tastes better stirred and not shaken. Try each method and decide for yourself. The suitable gins are Tanqueray, Beefeater, Booth's, Seagers, but not Plymouth, as it is not dry enough. If you are ordering this in a bar, don't be afraid to ask for your favourite brands – indeed, the same goes for the constituents of any mixed drink or straight-up drinks, such as Scotch, which come in many different brands and types. Alessandro Palazzi, bar manager of Dukes Hotel, uses frozen ingredients and omits the ice, as it dilutes the drink.

Fino sherry
There are several very good brands of this, which are readily available, such as East India Sherry, Emilio Lustau, Berry's Fino Jerez, Oloroso Viejo 30 years Hidalgo VORS (dated sherry). Serve the drier varieties slightly chilled, in *copitas* or sherry schooners.

French 75
This one was devised by a First World War French–American flying ace called Raoul Lufbery. He liked champagne but preferred it with a kick. To make this you take two ounces of dry gin, half an ounce of simple syrup and one ounce of lemon juice and shake that all over ice. You strain this into two chilled champagne flutes and top up with brut champagne.

Gibson Martini
This is a Dry Martini just served with a cocktail onion in place of the lemon or lime twist. There is a charming story that this derives from a teetotal host who, to avoid denying his guests the pleasures of their Dry Martinis and causing them embarrassment, had for himself glasses of chilled water laid on, distinguished, for identification purposes, by the presence of the onion in place of the lemon twist. Cocktail onions are, generally, insipid little things and far better, for the real Gibson, to run to a nice pickled shallot – but in a big glass.

Green Vesper Martini
Substitute Absinthe for the Lillet and lime peel for lemon.

Harvey Wallbanger
There are a couple of contenders for its invention but the nicest story is the legend that it was named after a Manhattan Beach surfer called Harvey who banged against the walls on leaving the bar (presumably with a six-foot three-and-a-half-inch white rabbit in tow) after a few of his favourite tipple. Take a highball glass of ice and pour in three parts of vodka and six parts of fresh orange juice and stir. Then float one part of Vanilla Galliano on the top and garnish with a glâcé cherry and an orange slice on a stick.

Horse's Neck

Originally, in 1890, this was just ginger ale and ice, garnished with a spiral of lemon peel. By the end of the first decade of the twentieth century it included brandy or bourbon. The modern formulation is one part brandy or bourbon, three parts ginger ale and a dash of Angostura bitters, poured over ice in an Old Fashioned glass and garnished with a spiral of lemon peel.

Kir Royale

Pour a measure of crème de cassis (blackcurrant liqueur) into a champagne flute and top this up with a reasonable non-vintage champagne, prosecco or cava, and enjoy! Plainly, do not use vintage champagne in cocktails. This cocktail is said to be named after a mid-twentieth-century French priest and long-time mayor of Dijon, called Félix Kir, in honour of his French Resistance activities, but the concoction has been known for longer. An ordinary Kir cocktail comprises crème de cassis and a white Burgundy called Aligoté.

Long Island Iced Tea

This cocktail seems to have originated at the (now demolished) Oak Beach Inn, Long Island in the late 1970s and is served in a highball glass: mix together, over ice, three parts each of vodka, gin, white rum, triple sec, tequila; five parts of lemon juice; six parts of gomme syrup and a dash of Coca-Cola and garnish with a slice of lemon. Drink this one sitting down.

Manhattan

This comprises a mixture of rye whiskey and sweet vermouth in proportions to suit one's taste, a dash of Angostura bitters, stirred over ice and strained into a Martini glass, garnished with a maraschino cherry on a stalk. It certainly hails from Manhattan and was probably first mixed there in the 1860s. Sometimes called the 'King of Cocktails', it was favoured by Frank Sinatra and the Rat Pack.

Margarita

As this is a tequila-based cocktail, firstly, frost some Martini glasses in the freezer and then edge the rims with lime juice and turn them upside down on a board of finely ground table salt to coat the rims. Take two shots of tequila, three quarters of a shot of triple sec and a shot of lime juice and pour into a shaker over ice; shake and serve.

Mimosa

This is the name of an American Buck's Fizz.

Mojito

This is an old Cuban cocktail, which may trace its origins back to a similar sixteenth-century local drink, named in honour of Sir Francis Drake, scourge of the Caribbean – '*El Draque*'. The modern version includes white rum, sugar or sugar cane juice, lime juice, ice and mint. Take three parts of lime juice, sprigs of mint and castor sugar (or cane juice) to taste and muddle them together; add to this four parts of rum over ice, in a highball glass, top up with soda and garnish with a sprig of mint.

Negroni

This is a famed Italian cocktail and ideal before a traditional Italian meal. It is said to have been invented by Count Camillo Negroni in Bar Casoni, Florence in 1920 when he asked for gin in his Americano in place of soda. So a Negroni comprises equal measures of dry gin, bitters – usually Campari – and sweet vermouth – such as Martini Rosso – served over ice with a twist of orange rind in an Old Fashioned tumbler. James Bond has one (made with Gordon's gin) in the short story *Risico*, from the *For Your Eyes Only* collection, although Bond's first drink in the first Fleming book (*Casino Royale*) is, actually, an ordinary Americano.

Noilly Prat

The first dry vermouth, dating from 1813, it is also called French vermouth. The dry version at eighteen per cent alcohol by volume is ideal for making a Dry Martini.

Old Fashioned

Mix a sugar cube, a dash of bitters and one tablespoon of water in an Old Fashioned glass; add a shot of blended whisky and stir with a twist of lemon and ice. Add a slice of orange and of lemon to the top and finish with a glâcé cherry.

Pastis and Anise

Until it was banned in 1915 in France, Absinthe had been produced by Pernod Fils and Ricard (now merged). After the ban, they turned their attention to the production of a similar concoction, omitting the dreaded wormwood. This included the famed Pernod, which is an anise-flavoured spirit normally at forty per cent alcohol by volume and best diluted with chilled mineral water in the ratio of one to five.

Pimm's No 1 Cup

This is *the* drink for mad dogs and Englishmen out in the midday sun: add appropriate measures per person to a large glass jug of ice, sprigs of mint, slices of orange, lime, lemon and chunks of cucumber (maybe even cherries, pineapple, grapefruit), and top it all up with a decent sparkling lemonade: a home-made real lemonade injected with gas by a soda-stream is the ideal. The result is not as innocent as it looks, so beware, and certainly sit under a shady tree!

Pina Colada

This is a drink that, more than any other, summons up vistas of azure seas and sparkling golden sands, edged with bendy coconut trees and spangled with bright parasols; shading girls with shining, golden thighs langorously stretched out on gaudy towels. But it has a conflicted history. The earliest version of all was just, as a straight translation suggests, strained pineapple. The first alcoholic version might have been produced by a Puerto Rican pirate called Roberto Confresi in the 1820s, to keep his crew happy. His drink comprised pineapple (crushed with the hilt of a cutlass), coconut cream (scooped out with a dagger's blade) and white rum – and so he would seem to pass the post as the creator of the first version of the modern drink, even though it doesn't sound like a typical pirate's drink of the Yo Ho Ho variety. However, his drink seems to have been lost to the world on his death in 1825, until rival claimants sprang up for its revival in the twentieth century. There are references in newsprint, between 1922 and 1950, to a drink with this name and general receipt. Apart from those, the Caribe Hilton Hotel in Puerto Rico claims, with astonishing specificity, that their barman, Ramon Monchito Marrero, invented it on 15 August 1954, but other places claim it as their own too, such as a restaurant called Barrachina, also in Puerto Rico, and that even has a plaque declaring that it had been the invention of Don Ramon Portas Mingot in 1963. Whatever the truth of its origins, you can make it as follows: take three parts of white rum, one part of coco cream and three parts of pineapple juice (or, better still, crushed pineapple) and blend it all together with pulverized ice until smooth and serve it in a goblet with a garnish of sliced pineapple, a maraschino cherry – and a smile.

Pink gin

This is, traditionally, the Royal Navy's choice in the wardroom; as such, Plymouth Gin (not so dry as London Dry), again the Navy's choice, makes the perfect pink gin. Swirl a few drops of Angostura bitters around in the glass, just to line it, and pour away the excess ('Bitters in or out, Sir?' 'Out, please.'); add your measure of gin and top up with ice-cold, still mineral water to suit. There is no need to stir this.

Pisco Sour

This is a South American cocktail, taking part of its name from the place where a grape liquor called pisco was first distilled in the sixteenth century, to avoid Spanish prohibitions on wine production. It is a cocktail over which there is much rivalry to this day between Chile and Peru but it seems to have been invented by one Victor 'Gringo' Morris in his bar in Lima in the 1920s. Take eight parts pisco; four parts lime juice; three parts simple syrup and one egg white and shake over ice or blend together. Strain the mixture into an Old Fashioned glass and sprinkle bitters over the foam: these may be either local bitters, such as Amargo, or Angostura.

Rob Roy

This is a variation on a Manhattan, which is made with Scotch whisky and named after the Scottish folk hero Rob Roy MacGregor (1671–1734). Adding Drambuie to a Rob Roy makes it into a Robbie Burns (1759–1796), named after the celebrated Scottish poet, author of many poems including 'Auld Lang Syne' and whose birthday is still marked with celebration on 25 January ('Burns Night'). At the supper, a large sheep sausage (traditionally cooked in a sheep's stomach) called a haggis is piped to the table and 'addressed' in a poem called 'Address to a Haggis'. Scotch whisky is the usual accompaniment!

Rusty Nail

This is a simple mix of nine parts Scotch and five parts Drambuie, served over ice, and gently stirred in an Old Fashioned glass.

Sake

This is Japanese rice beer – as it is brewed – but it tends to be called 'rice wine' and is a favourite with sushi. Normal grade table Sake is often drunk at body temperature – however, the grade of Sake to be drunk and the food to be eaten with it will influence the temperature at which it is offered and it might range from over ice to hot. Tamanohikari is a reliable brand, which includes different grades.

Sazerac

This is said by some to have been the first modern American cocktail, named by John Schiller in 1859 in New Orleans. The present-day version of this drink is as follows: you take an Old Fashioned glass and pack it with ice and allow this to stand. In a second glass you place a sugar cube and three dashes of Peychaud's Bitters to which you bring one-and-a-half ounces of rye whiskey and mix it all. You empty the ice from the other glass and line the glass with Absinthe,

Herbsaint or Pernod pastis. You then pour the mixture into this glass and garnish with a twist of lemon. Originally this was made with cognac instead of rye whiskey and the drink was named after the brand of cognac used: Sazerac-de-Forge et Fils.

Absinthe (also made by Pernod) was banned in some places for many years but it is again available and permitted and can be taken as a drink after the ritual preparation, which properly is described below. Absinthe is a highly alcoholic *apéritif* spirit infused with flavour from a usual minimum of five herbs such as green anise, Florence fennel (*Foeniculum vulgare dulce*), grand wormwood (*Artemisia absinthium*), Roman wormwood (*Artemisia pontica*), lemonbalm (*Melissa officinalis*) and hyssop (*Hyssopus officinalis*). It is traditionally 55 to 72 per cent by volume of alcohol (or 110° to 144° proof) and was banned in France from 1915, although manufacture continued elsewhere, such as in Spain, where Papa Hemingway combined it with champagne to make 'Death in the Afternoon': indeed! There is a business that sells pre-ban bottles of Absinthe and also modern versions at these internet sites: oxygenee.com/vintage and absintheclassics.com. The ritual preparation is: pour a *dose* of absinthe in a glass and place a sugar cube on a flat, perforated spoon. Rest the spoon on the rim of the glass and soak the sugar in iced water and slowly and, in a steady stream, run iced water over the sugar until the absinthe *louches* from peridot green to an opaque creamy colour and you have about three or four parts water to one part Absinthe. Then you drink it – but never alone, and never in the dark. Also just remember (while you can) that Absinthe makes the heart grow fonder – and the memory too. Now ... where was I?

Sidecar

... Ah, yes, in the sidecar, and certainly not driving, as was not one contender for *this* drink's invention, an American officer in Paris in the First World War. He was supposedly driven to a particular bar in a motorbike sidecar to drink the stuff (see Embury's *The Fine Art of Mixing Drinks*). Others attribute its invention to Pat MacGarry, head barman of Buck's Club in the 1920s, who made it up for an American officer who used to arrive at the club in a sidecar. It is made as follows. Takc two measures of brandy and one measure of triple sec plus one measure of lemon juice and shake them over ice. Strain into a sugar-rimmed cocktail glass and serve with a lemon twist.

Screwdriver

This is basically vodka (or gin) and orange juice over ice and, reputedly, derives its name from the practice of American engineers (presumably on grounds of economy) surreptitiously adding their own vodka to their bar-bought orange juice in the Park Hotel and then stirring the drinks with their screwdrivers. The modern receipt is to add one part vodka to two parts of orange juice over ice and stir. This is served in a highball glass, garnished with a slice of orange.

Stinger

This is simply half-and-half of cognac and white crème de menthe, shaken over ice and strained.

Tequila Sunrise

This drink was devised at the Arizona Biltmore Resort in Phoenix, Arizona (established in 1929 and once owned by the Wrigley's Gum manufacturing family). Besides being the place where this drink was invented, its pool is the place where composer Irving Berlin wrote several songs, including 'White Christmas'. The original cocktail comprised tequila, crème de cassis, lime juice and soda, over ice. The modern version is made by pouring three parts of tequila, six parts of orange juice and one part of grenadine syrup over ice, in a highball glass, and observing its sunrise colours before enjoying its taste, presumably at sunset rather than sunrise – but who knows, and, if you're actually at the Arizona Biltmore Resort, who cares?

Tom Collins

Probably first described in Jerry Thomas's book *The Bartender's Guide*, the modern receipt is to put ice in a tall glass and add a shot of dry gin and two ounces of lemon juice, together with a teaspoon of plain syrup; top this up with soda and stir; garnish with a twist of lemon and a glâcé cherry on a stick.

Vesper Martini

A little while ago, in response to a communication from me, the bar manager of Dukes Hotel in St James's, Alessandro Palazzi, telephoned me to deny that his 1950s' predecessor had invented the Vesper Martini, described in Ian Fleming's 1953 James Bond novel *Casino Royale*, although he confirmed that Dukes Hotel had been a favourite haunt of Ian Fleming and the 1950s' bar manager had used the phrase, taken up by Fleming for Bond, 'shaken, not stirred'. The true Vesper is a Martini served in a deep champagne goblet and comprises three measures of Gordon's gin, one of vodka and half a measure of Kina Lillet, shaken over ice and served with a thin slice of lemon peel. Gordon's gin has been reduced in strength since the original receipt was described (Tanqueray or Beefeater Crown Jewel is the correct strength) and the nearest drink to Kina Lillet now in production is Lillet Blonde (also called Lillet Blanc). Kina Lillet was first made towards the end of the nineteenth century in Bordeaux and was a fruit-and-spice-flavoured *apéritif* wine. The substitute lacks the bitterness of the original, deriving from the high presence of quinine, but you can correct this with a pinch of quinine powder. Quinine derives from the bark of a South American tree, called cinchona or, locally, kinakina (*Cinchona officinalis*), and is famously found in Indian tonic water, which was drunk with gin to keep malaria at bay. Kingsley Amis, in *The James Bond Dossier*, suggests that, in fact, Kina Lillet, with its quinine, would have made too bitter a drink and that Lillet vermouth (Lillet Dry) should have been used. Stolichnaya 100 Proof Vodka should be used in a Vesper.

The first thing that strikes me about all this is how many bar managers in all the hotels in all the towns in all the world would place a call just to *deny* the claim that his predecessor had (according to some urban myth) invented this drink, and deny it in the centenary year of Fleming's birth, with all the publicity surrounding the latest film *Quantum of Solace*, in which the cocktail makes another appearance? It is, by the way, interesting to reflect how a James Bond action movie can result from a short story about a faithless wife and the payback from her husband!

That Ian Fleming had a hand in the invention of the Vesper Martini is supported by John Griswold's *Ian Fleming's James Bond*: when Fleming started to spend the English winter in sunny Jamaica, he used to visit an elderly British couple in the early evening. At 6.00pm their servant would announce 'Vespers are served!', referring to a drink for the time of evening prayer – a sun-downer. This drink comprised frozen rum, fruit and herbs. Fleming's great friend Ivar Bryce maintained that this is where Fleming got the first name of the double agent in *Casino Royale*, Vesper Lynd. In the course of Fleming's writing this book, Fleming and Bryce experimented with various ingredients until they arrived at the receipt described in the book, and Fleming dedicated *Casino Royale* to Ivar Bryce with the words: 'For Ivar, who mixed the first Vesper and said the good word.' Griswold's book also mentions that a highly decorated Special Operations Executive operative from the Second World War, Krystyna Skarbeka (code name Christine Granville) GM, OBE, Croix de Guerre, may well have been the physical inspiration for the Fleming characters Vesper Lynd and Tatiana Romanova (*From Russia With Love*). In any event, Fleming named a fictional girl after a real cocktail and the fictional girl inspired the invention of another cocktail – the Vesper Martini – the best current version of which (under the name The Ian Fleming Classic Vesper Martini) the bar manager of Dukes Hotel assures me they make. I am inclined to believe him.

Vodka

Straight-up, chilled vodka is the drink for caviar and Stolichnaya 100 Proof is the best one generally available. There is no need to sprinkle some ground black pepper on Stoli to cleanse it of the fusel oils (largely acrid, amyl alcohol), as there is with cheaper vodka and Moonshine.

Whiskey Sour

One of the family of 'sour' cocktails; it comprises three parts bourbon whiskey, two parts lemon juice and one part gomme syrup, shaken over ice and served in an Old Fashioned glass, garnished with a maraschino cherry and a slice of orange. This drink dates from around 1870.

White Lady

There are various versions of this – some include egg white and cream and are fairly sickly. My favourite is as prescribed by Harry Craddock in *The Savoy Cocktail Book*: pour two measures of gin, one of triple sec and one of fresh lemon juice over ice in a shaker, shake and serve in a sugar-rimmed Martini glass with a twist of lemon. This version of the drink was invented in the Savoy's American Bar.

White Port

Chilled, clean, crisp and dry, this is a much-forgotten, but ideal, *apéritif*, especially before a fish supper. There are several good brands on the market, such as Quinta de la Rosa and their Finest Reserve. Serve chilled, in *copitas* or sherry schooners.

Something of British Beer and Ale

> No soldier can properly fight unless he is properly fed on beef and beer.
>
> John, First Duke of Marlborough

Real British beers and ales are appreciated largely in Britain. They are not always drunk as warm as those who mock us maintain but neither are they stifled by refrigeration as are many lager beers and, even now, extra-cold Guinness. There is no doubt that British beers and ales are an acquired taste, but one well worth persevering for. They typically come in at between three per cent and around six per cent alcohol by volume, although there are weaker and stronger ales and beers. Beer is one of the world's oldest prepared drinks and results from brewing mainly malted barley, yeast and (sometimes) hops. There is also beer from wheat or rice (as in Sake). Beer was especially important as small (or weak) beer in times and places when and where plain water has been unsafe to drink. Small beer even used to be taken for breakfast and the historian AL Rowse recounts (with a puritanical point) in his biography of Sir Arthur Quiller-Couch that he sometimes had beer for breakfast in the first half of the twentieth century.

Hops are sometimes added to the mix to give a bitter taste (hence 'bitter') and to act as a preservative. A famous example of this purpose is the high hop admixture in India Pale Ale (IPA), originally devised so that it would remain stable during the long sea voyage from Britain to India to refresh the members of the British Raj that other beers could not reach. However, this gives rise to a contradiction in terms as, properly speaking, the difference between the terms 'beer' and 'ale' is that ale has no addition of hops, when IPA has a high hop content! The distinction is further blurred by the comprehensive name of the 'Campaign for Real Ale' (CAMRA), formed as a reaction to the increasing commercialization, from the 1960s, of artificially gassed-up (sometimes tinned) cheaper beers and ales, peddled with catchy slogans.

From 1860, the Murree Brewery, at the famed hill station, started brewing its acclaimed beers in India and, despite the prohibition on alcohol for Muslims in what is now Pakistan, the Rawalpindi Brewery still produces beer and other alcoholic products for non-Muslims and foreigners.

There is no evidence that springs to my recollection that James Bond ever enjoyed a quiet pint in a country pub, or even in a Fleet Street boozer, from The George at the Strand end to The Punch at the Ludgate Circus End, but I have to say that this is, probably, his loss. No doubt Bond's tastes are modelled on Ian Fleming's and, apparently, when he worked on *The Times* Fleming used to make off to his club for luncheon. Interestingly, though, in 1963 when he was involved in a court case in the Courts in the Strand (concerning an allegation of plagiarism in relation to the *Thunderball* novel) he and his wife used to lunch in The George, across the road, so there is a vague possibility that Fleming *might* have had a glass of beer for lunch.

What are the main types of British beers and ales and examples of breweries that make them? The main types are: hopped bitters (including pale ales), porters and stouts (including dry Irish, chocolate, oyster, milk or oat) and mild or brown ale. The range is tremendous, comprising not just the large commercial ventures but also micro-breweries that might even be found in garden sheds and converted lavatory buildings, and it is far beyond the purpose of this book to go through all the breweries and their wares. But here are a few nice examples: Burton Breweries' IPA, Harveys IPA and Flowers IPA, all frothy, light and pleasant; Greene King IPA; Fuller's porter; Guinness, Beamish and Murphy's

Irish stouts; Courage Imperial Russian stout (formerly Thrales Entire Porter, made by the family of the first husband of Dr Johnson's Mrs Thrale); Rogue Ales' chocolate stout; Samuel Smith's oatmeal stout; Mackeson milk stout ('It looks good, it tastes good and, by golly, it does you good!') and Marston's oyster stout; mild brown ales from the Midlands and Newcastle: Newcastle Brown Ale; Samuel Smith's Nut Brown Ale; Greene King XX Mild; Theakston's Mild; Theakston's Old Peculier is a strong ale and so is Young's Winter Warmer. There is also St Austell Tribute ('tribute' being a reference to the commission payments that tin miners used to receive rather than to the town itself) and Hicks Special Draught from St Austell Brewery, a fine, nutty bitter beer. There is the Hogs Back Brewery in the home counties and Marston's have taken over Bass (formerly Bass Charrington). There is Courage Directors and Best bitter; there's Olde Bishop's Finger; London Pride; Waggledance (honeyed) and Summer Rose (scented with rose petals). There are Hall & Woodhouse Dorset Ales and those of Palmers, such as Copper Ale and Dorset Gold. Rather as with Scotch whisky, there are so many of these beers and ales that it is best to experiment, making mental notes of likes and dislikes as you go along, scientifically sampling away.

Are beers and ales largely for enjoying as social drinks or can they be successfully be matched up with food? It is worth noting that, according to Captain Jesse's biography, the great connoisseur Beau Brummell, exiled in France and reluctant to give up his little luxuries (such as fine snuff, maraschino liqueur, starched white cravats, eau de cologne and, allegedly, champagne-based boot-blacking), often drank a Dorset ale with his dinner and followed this up with a bottle of claret. This habit continued throughout the period during which he wrote his famous begging letters back to friends in England, complaining that he was compelled to eat 'bran bread' and asking his correspondents to try to comprehend (and therefore relieve) his miserable plight. There are some very good matches between beer, ale and food and it is not my purpose to mix and match for the sake of it, so I shall stick to these. Beef and pies: steak and kidney, steak and oyster, for example, go very well with strong ale, porter and stout and sometimes even contain these in the sauces. Curry is excellent with India Pale Ale and the Indian lager beers such as Cobra. Duck I should fancy with a good nutty bitter such as Hick's Special Draught. Seafood, especially shellfish, from oysters to lobster, go well with stout or its richer cousin Black Velvet. Beer-battered cod and chips and sweet or savoury pancakes would be well complemented by an IPA.

Something of Cider, Scrumpy, Perry and Mead

> I heard a sound as of scraping tripe,
> And putting apples wondrous ripe,
> Into a cider-press's gripe.
> Robert Browning

Cider and scrumpy are two of a kind and result from the fermentation, strictly with neither addition nor extraction, of apple juice. Scrumpy used to be made from *scrumps* or windfalls of apples. The cider industry is threatened (as is so much) by the vandals in the EU with their damned incentives to farmers *inter alia* to grub up their trees to produce acres of grain for the European grain mountains. However, so long as it remains with us, good British cider is better than poor European wine. Excellent farmhouse cider is infinitely preferable to the cheap champagnes that taste, like cardboard, of nothing much: sensual blanks.

Sir Arthur Quiller-Couch said it of words and I apply it to drinks too: 'Let us reject no coin for its minting but only if its metal be base.' In fact, you can apply this phrase to many things, and not just to words and to drinks.

Somerset, Devon, Herefordshire, Sussex, Kent, Cornwall and Norfolk are the main counties that have famous cider orchards. In Somerset on 17 January each year (old Twelfth Night) they 'wassail' the trees with verses to encourage them.

Cider has been made in Britain since the Norman Conquest, although apples were introduced into Britain by the Romans. Apples probably originated in the Caucasus with the natural hybridization of wild *Malus silvestris* and *Malus pumila*. Apples and pears are mentioned in Homer's *Odyssey* and Pliny mentioned auctions of fruit still on the trees; a practice that endures to this day in parts of Kent. The establishment of the Royal Horticultural Society (originally dating from 1804 and with its Royal Charter from 1861) caused a more scientific approach to hybridization and fruit production.

There is scrumpy, rough cider and farmhouse cider, besides the preponderance of the rubbish that is mass-manufactured from imported concentrate and artificially gassed up for sale in the supermarkets and all the mock-Tudor pubs. Presumably you drink that stuff with their dried-out, microwaved 'pub-grub'. The real McCoy can be got from small farmhouses where it is produced. For more information on cider sales and indeed for perry (pear cider), go to the About Cider and APPLE committee pages of camra.org.uk.

Perry has been made in Britain for as long as cider and there are many different varieties of perry pear trees, some with fantastic names: Merrylegs,

Mumblehead, Drunkers and Devildrink. Francis Showering of Shepton Mallet came up with the Babycham marketing brand and campaign in the 1940s, which popularized perry as *the* 1960s' bimbos' drink – although, perhaps, few people know what they are actually drinking.

Mead is an ancient alcoholic drink (maybe the most ancient alcoholic drink of them all), fermented from grain mash and honey, and, owing to the belief that a newly married couple should drink mead for a lunar month after their wedding (to aid fertility), the term 'honeymoon' evolved. It can range from dry to sweet and may be flavoured with fruit or herbs, for example, to make apple metheglin; soft fruits to make melomel or grape juice to make pyment, and it may be mulled, as wine, in the cold weather and at Christmas.

The Essential Dessert Wines, Digestifs and Liqueurs

Famed for its Martinis, the bar of Dukes Hotel in St James's also holds stocks of Cognac Bignon 1800, Impériale 1811 and Dom. De Bonnefont 1848, as well as Scotches such as Mortlach 1936, Linkwood 1939 and McPhail's 1950.

Amaretto

The famous, mainly almond, flavour of this Italian drink also derives from the stones of apricots and this concoction dates, maybe, from as early as the sixteenth century.

Armagnac

This is the oldest brandy distilled in France, although cognac has a bigger market share and bigger producers. It is distilled in the Armagnac region of south-west France and reputedly helps in the fight against cardiovascular disease: so, if ever an excuse were needed ...! There are named years and descriptions of grades similar to cognac. I have had the privilege to taste pre-First World War Armagnac and it seemed like drinking bottled sunbeams. There are several brands, such as Janneau, Delord and Domaine de Joy. Drink this straight up, after having warmed it in a brandy balloon in your hands.

Benedictine

Bearing the acronym DOM – Dominus Optimus Maximus – the receipt was, from the time of Dom Bernardo Vincelli in 1510, the carefully preserved secret of Benedictine monks, whose monastery must have been one of the most profitable around! I think that I detect the presence of honey and many aromatic herbs on a brandy base. Anyway, as a digestif, it is delicious in small amounts.

Calvados
This is the apple brandy of France, *l'eau de vie de cidre*, although Domfort includes thirty per cent pears in the process. There are various grades: Fine (over two years old); Vieux (over three years old); VO or VSOP (over four years old) and Extra VO (six plus years old). There are named years for exceptional production only but very often Calvados contains spirit admixed from an older distillation. There are several brands: a couple are Calvados Hors d'Age, Domaine Michel Huard and also Peyrat Associés VSOP.

Cannelle
This is a liqueur flavoured with cinnamon and was a great favourite with King George IV, but do recall before you take too much of this, or any drink come to that, that George IV died an early death from over-indulgence of several kinds, calling out (in apparent surprise), immediately before, to his page: 'What is this? It is death, my boy!' According to an account in the *British Medical Journal*, he then expired, in the act of nodding in acknowledgement at his physician, who entered the room.

Champagne demi sec
Half-sweet champagne is ideal with lemon tart or anything with an edge. Try the following non-vintage type: Louis Roederer Carte Blanche Demi-Sec NV.

Chartreuse
This was devised by members of the Carthusian order of monks. A text for an elixir, dated 1605, was found in 1720 and, by 1755, the elixir was, again, in production. Then came green chartreuse, the liqueur of health. There are green and also yellow varieties; the yellow is sweeter and both come in types called VEP, an acronym for the French for 'Ageing Exceptionally Prolonged'. So don't just gulp it down.

Cognac
Cognac is named after the principal town in the region of production in central France, is twice distilled and aged in Limousin oak casks. The products from top zones are called Grande Champagne and Petite Champagne; only certain types of grapes may be used and Ugni Blanc is the usual type. Before the mid- to late-nineteenth-century epidemic of *Phylloxera vastatrix*, which devastated France's vineyards, the main and best grape had been Folle Blanche and this had rendered an especially fine spirit from vines that traced their heritage back to Roman times. Now only about five per cent of cognac production derives from Folle Blanche. Occasionally, still, pre-epidemic cognacs come on to the market,

commanding astronomical prices. There are, sometimes, even bottles of the Great Comet vintage of 1811, when the grape harvest had been blessed by the appearance of a spectacular comet. There is a theory that some of the other great vintages have resulted from similar events. Cognac is 40 per cent alcohol by volume and 80° proof. Its basic grading is: VS means very special and the youngest brandy used (dating from 1 October of the year of harvest) is at least two-and-a-half years old; VSOP means very superior old pale and the youngest brandy must be four-and-a-half years old; and XO means extra old, when the youngest brandy can be no less than six-and-a-half years old, but is often much more, as it is in Napoleon and Hors d'Age Cognac. Some great cognacs are available besides the run-of-the-mill types we all know: L'Or Martell is a minimum of 50 to 60 years old, Louis XIII from Rémy Martin is around 55 years old and L'Esprit de Courvoisier contains *eau de vie* up to 200 years old. Consume as Armagnac.

Cream sherry
This is unfairly scorned as an abstemious, aged aunt's Christmas tipple. But there are delightful types available, including Berry's 'Bishop's Mead' Oloroso Cream, to bring a gentle glow to venerable cheeks.

Crème de Cacao
This is a delicious drink flavoured with cocoa bean and the vanilla orchid. There are two varieties: clear syrup and chocolate-coloured.

Crème de Menthe
This is a sweet, mint-flavoured liqueur and may be clear or emerald green in colour. It is used as an ingredient in several cocktails and as a digestif.

Drambuie
Apparently the name derives from the Gaelic for 'the drink that satisfies' and this combination of whisky, honey and herbal infusion does not disappoint. Legend has it that the receipt was given by famed toper Bonnie Prince Charlie to his saviour after the Battle of Culloden in 1746. Captain MacKinnon kept it in the family, which still produces it.

Galliano
This was formulated around 1895 by Arturo Vaccari in honour of Italian troops, led by Giuseppe Galliano, in a hopeless battle against a vastly greater Abyssinian force. It has a sweet and sour flavour.

Grand Marnier

One of the best triple secs (thrice distilled), although the brand name Cointreau may be more recognized: it was devised, in 1880, by Alexandre Marnier-Lapostolle as an infusion of bitter oranges (Bigarade, from the island of Curaçao) in brandy and named 'Grand Marnier' (jokingly) by hotelier César Ritz. There are also many other brands of Orange Curaçao.

Madeira

This is the stuff of legend and of a humorous song, of which more anon. Firstly, this fortified Portuguese wine comes from the island of Maderia and has been produced there since the sixteenth century. There are four main types, ranging from sweet dessert to dry *apéritif*: Malmsey, Bual, Verdelho and Sercial (the last served chilled, as amontillado sherry). This wine is treated with heat in a unique process to stabilize it to endure the long sea voyages that it used to undergo all round the world – notably to North America, where it remains in great favour. It is fortified with plain grape spirit. There are various grades, including Reserve (aged five years or more), Special Reserve (aged ten years or more), Extra Reserve (aged fifteen years or more) and Colheita (actual single vintage but not aged for the minimum of twenty years for the actual vintage [also called Frasquiera]). As long as Colheita is actually labelled 'Colheita' it may carry the vintage label. Madeira is a most stable and long-lived wine.

George Plantagenet, Duke of Clarence (1449–1478) was the brother of King Edward IV and King Richard III and conspired against King Edward. He was executed privately in the Tower of London (according to legend) by being drowned in a butt (477.3 litres) of Malmsey wine. But what a way to go! Blandy's make a variety of Malmsey called Duke of Clarence to this day.

The Flanders and Swann song about a maiden's downfall includes the lines:

> Have some Madeira, m'dear,
> It's very much nicer than beer ...

Maraschino

This is a Dalmatian drink, dating from the sixteenth century, made from the marasca cherry. It bears an Italian name and is shipped out of Zadar. It was also one of George IV's favourite tipples and, besides the snuff that Brummell sent George IV on his fleeting visit to Calais during exile, he also sent a bottle of aged maraschino. The Luxardo distillery, dating from 1821, makes a well-known brand – it takes its name from Girolamo Luxardo, who had been the Sardinian Consul to Zadar and started this distillery, which continues.

Marsala

The most famous wine of Sicily and, apart from olive oil, *La Cosa Nostra* and Vito Corleone, Sicily's most famous export. It comes from around the town of Marsala and is a sweet, fortified wine, first noticed commercially by wine shipper John Woodhouse around 1796. It is served chilled as an *apéritif* with cheeses, or at room temperature as a dessert wine. There are various grades and types. One very good all-rounder is Marsala Superiore Riserva 10 Anni Marco De Bartoli, Sicilia.

Marula fruit cream

This is spirit and cream infused with the small yellow berries of the Marula tree (of the mango, *Anacardiaceae*, family), which grows wild in the southern regions of Equatorial Africa and is known there as the 'Elephant Tree' as its delicate sweet fruit is beloved of that animal. There is a brand of liqueur called 'Amarula'.

Muscat de Beaumes de Venise

This wine comes from the south east of the Rhône Valley and is one of two main wines produced there: the other is the Côtes-du-Rhône-Villages, a red wine. The one that we are concerned with here is the *vin doux naturel*, which is the fortified white dessert wine, produced in the region for centuries. Try these to start: Domaine de Durban and the Domaine de Durban, Leydier.

Port

Famously passed around the table after the ladies have retired (it used to be, anyway) and drunk with nuts or stilton cheese, this is another fortified wine beloved of the British. It comes from the Douro Valley in north Portugal and is shipped out of Oporto, having been fortified with brandy before the fermentation process is complete. This brings that process to an end and the unfermented sugars remain to sweeten the wine. The best of it is aged in barrels, but there are several different types, besides the White Port mentioned under the section on *apéritifs*, above. There is Tawny Port, which gets its nutty flavour from being aged in wood; there is Ruby Port, the cheapest normal type; Reserve or Vintage character is better. The Late Bottled Vintage is just that – bottled later than classic vintage and filtered before bottling, making this Port useful in the catering trade as it is not necessary to decant it and it is possible to re-cork it and keep it. There is Crusted Port, which comprises blended vintages (and needs to be decanted), and there is proper Vintage Port with classic vintages such as (especially) 1963 and 1970, and all these come under great names such as Berry's, Dow, Graham, Taylor, Fonseca, Cockburn's and Croft. Here is a selection: Berry's Crusted Port; Berry's St James's Finest Reserve Port; Graham 1966 Vintage Port and Dow 1977 Vintage Port.

Recioto della Valpolicella

This Venetian *passito* is an ancient Italian dessert wine and excellent with chocolate. The name derives from the Italian *orecchie*, 'ears', as originally only the best 'ears' from each bunch of grapes were used to make this wine. Try Recioto della Valpolicella, Agr. Corte Sant'Alda. The over-fermentation (by oversight) of a quantity of this wine gave the world the dry and bitter Amarone della Valpolicella, which (described by him as a 'big Amarone') is the wine that Hannibal-the-Cannibal Lector actually drinks with the human liver in the book the *Silence of the Lambs.* It is changed to a 'nice Chianti' in the film as many have heard of Chianti but few of Amarone. *Animal* liver or game might indeed be nicely complemented by an Amarone.

Riesling

This embraces many wines from the simply bland to the truly sublime. Two great sweet examples are Nackenheimer Rothenburg Riesling Beerenauslese, Gunderloch 2002 (medium sweet) and Bernkasteler Badstube Eiswein, Sebach-Oster 2001 (sweet).

Sauternes

This is produced in the Graves region of Bordeaux and is made from Sauvignon blanc, Semillon and Muscadelle grapes with Semillon predominating for Sauternes; whereas Sauvignon blanc predominates in the drier white Bordeaux wines. The sweetness derives from the existence of noble rot, described under Tokaji below. Château d'Yquem is the most famous and costliest of the wines produced in this region. Interestingly, if the noble rot fails to develop, dry white Bordeaux wine results and is sold accordingly. Although I have listed Sauternes amongst dessert wines, it is also the classic accompaniment for *foie gras*. Some good examples of this wine are (for the economical) half a bottle of Château de Fargues and (for the aspirant to the high life) half a bottle of the Château d'Yquem 1990, 2005 or the sublime 1967 or 2001.

Sloe gin

This is made by infusing sloes (the fruit of the blackthorn *prunus spinosa*) in gin with sugar. Obtain your gin and from each bottle remove half the gin and replace with 150 grams of fine sugar and the sloes, which you have pricked all over to let the juices out. The best sloes are obtainable from the hedges in October or November, after the first frosts. You then seal each bottle up and keep agitating the bottles daily for a couple of months, then occasionally. You could use this drink after a couple of months – but far better to leave it a year, strain and rebottle it all and enjoy! You can buy commercially produced sloe gin but it isn't half the fun of making your own.

Tokaji Aszú

Tokaji wine from the Tokaji region of Hungary has been made since the sixteenth century. The legend is that after the Ottoman Turks had finished their raid and gone home the locals were left with grapes rotting on the vines, and so, with little choice, they still made their wine, which turned out to be very sweet and, overall, very good. This wine derives from *la pourriture noble* or the noble rot that sets in as the grapes are left on the vines. This is caused by a fungus (*Botrytis cinerea*), which concentrates the sugars; the fog of the region, resulting from the confluence of two rivers, also helps here as the atmosphere becomes more humid. The dessert wines that are produced are noted for their longevity and Louis XIV of France called Tokaji 'the wine of kings and the king of wines'. The corks are changed only every twenty-five years. Here are a couple to get you started; the first expensive and the second not: Berry Bros & Rudd's Tokaji, 6 Puttonyos, Oremus and their Royal Tokaji, 5 Puttonyos.

Triple sec (Grand Marnier, Cointreau etc)

This is described under Grand Marnier, above.

Vouvray

This wine is very good with sole and other fish, especially with a rich cream sauce; it also goes very well with a creamy cauliflower cheese or lasagne. A nice type is Vouvray Le Mont, Demi-Sec, Domaine Gaston Huet.

Other Drinks

Advocaat (Egg Flip or Eggnog)

This is a very old drink and is known in many places, most famously Holland. In the middle ages in England it was called posset. To make this, beat six egg yolks in a bowl and beat in five ounces of fine sugar, adding also twelve fluid ounces of brandy and four fluid ounces of dark rum plus two pints of milk and a pint of cream. Take the separated egg whites and beat until peaked and fold into the mixture. Then whip a pint of cream and two ounces of icing sugar in a bowl as a topping to each measure and grate nutmeg over each glassful.

Hot toddy

This is a fairly flexible drink. My own version comprises a base of boiling water into which you stir a tablespoon of good honey and a generous measure of any good blended Scotch whisky, or an Irish whiskey, rye or bourbon or dark rum, together with the juice from at least one large lemon or at least two limes. If taken at the first hint of a head cold, together with a pinch or two of mentholated snuff in the nose (all the makers mentioned in Chapter 6 make mentholated and other medicated snuffs), there is a very good chance that the cold will immediately become symptomless. Then run for cover.

Mulled wine

This is a cold winter's day 'must have'. There are no hard and fast rules as to ingredients but, obviously, you will not use vintage wine – although neither must you use any wine that you would not be prepared to drink unmulled; just as you should never cook with any wine that you could not face to drink otherwise. The reason is simple – horrible ingredients remain horrible whatever you do with them and if you used undrinkable wine you would simply end up with nasty mulled wine. Red wine is usual and even a Ruby Port might be an idea. Take this by the pint and measure out a cup of water for every pint of wine. Boil up cinnamon sticks, cloves and nutmeg in the water and, after five minutes' simmering, add the wine and return to the boil. Bring off the stove and place it in the serving vessel, together with an orange treated in this fashion: the orange should (as a matter of honour) have been peeled in *one single spiral of peel*; this is dropped into the drink and the peeled orange is then spiked all over with cloves and placed in the drink too. Serve immediately. Just one point (made by Mrs Beeton): it is best to use a vessel for preparation that is not used for any other purpose – this avoids tainting the taste.

Rum punch

This is an ideal Christmas party drink. The name derives from the Urdu/Hindi word for five – *panche* – because the drink was from India and originally contained five main ingredients, alcohol, sugar, lemon, water and mixed spices. There are many varieties of this drink but the best-loved uses dark rum as the alcohol.

Tom and Jerry cocktail

This is not the usual modern idea of a *cocktail* at all, as, for a start, it is hot: take three egg whites and beat to peaks. Beat the yolks and mix in three tablespoons of fine sugar, half a tablespoon of allspice, half a teaspoon of cinnamon and half a teaspoon of cloves; fold the egg whites into the egg yolk mixture and pour two tablespoons of this mixture into each of four mugs and to each add one ounce of brandy and two ounces of dark rum. Top it all up with hot water or milk and, after a brisk autumn walk through the leaf-strewn woods (maybe collecting sloes), get yourself close by that log fire and the crumpets on the toasting forks!

Other winter warmers

For outdoors in the cold and wet, I have a couple of recommendations: the first is a thermos flask of black coffee and whisky and the second is a thermos of Bovril and amontillado sherry. The first of these was, sometimes, favoured by James Bond on cold outdoor missions, such as that in *For Your Eyes Only*, although his use of a quarter coffee to three quarters bourbon seems a little OTT. The second is the recommendation of Noël Coward, surprisingly convincing as windswept Captain Kinross, Commander of HMS *Torrin*, in his stirring wartime propaganda film *In Which We Serve*, co-directed with David Lean.

Some Great London Vintners

> I often wonder what the vintners buy,
> One half so precious as the goods they sell.
>
> Edward FitzGerald, from the translation of the *Rubaiyat of Omar Khayyam*

There are many off-licences in London, but there are not that many great vintners. Here is a handful for the truly discerning.

Berry Brothers & Rudd

One of the oldest vintners around, Berry Bros & Rudd (which is still in family ownership) was established by the Widow Bourne in 1698 at 3 St James's Street as a coffee chandler and the sign of the coffee mill still hangs outside their shop.

Inside you can see the giant coffee scales and beam, which did alternative service as human scales for their customers. They have records showing George 'Beau' Brummell's weights through a certain period of his changing fortunes and, intriguingly, they also have a purported record of his weight supposedly taken sometime after his enforced exile for debt in France, suggesting that he might have returned once after his exile. However, it is possible that this was a prank by a bored clerk as Brummell would have been unlikely to have shown his face with the risk of imprisonment for debt still hanging over him! Although there was, even then, provision for time-barring of actions for debt, it did not apply to periods spent abroad.

Since the reign of George III, Berry Brothers & Rudd have held royal warrants as vintners. In 1923 they first blended the famous light-coloured Cutty Sark whisky, named after the famous tea clipper built in 1869 and undergoing restoration. This vintner now, besides listing ninety-three web pages of fine wines, also carries an enviable stock of single malt whiskies and has branches in Hong Kong and Dublin as well as running two wine schools. There is even a fine dining venue in the cellars of the St James's Street premises.

Alexander Hadleigh

Alexander Hadleigh is another relative newcomer and a fine independent vintner with a wide-ranging stock of vintage classics that covers all price ranges, principally priding itself on value for money. It was founded as a small select outlet in 1973 and became a limited company in 1984 when it began warehouse sales to the general public. It also now also carries the types of spirits and fortified wines that most vintners carry, including seriously good vintage Cognacs and Armagnacs, some even predating the Second World War.

Justerini & Brooks

Justerini & Brooks was founded in 1749 by Giacomo Justerini who originally came to London in pursuit of a famous opera singer Margherita Bellino. Although his suit of her failed, he soon found himself in possession of a fine vintner's business, and this has been continued by securing every sovereign's warrant since George III and with sales of the business, first to George Johnson in 1760 and then to Alfred Brooks in 1830 (who added his name). The world-famous J&B blended Scotch whisky was one of the popular choices in the USA after the abolition of Prohibition in 1933 and continues as a world brand leader. This firm operates a worldwide business and can supply anything that any wine-lover could reasonably require from Bordeaux to Champagne and Barolo to Tokaji, not forgetting the New World and, especially, the fabulous wines now coming out of Argentina and Chile.

Majestic Wine Warehouse

This is a chain with many branches, priding itself on supplying, through a warehouse system, mixed cases at the best available prices. It is the biggest wine retailer in the UK with 144 stores. The only slight downside is that there is a minimum order of a dozen-bottle case, but they can be mixed bottles, and any mix. There is a useful exception to this rule for gift bottles, subject to special charges. Majestic also runs regular wine tastings and has won many recent awards in the industry.

Oddbins

Oddbins is a relatively new boy on the block in terms of vintners. It had its beginnings with a small enterprise begun by Ahmed Pochee in 1963 when he started selling bin-ends to businesses in the West End of London. His successful start built a business that was bought out in the 1970s by Dennis Ing and Nick Baile, who opened the eyes of the British public to the possibilities of wines from Portugal and the South of France. It was also at this time that it began expanding into the quality countrywide chain store that it has become. In the 1980s it was bought again by Seagram and reached a total of 100 shops, being one of the first to introduce Australian wine on to the shelves. Now Oddbins hosts two wine fairs a year; one in London and the other in Edinburgh. It continues to build its reputation for innovation and the introduction of fresh tastes.

thewhiskyexchange.com

Although not strictly vintners, thewhiskyexchange.com is an online venture that does what it says on the tin – it sells whiskies from all around the world: Scotland, Ireland, America, Canada, even Japan. Begun by brothers Sukhinder and Rajbir Singh in 1999, they trade from Park Royal in west London and export all over the world. They stock in the region of 1,500 whiskies as well as a large range of other spirits including brandies and rums.

Sweets (Candies)

Everyone's a Fruit and Nut case.

Advertising slogan

Some men never grow out of the sweet-toothedness of boyhood. As I hit my half century, I am certainly one of them. I regularly used to eat four ounces of sweets (about a hundred grams) in well under half an hour and could still very happily do this now. On one occasion (and as a dare) I got four regular-sized Mars bars into my mouth at once, and managed to eat them. Loose sweets in jars, which have to be measured out, are undoubtedly the best to satisfy the craving for the tastes of childhood.

The sweets in jars used to be dispensed into proper white, paper bags, which were then closed with a somersault and twist, but even this has changed and most places now use thin plastic bags that they just knot up and even in this:

> The new world still is all less fair
> Than the old world it mocks.

Gums

These are sweets made from animal or vegetable collagen agents, including: gum arabic, gelatine, agar-agar, pectin and modified starches, called penetroses, together with sugars, starches, flavouring and colouring agents. Gelatine is largely derived from animal bones, cartilage and tendons.

Boiled sweets and toffee

Boiled sweets are made with low-ash content, refined sugar and glucose syrup, flavourings and colourings. The central ingredients are high-boiled to produce a super-cooled liquid, which is solid at normal ambient temperatures. Toffee and fudge are produced in a similar manner, except that milk and fat are added to the process and fudge is not so high-boiled.

Brands

There are still the sweets that Churchill insisted must remain available in the ration book during the Second World War, such as Rowntree's Fruit Pastilles (launched in 1881) and Fruit Gums (launched in 1893) and, if anything, these have actually improved over the years. There is too one company that still manufactures the Lion Brand of loose gum and boiled sweets, as well as a big range of their own – Maynards (bless them!). But the danger is that many of the little independent shops (confectioners and tobacconists and newsagents) that sell them are under threat (and actually disappearing right now, even as I write) and I just hope that a significant number can forever struggle against the economic forces of the so-called 'supermarkets' and that there will forever be enough British children of taste and discernment in these things to support them. Among my favourite sweets are American hard gums, striped mint humbugs, lemon sherbets, midget gems, liquorice and butterscotch gums (preferably one of each eaten together), aniseed twists, the winter mixture and Haribo liquorice torpedoes. Liquorice comes from the root of *Glycyrrhiza glabra*, a vegetable plant, which is boiled to extract the essence.

There are also other specific types, such as Maynards Wine Gums, Jelly Babies and Jelly Buttons, and although Callard & Bowser toffees (ordinary caramel and liquorice and treacle flavoured) have been taken out of production by a foreign firm that took them over, there is still great toffee from Walkers and Thorntons and Sharps and, when all is said and done, who would honestly deny the innocent indulgence of a Barrett's Sherbet Fountain? The satisfying 'fizz' in sherbet derives from an endothermic reaction between sodium carbonate and weak citric acid that is triggered by saliva in the mouth. Soft-centred, fruit-flavoured boiled sweets are also still made by Maynards, such as their blackcurrant and liquorice variety. Good confectioners also sell Fisherman's Friends, which are wonderful for a walk in the cold, and the tinned travel sweets sold by pharmacies and at airports really do help to keep sugar levels up on long journeys.

Nougat

Real Montelimar almond nougat might have been introduced by the Greeks to Provence and it became called *nux gatum* and *nougo*. The almond trees, which later became acclimatized to Provence, added their contribution to the manufacture of nougat and the nougat from Montelimar remains the world leader. Nougat is an aerated, high-boiled syrup with added fat, which is stabilized by a whipping agent, such as egg albumen, gelatine, milk or soya protein, in combination with starch or gum arabic, with optional added nuts or fruit and nuts. Consistency can be controlled and even crumbly nougat is available, but I think that the long-chewing type is the very best.

Indian sweets – mithai

Receipts for Indian sweets rely heavily on milk, sugar and condensed milk and production by frying. Three great ones to try (if you have not already) are, first, *Laddu*, which is flour and the other staple ingredients, dipped in syrup. *Jalebi* is a ring of deep-fried sweet, orange batter, also dipped in syrup, and *Gulab Jamun* is a milk-based dough, scented with rosewater again, dipped in syrup. There are many suppliers in and around London (and other places): one that I recommend is Ambala.

Turkish Delight

Turkish Delight or *rahat lokum* is a confection made of starch, cream of tartar and sugar, flavoured with rosewater, lemon or pistachio and dusted with icing sugar. It has been produced in Turkey since at least the fifteenth century and the current principal Turkish producer is the Ali Muhiddin Haci Bekir company in Turkey.

Marshmallows

Originally, these sweets contained extract from the root of the marshmallow plant (*Althaea officinalis*). Now they result from a beaten mixture of gelatine, sugar, syrup, seasoning and vanilla flavouring. These are best eaten toasted, and to do this, place a marshmallow on a toasting fork and rotate it over hot coals (*not* in the flames) for half a minute, until browned, and consume immediately. There are receipts for actually making marshmallows at home but they are (just) beyond the scope of this book.

Chocolate

What you see before you, my friend, is the result of a lifetime of chocolate.

Katharine Houghton Hepburn

There is a growing craze for grown-ups' bitter chocolate – or should that be for bitter grown-ups' chocolate? The thing is, many grown-ups don't know anything like as much about sweets as children do, and so, when the EU chocolate *cognoscenti* start comparing notes over their seventy-per-cent-plus cocoa-content chocolates and bullying the rest of us into accepting that the chocolate of our youth was not chocolate at all, we should, with a loud, clear voice, declare that everyone should be free to be a Cadbury's Fruit and Nut case or the Milky Bar Kid just as we should be free to indulge in an occasional facefull of jelly beans without being warned and lectured about the dental consequences.

Still, we should also be cosmopolitan and catholic in our tastes and prepared to admit that there are times when a sophisticated, bitter chocolate has its place in the scheme of things.

The seeds of cacao (*Theobroma cacao*) have been made into chocolate for thousands of years in South America. The modern production of it involves the harvesting and fermentation of the seeds from three main varieties of bean – *criollo*, *forastero* and *trinitario*. These are then roasted and the cacao 'nibs' are ground up to make into a liquid. Then the cocoa solids are separated from the cocoa butter. The blending of these with other ingredients results in dark chocolate – the purest form – milk chocolate and white chocolate. Milk chocolate contains also dairy products and sugar and white chocolate contains dairy products and sugar and cocoa butter but not cocoa solids. Conching takes place next, and this is a very refined grinding process to give the product the familiar, smooth texture. Finally, there is tempering, to prevent crystallization.

Here are some great modern makers and suppliers to try out. First, there is William Curley, who makes a great House 70% Dark Chocolate (cocoa) bar and then there is Paul A Young and his 'Artisan' bars, as well as the massive selection of bars and individual chocolates carried by Rococo Chocolates with their three London shops and other outlets. Besides these, there are (amongst several others) Leonidas Belgian Chocolates, Charbonnel & Walker, and Prestat and Chocolat-Chocolat over in Bloomsbury. There is also the ninety-nine-per-cent cocoa chocolate made by Lindt.

Tea

> There are few hours in life more agreeable than the hour dedicated to the ceremony known as afternoon tea.
>
> Henry James

The tea plant *Camellia sinensis* largely originated in China, although it was indigenous to Assam in India too. Tea drinking seems to have been known in China for more than 5,000 years. By the third century AD, the character *ch'a* had been developed especially for it. During the Sung Dynasty (AD 960–1279) it was introduced to Japan, where a new tea ceremony paralleling the Chinese version developed. It was during the Ming Dynasty (1368–1644) that the brewing of leaves started and then that the first Europeans tasted tea.

The (English) East India Company had its first Royal Charter under Elizabeth I and enjoyed a trade monopoly over the East Indies, although the early trade comprised spices and textiles. Its activities continued through the Commonwealth of Cromwell and into the reign of Charles II, even developing a military wing to bring trade by conquest. Catherine of Braganza was a Portuguese princess who became Charles II's wife. She brought her love of tea (resulting from Portuguese expansionism) with her and it soon became fashionable. The East India Company's first importation of 100 pounds of tea occurred in 1664, and this was China tea purchased from the Dutch in Java. By the eighteenth century most of the population at least knew about tea. However, duty on tea meant that many enjoyed it infrequently and often second-hand. By 1720, Fortnum & Mason were importing significant amounts of tea and customers (including officers' messes) had their own blends created from the nineteenth century onwards.

By 1750, Britain was importing nearly five million pounds of tea a year. The high price (resulting from the monopoly) and a high tax led to smuggling. Eventually, the Commutation Act of 1784 reduced the tax but, meanwhile, the East India Company had started exporting tea to the American colonies and imposed a tax of three pence a pound. When the company's ships arrived in Boston in 1773 the Boston Tea Party resulted as Bostonians, dressed as Native Americans, boarded the ships and jettisoned the cargo of 324 chests of tea (enough to make 24 million cups) in protest at the tax. This was an incident that occurred near the beginning of the American War of Independence. By 1834 the East India Company had lost its trading role and it had become just a government agent but, despite that, it decided to try to cultivate tea in India, and Assam was the subject of the first experiment. In 1838 twelve cases of Assam tea were produced and most were auctioned in London.

The heavy taxation of the Indian population by the East India Company and local flashpoints of protest led to the Indian Mutiny of 1857. Once this bloody and terrible affair was over, the East India Company was replaced by the government of India under its first Viceroy, Lord Canning. By 1888 Indian tea production exceeded British imports from China, as other districts (Darjeeling being the next) planted tea.

The romantic age of the tea clippers was a part of all this, involving hard-fought races home, around the Cape of Good Hope. One of the earliest was between the *British Challenger* (built in 1851) which, in 1852, raced the American clipper *Challenge* from China to England and won by two days. Because premiums were paid for the first tea home there was an economic point in these races. One of the most famous races of all was that between ten clippers that set out together from Fouchow in 1866. Two of them (*Taeping* and *Ariel*) reached the Thames Estuary at exactly the same time, after ninety-nine days at sea, and the race between them was declared a dead heat and the premium split. Of course, the race from Shanghai to England in 1872, between *Cutty Sark* and *Thermopylae*, is also legendary: Cutty Sark got 400 miles ahead but actually lost the race because she had sustained damage to her rudder, but she still made a respectable time and, of course, she lies in dry dock at Greenwich (being repaired after a disastrous fire) as a great monument to all these ships and the men who sailed them:

> They are grander things than all the art of towns;
> Their tests are tempests and the sea that drowns.
> They are my country's line, her great art done
> By strong brains labouring on the thought unwon.
> They mark our passage as a race of men –
> Earth shall not see such ships as those again.

From John Masefield's poem 'Ships', part of
which is engraved on a plaque beside her.

I have a small piece of *Cutty Sark*'s pitch pine keel, removed during a restoration, here beside me as I write, and it actually tastes of the oceans through which she ploughed – and of tar.

01. Military-backed faux ivory hairbrush, from Taylor's.

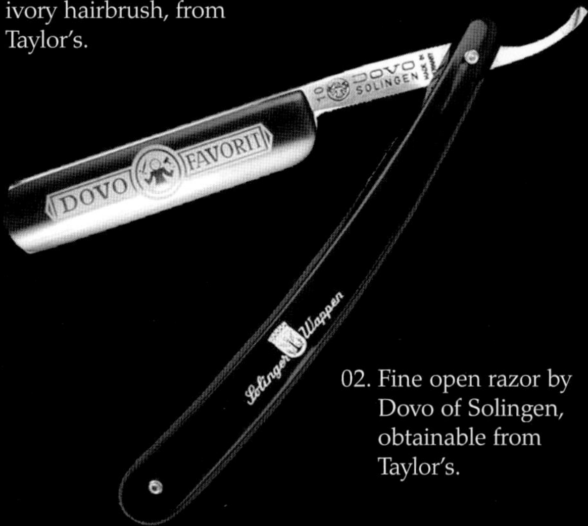

02. Fine open razor by Dovo of Solingen, obtainable from Taylor's.

03. Badger shaving brush from Taylor's.

04. Shaving cream, from Taylor's.

05. Boxed set of grooming items by Taylor's.

06. Bespoke slipper from the W S Foster - Henry Maxwell collection.

07. Floris Special 127.

08. Cameron separate stiff collar from Luke Eyres.

09. Evening gloves by Budd. Photograph by courtesy of Kenneth Lim.

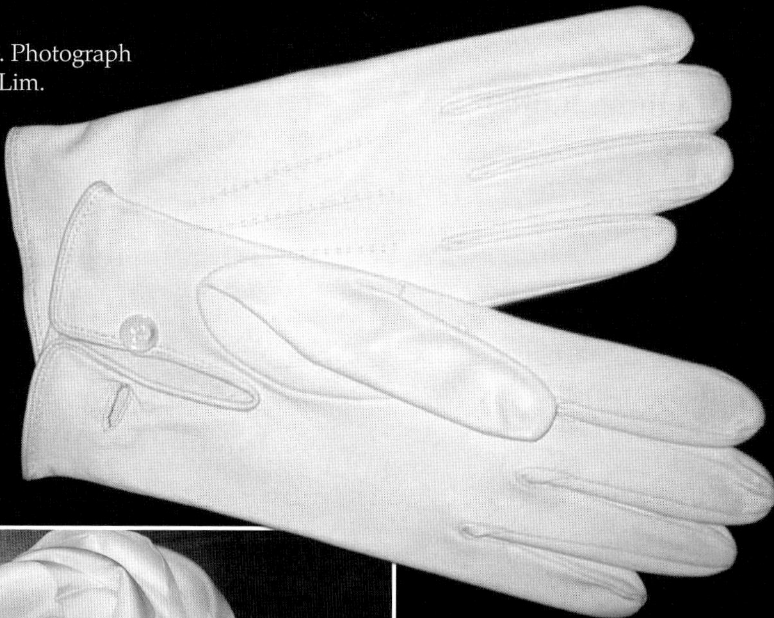

. Evening scarf by Budd. Photograph by courtesy of Kenneth Lim.

11. Smoking hat, from James Lock & Co.

PLATE 18.—SEMI-DRESS COAT STYLES

VESTON "SMOKING." SACCO "SMOKING."

12. Dinner jacket styles, as illustrated by pattern expert J P Thornton, circa 1911-1913.

13. Contemporary photograph of the beautiful Cora Brown Potter, showing a tattoo of the Prince of Wales's feathers on her left upper arm. Original photograph by Lallie Charles.

14. Snuff handkerchiefs by Turnbull & Asser.

15. A magnificent, minute repeating, split seconds chronograph (or double chronograph), with eccentric meantime dial, dated 1882, by Charles Frodsham & Co, which owns the copyright in the photograph. This watch was bought by New York banker J P Morgan for his butler, on the occasion of his marriage. The slide on the side activates the repeater. The double chronograph mechanism has two seconds hands. One button releases both hands and the other stops and also returns to zero. This device enables the simultaneous timing of two different events to one fifth of a second.

16. |A pocket knife by Charles Bennica, showing Damascus work - etching over layers of different steels, to create decorative patterns. Photograph by courtesy of J. Delage.

17. Selection of umbrella handles by James Smith & Sons.

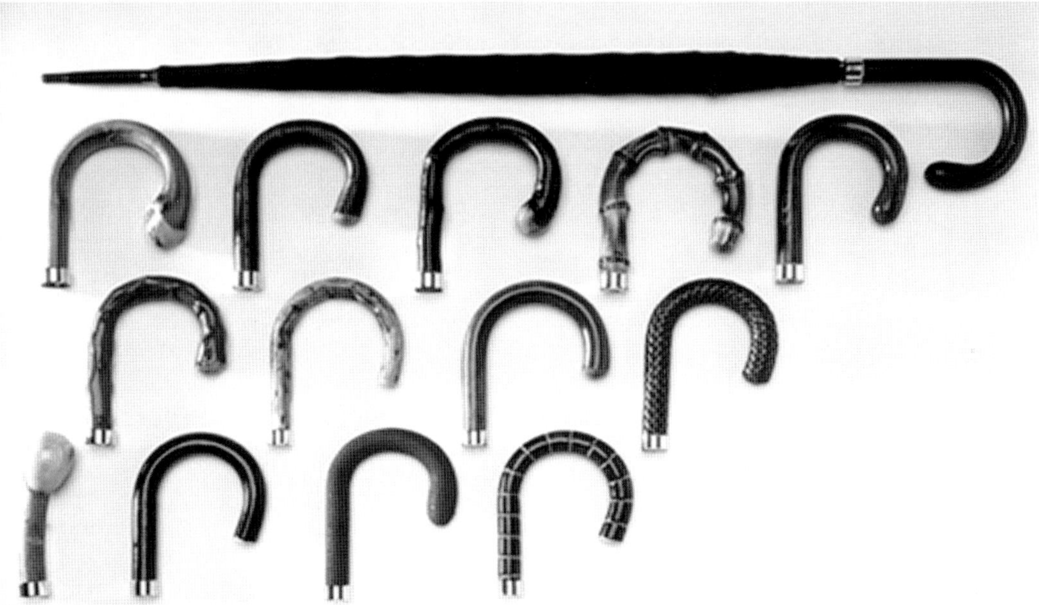

18. Orchid Cymbidium West Down. Photograph by courtesy of Liz Johnson.

19. A bottle of pre-ban Absinthe. Photograph by courtesy of oxygenee.com.

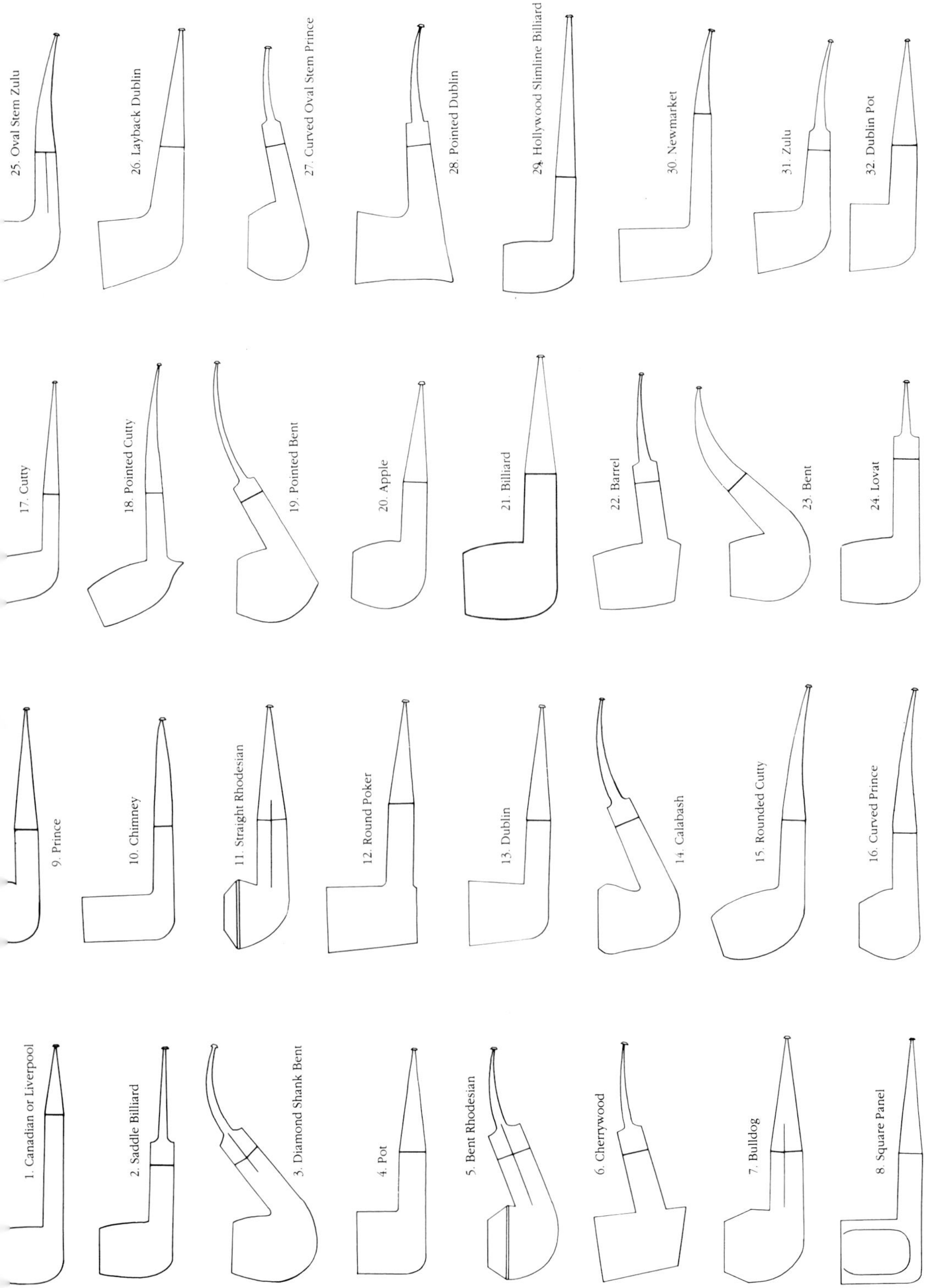

20. A chart of pipe shapes, from James Upshall.

21. In this picture: at top left, Peterson,'Sherlock Holmes Collection, Dr Watson'; top right, Astley 'Tankard'; lower right, Dunhill'Shell', and lower left, Butz Choquin, briar'Calabash de luxe'. Photograph by courtesy of C. Paul Taylor.

22. Selection of twelve principal cigar vitolas. Photograph by courtesy of Hunters & Frankau.

23. An open, 'dressed' box of Havana cigars. Photograph by courtesy of Hunters & Frankau.

24. The author's own remaining Benson & Hedges' Cairo Cigarettes. Photograph by courtesy of Laurence Mann.

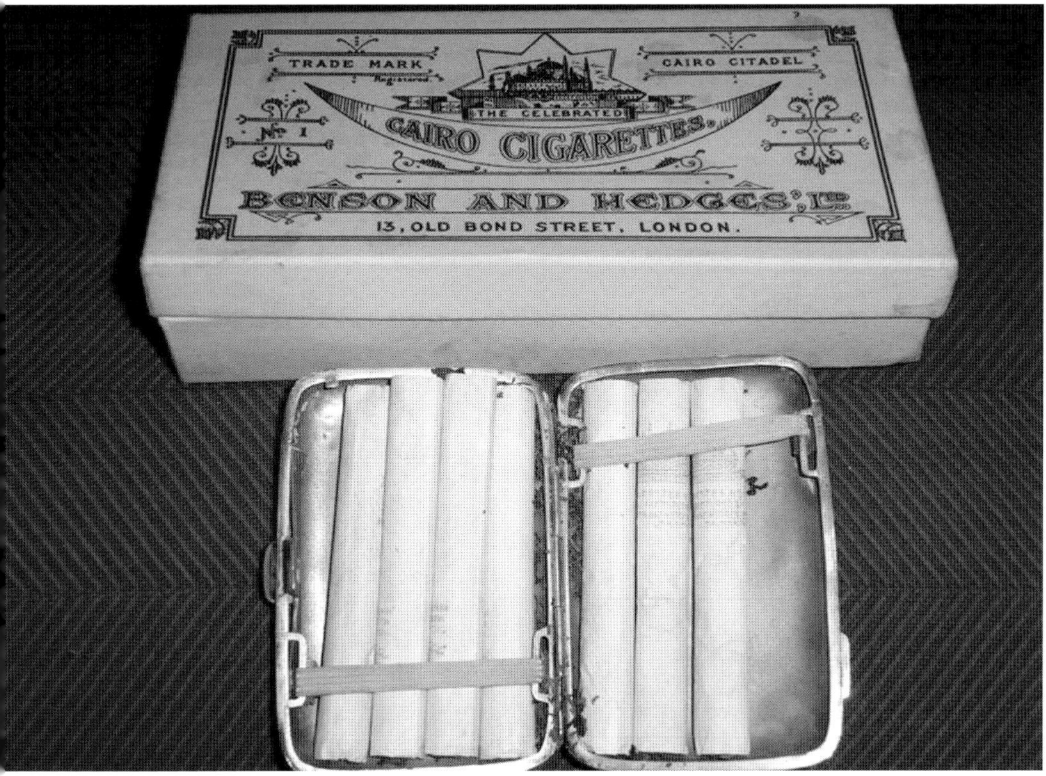

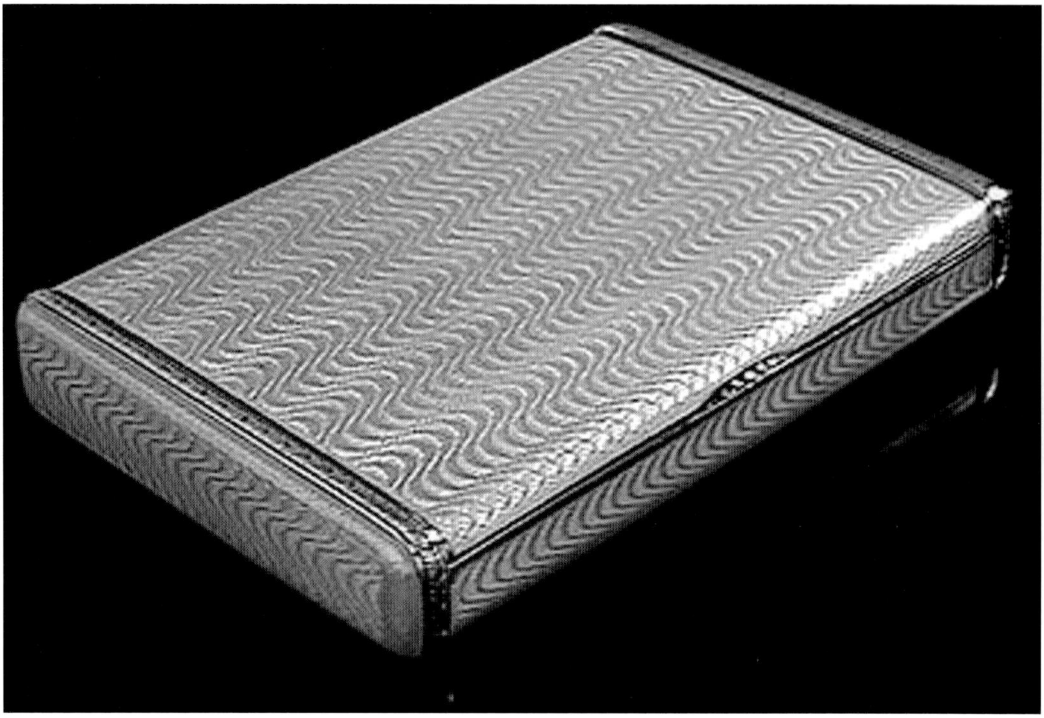

25. A parcel-gilt silver cigarette case, enamelled over a moiré guilloché ground, with diamond-set catch and laurelled gold banding, by Fabergé; Workmaster André Adler, St Petersburg (1908-1917). Photograph by courtesy of RomanovRussia.com.

26. A gold, samorodok-finished cigarette case, with oval, cabochon-cut ruby catch, by Fabergé; Chief Workmaster Henrik Wigström, St Petersburg, (circa 1910). Photograph by courtesy of Bentley & Skinner (Bond Street Jewellers) Ltd.

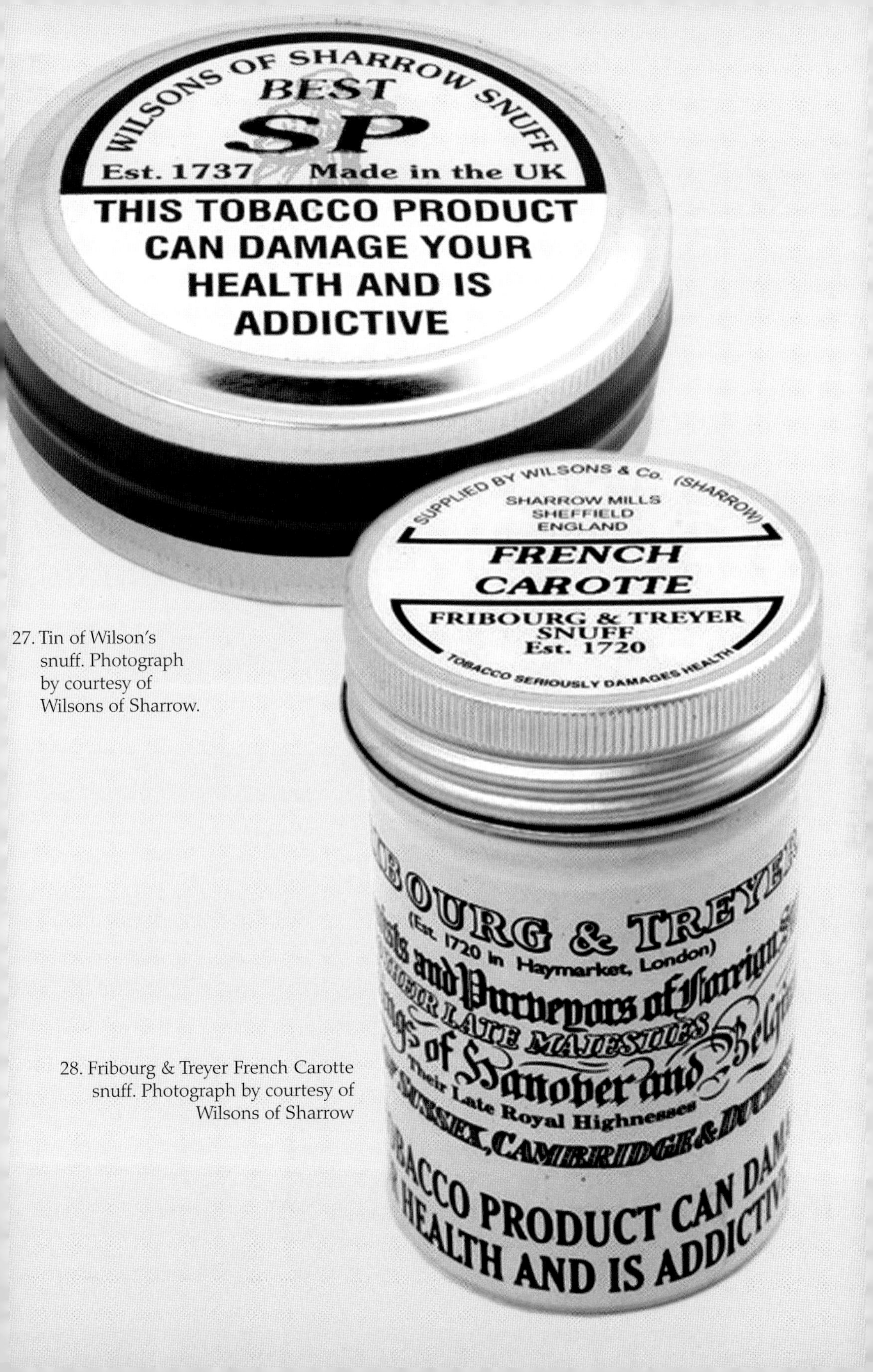

27. Tin of Wilson's snuff. Photograph by courtesy of Wilsons of Sharrow.

28. Fribourg & Treyer French Carotte snuff. Photograph by courtesy of Wilsons of Sharrow

29. Crockford's dining room.Photograph by courtesy of Genting UK.

30. Tom and Jerry fighting on the south side of St James's Square, from a Regency cartoon in the works of Pierce Egan.

31. Beau Brummell (left foreground) "Deep in conversation with the Duchess of Rutland", in Almack's ballroom, from a cartoon by Grego.

32. Cigarette case, enamelled in green and white, over a guilloché ground, with orange hessonite garnet-set catch and laurelled gold banding, by Fabergé; Chief Workmaster, Henrik Wigström, St Petersburg (1903-1908). Photograph by courtesy of Wartski, London.

33. Ladies' vanity case, by Fabergé; Chief Workmaster, Henrik Wigström, St Petersburg (1908-1917). Photograph by courtesy of Bentley & Skinner (Bond Street Jewellers) Ltd.

After the Suez Canal was opened in 1869 the days of the tea clippers were numbered, as steam ships could bring the cargo back in a shorter journey and the clippers, including *Cutty Sark*, then turned to other trades, such as bringing home Australian wool.

The London Tea Auction, for auctioning the tea from many different countries, was a British institution between 1679 until its closure on 29 June 1998, but modern methods of communication (especially the advent of the internet) killed it off and the proceeds of the very last auction were given to charity.

The principal tea-producing countries are China, India and Sri Lanka, Kenya, Malawi and Zimbabwe. I go a little into the production methods of colognes, some drinks and tobacco in this book, but I feel that, in relation to tea and coffee, this is of less interest and do not go anything like as far. However, it is right to point out that the particular characteristics of different teas and coffees are just as dependent on soil, climate and processing as the particular characteristics of different tobaccos and wines.

In the Edwardian era Fortnum & Mason created in-house blends such as Old Silver Teapot and Queen Anne. In the 1920s and 1930s they offered a service by which customers could send samples of their drinking water for analysis and the firm would then send small packets of tea that was compatible with the water for the customers to sample and select.

China teas include the black teas from Fujian Province – smoky Lapsang Souchong, dried over pinewood fires – developed largely to stabilize the tea for voyage as green teas could not withstand it. This is similar in original purpose to the fortification of some wines, as already noted, to stabilize them for long journeys. Then there is Keemun (from Anhui Province) and Yunnan, which is great as a breakfast tea (and one of the China teas that can take milk).

There are the green teas. These also all come from *Camellia sinensis* but the teas have to be handled carefully as they are harvested before they are subjected to processes to prevent oxidization: for example, gunpowder green (also called Twanky), from Pingshui in Zhejiang Province. Pelletted green tea is graded from pinhead size to peahead size. Green teas are 'fired' by steaming, roasting or baking to kill the leaf enzymes and this prevents oxidization.

There is Oolong tea from Fujian Province and Taiwan, which is semi-oxidized and a great tea to enjoy with a Chinese meal and it is far better, to my mind, than the usual offering of jasmine-scented tea. One is called Tie Kuan Yin Oolong: 'Tea of the Iron Goddess of Mercy'.

There are also Pouchong teas (lighter than Oolong), white teas, Puerh teas, compressed teas and scented teas (including Earl Grey tea, scented with oil of Bergamot).

The Indian teas include, of course, Assam and Darjeeling – both first and second flushes (or harvests of the shoots), each giving different characteristics to the resulting tea. Generally speaking, only women harvest the most delicate leaves! There is also Nilgiri from Southern India.

Sri Lankan tea is still called Ceylon tea. The first tea to be planted there was Dimbula, when the coffee failed in 1870. This is crisp and strong and refreshing. Others include Kenilworth, Uva, St James and Nuwara Eliya, as well as many blends.

Often the term Orange Pekoe is seen and some believe that it is a variety of tea. It is not: it is black tea made with a medium-grade leaf, and the term is applied to Indian and Ceylon teas (hence the term Broken Orange Pekoe, or BOP, meaning broken leaves). BOP Fannings are finely broken and popular as this lessens brewing time. There are other acronyms too, such as GFOP, meaning Golden Flowery Orange Pekoe. This and Finest Tippy Golden Flowery Orange Pekoe are especially fine teas and expensive because of the care that goes into their harvesting and production. Dust grade goes into many of the cheaper tea bags.

There really are advantages in pre-warming a teapot and allowing the tea to brew in the pot for around five minutes before drinking it. Moreover, it is as well to have a jug of hot water on standby and to top up the pot immediately after the first few cups have been poured. China tea is seldom drunk with milk and many true connoisseurs would not take it in any tea at all.

Apart from the delights of drinking tea, it is rich in anti-oxidants, called flavonoids, which combat heart disease and cancer. To gain maximum benefit from its health-giving qualities, the ideal rate of consumption for an adult is four cups of tea a day.

From the time of the earliest imports of tea into Britain, there have been tea caddies, originally small locked chests to keep this expensive commodity safe. They were often made of precious woods such as mahogany and walnut and ornamented in veneers of other woods or covered in mosaics made of mother-of-pearl, ivory and tortoiseshell, and these caddies are still available from antique shops and auctions. Of course the tea merchants also stock modern tea caddies, often in hardwoods or even decorated metal tins. The word 'caddy' derives from the Malay 'kati', which is a unit of weight around three-fifths of a kilogram.

Coffee and the plethora of popular, soft, cold drinks that have seduced a generation have meant a decline in tea consumption in Britain but it is still very significant and it is to be hoped that it will continue to be seen as the national beverage and that future generations will still feel moved to make time and space in the day for the proper preparation and consumption of the cup that cheers.

In recent years, their archivist Dr Andrea Tanner tells me, Fortnum & Mason have noticed an increasing interest in hand-tied flowering teas and in white tea. They also sell the only tea grown in England, from the Tregothnan Estate, in Cornwall.

Famous British tea merchants include: Fortnum & Mason, Harrods, Jacksons of Piccadilly (still manufacturing but no longer in Piccadilly), Twinings of London, Whittard of Chelsea and also allabouttea.co.uk.

Coffee

I have measured out my life with coffee spoons.

TS Eliot

Legends aside, it seems that coffee originated in Ethiopia, where it still grows wild. From there it was taken to Yemen and cultivated from the sixth century AD. The first coffee houses appeared in Mecca and Cairo. The Arabs jealously guarded fertile seeds and refused to export them. In the middle of the seventeenth century an Indian Muslim pilgrim to Mecca called Baba Budan smuggled some fertile seeds out of Arabia and took them to Southern India, where the resulting plants flourished. The Dutch took coffee to Java where it also quickly became established. In 1715, Louis XIV of France received the gift of a coffee plant from the Dutch. It had travelled from the Arabian port of Mocha to Java and then to France and, to house it and keep it free of frost, Europe's first greenhouse was built. It was called the 'Noble Tree' and from this one tree are sprung millions upon millions of *Coffea arabica* coffee plants, including those in Central and South America.

It was Brazilian Don ('Juan') Francisco de Mello Palheta who, in around 1727, charmed the wife of the Governor of French Guiana so well that she sent him seeds and cuttings of coffee plants to enable him to start the process that, eventually, led to the lyrics of the song entitled 'There's an Awful Lot of Coffee in Brazil!' In 1893, coffee from Brazil was planted in Kenya and Tanzania, very near to Ethiopia, from where coffee had taken the world by storm.

The coffee plant is a woody perennial in the *Rubiaceae* family. There are two main species: *Coffea arabica* and *Coffea canephora*, the latter is also called robusta coffee and is inferior. The plants have tremendous root systems and produce a very great deal of oxygen.

The process of roasting the beans, after harvesting and drying them, holds the secret to a fine cup of coffee. The method of roasting affects the aromatics and the acids to enhance flavour, acidity, body and aftertaste. The final treatment in this process results in the caramelization of the sucrose content and produces the dark brown colour of the roasted beans; over or under-doing the roasting makes or breaks the final product.

Coffee should be ground ideally no more than two minutes before it is to be brewed or staling (by oxidization) quickly begins. Burr grinders are better than blade grinders, as they produce more even grounds. Different brewing methods need different grinding sizes. The smell of the grounds before brewing is the famous 'fragrance'.

Some say that the best coffee produced in the world is Jamaican Blue Mountain. It is certainly one of the most costly; not least because it is produced in such tiny quantities.

Espresso coffee has become an increasingly popular way in which to take coffee. The modern espresso derives from the invention of Luigi Bezzera in 1901. There is still also the mocha pot, which is good for home use. It comprises a pot into which is placed the water and above this is a valve and a chamber in which is put the ground coffee and above this is another pot (with a spout) into which the liquid coffee is forced by pressure through the valve. According to an article in the *Economist* on 20 December 2001, the Università del Caffè Illy in Trieste (something of an espresso laboratory) serves amongst the best espresso in the world.

One reason why coffee has taken a larger and larger market share against tea is that tea was rationed in the Second World War and coffee was not and people gradually started substituting coffee for tea; although it might also be noted that Fortnum & Mason supplied coffee to Oxford University as long ago as the early eighteenth century.

Great London coffee merchants include: Algerian Coffee Stores, Camden Coffee Shop, Fortnum & Mason, Monmouth Coffee Company and Whittard of Chelsea.

CHAPTER 5

Matching Food and Drink

As founder of the Wine and Food Society André Simon said:

> Food without wine is a corpse; wine without food is a ghost; united and well-matched, they are as body and soul, living partners.

Apart from the things that I have already said about it, it seems appropriate to make a little more mention of matching food and drink but, this time, mainly food and wine. In a reasonably logical order, here are a few ideas:

Caviar

Traditionally, in Russia, this is eaten, on blinis, with a chilled vodka accompaniment, although in western Europe often champagne is drunk instead. Proper caviar is the roe of the primitive sturgeon fish, of which there are twenty-five species worldwide. The best comes from the Black and Caspian seas. There is Beluga (*Huso huso*), which can live for up to 150 years. This has the largest eggs, ranging in colour from dark (Royal Beluga) to lighter (Royal Pearl) and is the most expensive caviar normally available. Then there is Oscietra (*Acipenser persicus/gueldenstaedtii* and *nudiventris*), which can live for about fifty years. The golden type of this is very rare and costly (more so than Beluga) and is called Imperial caviar. Sevruga (*Acipenser stellatus*), can live for thirty years and yields the smallest eggs.

Escargots

The larger type of edible snail is the Roman snail or *escargot de Bourgogne* (*Helix pomatia*) and this is harvested from the wild and also extensively farmed and often eaten in a rich butter and garlic sauce. With this an aged, oaked Chardonnay is ideal. Sometimes it is eaten in pastry parcels and with these a Beaujolais or a light red Burgundy would go nicely.

Soups and foie gras

Often a complementary dry sherry, especially with consommé, is a good match but with *foie gras* there is really only Sauternes.

Egg dishes

Typically, this might be a soufflé, a quiche Lorraine or an omelette Arnold Bennett. This is not an easy match to make and needs a gentle touch. The best that is readily found is, probably, an unoaked Chardonnay.

Ham and pork

These are fatty meats and so you probably need a wine that is low in tannin and high in acidity to cut through it. Therefore a Beaujolais or a light red Burgundy (maybe Volnay) might do very well. For a cassoulet, a fruitier Beaujolais, such as Morgon, would make a fine match. A Chablis or, if red is preferred, a red Australian Shiraz goes nicely with pork bangers – unless it is at breakfast when, of course, it is going to be champagne, or Assam or even Yunnan teas.

Roast beef, bifstek, lamb

Here you can hardly beat a good red Bordeaux or 'claret'. There is the reliable Berry's Extra Ordinary Claret as a good staple wine; moving up, there is Château Batailley 2000, 2004 or, if you are really pushing the boat out, there are very fine wines, such as Château Lafite Rothschild, Pauillac, 2005. Other wines that might be considered here include red Rioja, Amarone and Barolo.

Liver and kidneys

Bouzy Rouge is the best known still, red champagne. It was chosen by Louis XIV for his coronation banquet. Made from old vines of Pinot Noir, grown mid-slope, matured in oak casks and, when poured, opening up as smoothly as a Rolls Royce Silver Cloud III Continental saloon, there could hardly be a better choice here for liver and kidneys of veal or chicken. Another good choice with *chicken* kidneys is a fine amontillado sherry. For lamb's liver or kidneys you might need a red Rioja, a claret, an Amarone or a Barolo.

Chicken, duck, cuisses de grenouilles and game

The modern red Burgundies or a medium-bodied Priorat come in useful for chicken and duck and even partridge and *cuisses de grenouilles* (maybe even going as far as a Rioja, such as Propiedad, for garlic-flavoured *cuisses de grenouilles*) but for most roast wildfowl and game (including venison and hare) it is often difficult to beat a good claret. If you must have a white, an oaked Chardonnay, preferably with some ageing, is acceptable. *Coq au vin* is traditionally cooked in, and eaten with, a wine from the same region as the chicken it is to complement, but even if you are not fortunate enough to have access to birds from Bourg-en-Bresse, a good Beaujolais will be an excellent choice. Also, *always* remember that if wine is not fit to be drunk it is not fit to be used in cooking either!

Fish

Many fish go well with a dry Italian white wine, such as a Pinot Grigio or a Trebbiano di Lugana, a white Burgundy or Chablis. However, with grilled salmon, tuna and red mullet, the light New Zealand Pinot Noirs (or even a red Burgundy such as Volnay) is a good choice; whereas for tuna in a Salade Niçoise you are going to need a Provençal heavyweight to cut through the oil. For Gravadlax or smoked salmon, one could do little better than a Blanc de Blancs champagne or a dry Alsace. Shellfish present a different challenge and with crab meat a white Graves is the thing; langoustines and prawns take a good white Burgundy and for lobster (plainly cooked or in a salad) you could hardly do better than champagne or Chablis. A Chilean Sauvignon Blanc is a perfect foil for scallops and an aged Muscadet complements *moules marinières*, as does a Belgian Witbier. I have already mentioned the merits of Black Velvet with shellfish, including oysters.

Chicken or fish in rich creamy sauces

Most chicken or fish in a rich creamy sauce benefits from a white Graves or a Vouvray wine accompaniment, even a sweet Riesling, and much the same could be said for cauliflower cheese and lasagne.

Tomato-based sauces

Here you need weight and tannin and there is no point in pushing the boat out in terms of cost. Another thought is that to insinuate a wine's favour with a sauce (indeed any sauce) one simply includes a dash of it in the sauce to begin with. It was great Edwardian cook and hotelier Rosa Lewis who began the introduction of wines into English sauces; maybe as a result of her former employment with the Duc d'Orléans and the Comte de Paris. She seems to have begun the process by adding a dash of sherry to the consommé and gradually converted a whole generation. To complement tomato sauces, suggestions might be Syrah, Primitivo and Zinfandel, Grenache and Merlot wines. A commonplace accompaniment is a white Viognier.

Traditional English puddings and pies

For certain traditional English dishes, such as steak and kidney pie or pudding (a 'baby's head') and fish and chips, as already mentioned, beers, ales and cider are often a fine accompaniment.

Cheeses

For many non-blue cheeses, a good Chardonnay is hard to beat, but for the blue cheeses there is, famously, Port for Stilton and Sauternes for Roquefort. Bual Madeira or Port sets off Gorgonzola and for Dolcelatte there is Amarone. Goats' cheeses are rather nicely complemented by a Pouilly Fumé. Fine English cheddar is good with a claret or a Rioja or (my favourite) a good farmhouse cider and, with many smoked cheeses, an Alsace Gewürztraminer is just the ticket. A Camembert will take a Pomerol and a Brie a nice Chablis. Bouzy Rouge advances the sweet nuttiness of a Gruyère or a Comte.

I must just mention the great cheesemongers in Jermyn Street, Paxton & Whitfield. The partnership dates from 1797 but in fact the business dates from one started in 1742 at Aldwych by Sam Cullen. They are not just the best cheesemongers in London or even the best cheesemongers in England: they are amongst the best cheesemongers in the world. Churchill said of them:

> A gentleman only gets his cheese from Paxton & Whitfield.

Desserts and puddings

Many desserts and puddings will be set to advantage by a sweet Muscat but there are a few others: Black Forest Gâteau is, traditionally, eaten with coffee, as the Kirshwasser, which is an essential ingredient, will undermine anything but an extremely robust sweet white wine, such as a late-harvested Riesling. A heavy chocolate pudding such as Death by Chocolate will easily take a Port, although a Tannat, the grape of Madiran, and also grown in Uruguay, is able to add an additional dimension to a chocolate-based pudding. Recioto della Valpolicella is another great wine with chocolate. Sauternes is good with crème brûlée and for vanilla ice cream there is the often over-looked Oloroso cream sherry: pour it on, too. Treacle tart will take nicely a Sauternes, a sweet Muscat or a Tokaji. The apple and lemon tarts and puddings go well with sweet German wines and for fruit salads and summer puddings, Eton Mess and so on there is Moscato d'Asti or sweet champagne. A Sauternes is ideal with Tarte Tatin and a Muscat de Beaumes de Venise chimes in well with sweet banoffee pie. For vanilla-flavoured puddings, there is the delectable Moulin Touchais, but since they guarantee it for a century, you might like to choose one that it is older than that. Port goes rather nicely with nuts.

One thing to be noted is the increasing popularity of organically produced wines, even some that are certified as 'organic' and 'bio-dynamic'. An organically produced wine is one that meets the standards set by bodies established for the purpose of monitoring viticulture in various countries and a bio-dynamically produced wine is one that meets even stricter standards, including standards applied to the tending of the vines in accordance with astronomical cycles. There are even certain systems of certification of the methods used. Another thing is the increasing awareness of the small producers of wines, such as champagne, of the merits of the slogan 'It pays to advertise.' The wine of a very small producer, Diebolt-Vallois Fleur de Passion 1995, has had a good press; another is that of Jacques Selosse under the tight bio-dynamic guardianship of Anselme Selosse.

On a final note:

An aphrodisiac menu

There are a great many myths about aphrodisiac foods, the term deriving from the name Aphrodite, the ancient Greek goddess of love, born out of the sea on the island of Cyprus. They range from freshly shucked oysters in their shells and conch chowder to the ground beetle powder of Roald Dahl's fictional Uncle Oswald and, of course, rhino horn. Maybe, some of them *have* been known to work, but on the placebo basis: one genuinely thinks that the foods are aphrodisiac and therefore they become it! Honey has been reputed to be aphrodisiac since ancient times and, as already noted, the old alcoholic drink mead is made from honey. So, mead shall be the drink to precede this menu as an unusual *apéritif*.

Plain fresh oysters, retaining the juices and doused in Tabasco (or other hot pepper sauce), lime juice and black pepper and eaten with wholemeal bread and butter shall be one *hors d'oeuvre* and steamed asparagus with Cornish butter (sticky on the fingers) and pepper shall be the other choice. Both shall then share, with the same spoon, a bowl of clam chowder.

We shall choose a bottle of Diebolt-Vallois Fleur de Passion 1995 to take us from the *hors d'oeuvre* through the main course.

The main course itself might comprise a peppery rocket salad, dressed in extra virgin olive oil, lime juice, Balsamic vinegar and black pepper and thin slices of hot ginger. Instead of bread rolls we shall have saffron buns (saffron from the innocent-looking little crocus is allegedly aphrodisiac and costlier, by weight, than gold) and, whether we choose a cold lobster or steamed langoustines in garlic and butter, we must find room for strong black truffles and tomatoes. If, however, we have more oysters, this time they shall be cooked in ginger and spring onions. In Brazil, boiled quail eggs are considered highly aphrodisiac, so we shall have a side-plate of these too.

For pudding we shall have a choice of passion fruit mousse (made of beaten condensed milk, fresh cream and passion fruit seeds) eaten with a great Sauternes and Death by Chocolate or a chocolate bombe, eaten with a couple of glasses of Taylor's 1970 Vintage Port. To finish we shall abandon even the great British cheeses in favour of peaches and apricots, which contain anhydrotoxins, also supposedly aphrodisiac. But if you have the time and the patience for a cheese, choose Gruyère or a Comte because that way you can send her eyes crashing through the ceiling with the dissolute-sounding Bouzy Rouge.

If we need to take something to the bedroom, maybe it should be banana fritters in Cornish clotted cream and two crystal brandy balloons of pre-1914 Armagnac, a dish of Belgian cherry liqueur chocolates and a spoonful of ginseng. Let's just hope that the headboard is soundly secured – and not too close to the wall …

For the morning there must be a chilled bottle of Veuve Clicquot Grande Dame Rosé Champagne, Vintage 1996, and two deep goblets, and my idea of 'the ideal breakfast' that I describe in Chapter 4 wheeled in … not a moment before 10.00am.

Chapter 6

Smoking and Snuff

A million surplus Maggies are willing to bear the yoke;
And a woman is only a woman, but a good Cigar is a Smoke.
Light me another Cuba – I hold to my first-sworn vows:
If Maggie will have no rival, I'll have no Maggie for Spouse!

From 'The Betrothed' by Rudyard Kipling

The sentiment is famously put, but I have always thought that there are some who could turn it on its head!

Tobacco

A short introduction to the history of tobacco

According to a paper by Herbert H Tidswell MD called *The History and Antiquity of the Tobacco Habit*, at least two species of tobacco grew from time immemorial in China and Hindustan and tobacco had been similarly known in Burma; while in Persia, tobacco had been known from at least 1260. The extent to which tobacco had actually been in *use* in the east before Columbus returned with his accounts of tobacco smoking in Cuba in 1492 is a matter of debate. The scientific name of the main genus is *Nicotiana tabacum* and it is named after Jean Nicot de Villemain who, as French Ambassador in Lisbon, sent it to the French Court in 1560. He believed tobacco to be a cure for a range of ailments.

The Mayans and Aztecs had smoked tobacco thousands of years ago and all are familiar with the Peace Pipe of the North American Indians. The word 'cigar' derives from the Mayan word 'sikar' meaning 'to smoke' and, in their first use in England, cigar was spelt 'segar'.

This is all a long time before Sir Walter Raleigh promoted its use in England, as a purported cure for dyspepsia. The first recorded English seizure of a Spanish tobacco ship was in 1565 and Raleigh introduced tobacco to the court of Queen Elizabeth in 1586. However, a colleague of Christopher Columbus called Rodrigo de Jerez became, in 1493, the first European to smoke elementary cigars from Cuba, and when he pulled the stunt in Spain he was imprisoned by the Inquisition, becoming the first victim of a smoking ban!

It seems likely that one of three seamen was the first to import tobacco into England in the mid-1500s: Sir Francis Drake; Sir Richard Grenville (of the *Revenge* fame); or Sir John Hawkins, a slave trader. Of course, Raleigh's slightly later promotion of tobacco remains in the public imagination and he is credited with the actual introduction of tobacco to England. His enthusiasm for it might have also had *something* to do with his own investments in tobacco plantations in the American Colonies.

During the late seventeenth century plagues of London, smoking was thought to be a preventative measure, and smoking by boys at great schools, such as Eton and Westminster, was *obligatory*.

Early reception

Pipe smoking was the early British way of smoking from the sixteenth century. Even the early reception of smoking was mixed: King James I hated it, tried to stop it and, failing, taxed it heavily. He later relented, even to the extent of granting a Royal Charter to a City Livery Company in 1619 (revived in the twentieth century as the Worshipful Company of Tobacco Pipe Makers and Tobacco Blenders) but not before he had written his 'Counterblast to Tobacco'; White's Club has never permitted it; the House of Commons soon banned it (in the Chamber); and Charles Lamb, on his doctor's orders, 'left off smoking' and wrote his famous (and ambivalent) *Farewell to Tobacco*, addressing it as 'Great Plant'. Observations have ranged from disgust –'feast for the fiend' – to delight – 'cornucopia of all earthly pleasure'. Elsewhere, smoking found much opposition: in Russia, Persia, India and Turkey harsh, even capital, penalties were meted out. Two popes published bulls against it, promising excommunication.

Cigars became an increasing alternative to pipes in Britain after the British soldiers returned from the (Iberian) Peninsular War (1808–1814) and, although cigars had been manufactured in Spain, using Cuban tobacco, from the eighteenth century (forty years before organized manufacture began in Cuba), it was 1820 before cigars began to be manufactured in Britain; although Fribourg & Treyer's records show a sale of '2lbs of Havannah Segars' as early as 1800. The soldiers from the Crimea campaigns (1853–1856) brought back the habit of cigarette smoking but again Fribourg & Treyer got there first with a supply of hand-rolled cigarettes in 1852. The first actual cigarette factory opened in Walworth in 1856, again using hand-rolling. In 1857 the medical magazine *The Lancet* first raised the question of the effects of smoking on health.

By 1880 cigarette smoking had become firmly established in Europe and in 1908 British legislation was enacted to prohibit the sale of tobacco to persons under the age of sixteen years. It certainly did not stop them all. In 1933, powers were added to all police and park keepers to confiscate smoking-related items. Since October 2007 the age limit, in the UK, has been raised to eighteen.

In 1990 the EU made a directive banning the supply of cigarettes containing more than fifteen milligrams of tar in each cigarette. The playwright John Osborne, a devotee of an occasional Turkish cigarette – 'Untipped, robust and fragrant they always seemed to me the only tobacco worth smoking and one of life's few and reliable pleasures' – found that they were no longer permitted and wrote a coruscating letter to *The Times*. He ended with the salvo:

> As a schoolboy I narrowly escaped from 'European' bombs on my doorstep. I can forgive this eagerness, but not the compounding of the insult by dashing the tobacco from my lips forty years on.

The Times supported his position in a leading article, entitled 'A Whiff of the Orient', saying: 'The EU should permit people to design the route to their own demise – and if they want to go out stylishly, in plumes of Turkish smoke, let them.' But, of course, it did no good. Osborne, though, wrote to me and said that as a result of his letter he had been sent so many boxes of Turkish cigarettes from Turkey that they would 'keep me going almost indefinitely' – well, until he died in 1994, anyway.

What Osborne would have made of the ban on smoking in public, introduced in 2007, heaven alone knows. Moreover, the Pipe-man of the Year Award was discontinued after 2003, as the organizers had, by then, been brow-beaten by tub-thumping Tin Hitlers into fearing that this harmless caper might actually be *illegal*. This modern world is certainly forgetful of Ben Jonson's observation that:

> The pipe marks the point at which the orang-utan ends and man begins.

Indeed, it might even be suggested that the orang-utans are, to an uncomfortable extent, now in control; while their compliant victims are on prescription drugs for depression.

Main types of tobacco

The main types of tobacco are: **Virginia**, which is fire-cured and light; **Burley** (including **Perique**), which is mainly air-cured, darker and stronger. Then there is **Oriental**, which is grown in the Balkans, Turkey and the Middle East. This is sun-cured and found in Egyptian- and Turkish-style cigarettes, which sometimes also include **Latakia,** a strong, dark, fire-cured tobacco originally from Syria, which needs to be mixed to be palatable. **Corojo** and **Criollo** (and further varieties developed from them) are Cuban cigar tobaccos, deriving from *Tabaco negro cubano*. Plainly, just as with wine, the soil, altitude and climate all play a part in the creation of the different characteristics of the various types of tobacco; as does the method of treatment, after harvesting, which creates tobaccos with characteristic fragrances, such as **Cavendish**.

A tobacco mixture is just a mixture of different tobaccos; strictly, a blend is a mixture that has been subjected to steam-pressure treatment.

Curing methods

The main curing methods are air-curing, sun-curing; flue-curing (by heat introduced over the tobacco through flues) and fire-curing.

Pipes

There are jars of jelly, jars of jam,
Jars of potted meat and ham;
But welcome most to me by far
Is my dear old tobacco jar.

Old verse from a tobacco jar

Introduction to the history of pipes

The earliest pipes in general use in Europe from the sixteenth century onwards were clay pipes made of kaolin or porcelain clay, of the same type used in many applications from medicines, toothpaste, paint and paper to porcelain. Originally, these pipes were of the basic, familiar design in a range of shapes and lengths, although later on they were sometimes made to incorporate decorative features, such as animal heads. In the early days, as tobacco was a costly commodity, the bowls were small. By the turn of the seventeenth century pipe-smoking had spread to Europe and across the east and Holland became the chief centre of clay pipe production.

Meerschaum pipes

These are, nowadays, largely made near Ankara in Turkey from a type of soapstone composed of white hydrous magnesium silicate that may be an ancient compressed compound of crushed sea shells and, in fact, '*Meerschaum*' is German for 'seafoam'. In the eighteenth century the centres of production were

Vienna, Germany and Switzerland. These pipes are, by tradition, highly decoratively carved, often bearing animal and even human head shapes and features. As they age with use they grow darker in colour. The material is very light and porous and so is both handy to hold and use and it also absorbs the tar from the tobacco. Moreover, since the material does not burn, you do not need to carbonize it (as you do a briar or corncob pipe) to protect it.

Briar pipes

The archetypical British gentleman's smoking accessory is the briar pipe. Curiously, these were not originally of British manufacture but from France. Pipe-makers such as the French Comoy family, based in Saint-Claude in eastern France, who had started off making pipes from clay, boxwood and beech, turned to briar (*bruyère*).

Henri Comoy (1850–1924) and his son Louis discovered that the wood to be obtained from the root of the white heath bush (*Erica arborea*) rendered by far the best wood for making pipes: naturally dried and matured, this wood has all the characteristics necessary to breathe and provide a cool smoking experience. Briar pipes are made from selected, roughly cut chunks of white heath root that arrive as '*Ebauchons*' (cut to maximize use of the briar burl) or (for the high grade pipes) as '*Plateaux*', which are cut from the top of the burl, to make the best of the grain.

In 1879 Comoy moved to London and set up a small factory at Seven Dials, near Cambridge Circus. The company became called H Comoy & Co Ltd. By 1895 demand for their product had grown to such an extent that they moved the factory to larger premises in Clerkenwell and they stayed in that area until they eventually moved out to Aldershot in 1950. In 1980 the family firm sold out but these pipes are still made by the inheritors of their rich tradition.

Some have sought to explain the attraction of the briar pipe for the British gentleman on the basis that plain clay pipes were seen as essentially working-class accessories and hardly the sort of thing to be seen walking around and smoking; moreover, they were frail and liable to snap. The reasonably ready alternative of the ornately carved *Meerschaum* was equally unacceptable as it appeared too flashy so, to appeal to the combined desire for a good smoke and sturdy, understated elegance, Comoy had hit the nail on the head. Another type of pipe – albeit of a bucolic appearance – is the corncob, which, if well made, can also deliver a surprisingly good, cool smoke.

Alfred Dunhill opened his first pipe shop in Duke Street, St James's, in 1906, as an add-on to his increasing business in motoring accessories (Dunhill's 'Motorities'). The fame of these excellent pipes soon became worldwide and so he later opened international shops. The famous white spot was introduced as a logo in 1915 and Dunhill devised a windshield pipe and also invented the sandblast or 'shell' finish in 1917. Later they introduced other finishes and took to soaking the rough briar in olive oil as part of the curing process. All Dunhill pipes are date stamped and recorded. Famous customers have included the Duke of Windsor. Dunhill also took over the Charatan brand name and still make these pipes too, but not all Dunhill and Charatan pipes are handmade.

The justly famous, relatively recent, small firm of James Upshall began when the managing director of the old firm of Charatan & Co decided to set up his own pipe-making business at Tilshead in Wiltshire in 1978. Barry Jones, Upshall's head pipe carver, is acknowledged as one of the very best of the modern pipe-makers and had been apprenticed at Charatan's. The name James Upshall derives from the name of an ancestor of Colonel Barnes, who established the company. Upshall pipes come from Greek white heath briar and the material is naturally dried and matured and the pipes are all completely hand-turned. They are in great demand the world over as maintaining the tradition of fine artisan craftsmanship, in an age during which many fine crafts are gradually being lost.

Other good current makers include: Alberto Bonfiglioli, Ashton, Bari, Butz Choquin, Castello, GBD, Herbert Love (Glasgow), Nording, Peterson (Dublin), Savinelli, The Royal Dutch Pipe Factory, Stanwell and Talamona Oltrona.

The various names for the shapes of pipes that are currently available (across the board but especially from James Upshall) are to be found in the diagram from James Upshall in plate 20.

The finishes vary between bark, sandblast, black dress and smooth and there are different grades of pipes according to the configuration of the grain. In ascending order of desirability, they are: cross grain, flame grain, straight grain and perfect high grade (a very few specimens enter this grade as the straight grain in the briar has to feature in both the bowl and the shank – the piece that joins the mouthpiece).

Calabash pipes

These were famously smoked by screen actors such as Basil Rathbone in their early portrayals of Sir Arthur Conan Doyle's fictional detective Sherlock Holmes. The books do not mention calabash pipes as Holmes' particular favourite but, owing to the strength of the screen image, significantly perpetuated in the tiling at Baker Street underground station, this pipe is now firmly embedded in the popular imagination as *the* Sherlock Holmes' pipe. The calabash describes the bowl of this pipe – or the apparent bowl – which is fashioned in Turkey out of an

African calabash gourd from the plant *Lagenaria siceraria*. This is a type of dried vegetable that is often also used to make storage receptacles of various kinds. The calabash is lined with a *Meerschaum* pot perforated at the bottom to allow the smoke through into the cooling chamber of the calabash before it is inhaled. These pipes are always made in the traditional bent shape. 'Calabash' is also a term for the same shape of pipe fashioned out of briar.

Anatomy of a pipe

Most briar tobacco pipes comprise the following parts: the bowl and the shank. In a briar pipe this is all one piece; the stem might be joined to the shank under a silver or gold band or 'spigot' – then there are the bit and the lip (the mouthpiece end).

Selecting pipes

The selection of a pipe is an individual matter in terms of size, quality, materials and appearance. However, you might as well also bear in mind when and where you will be smoking it. If it is a pipe for use in an armchair at home, you might run to a larger or a longer pipe (such as a Church Warden) than the pipe that you take with you on country rambles, for which a bent, a billiard or a bulldog is ideal. Always test the balance and feel of a pipe and decide not just on how it looks but how comfortable it is to hold. The traditional way of holding a briar pipe is with the thumb pointed up at the back of the bowl, the bent index finger gripping the front of the bowl and pointing downwards.

Running in a pipe

When you buy a new *briar or corncob* pipe, you need to run it in by gradually building up a layer of carbon on the inside of the bowl to protect the wood. You need to do this by beginning with a small amount of tobacco, maybe a quarter of a bowl, and gradually build this up, over eight to a dozen smokes, to a full bowl and after that smoke it gently once a day for a week until it is nicely encrusted. For actually filling the pipe, see the next paragraph.

Lighting and smoking a pipe

Rub the tobacco, if necessary, and place it by sprinkling (*not pinching*) it into the empty bowl of a run-in pipe until it is three-quarters full of tobacco – but keep the tobacco springy. Tamp it down, test the draw and carefully fill it right up so that there is a slight mound and tamp again. Proceed next to what is called the 'false light': light the tobacco with a circular motion and take light and small puffs; cover the pipe bowl with a matchbox, puffing away a little, and then tamp it down, with a tamper, so that the tobacco goes out. Then you go to the 'true light', lighting up as before with the circular motion and using the matchbox to encourage it until it is going. Then, only practice can tell you how to smoke it through. Don't puff like crazy or it will just burn out; don't tilt the pipe up or the tar will run into your mouth and don't smoke to the bitter end or you'll be sick. You are bound to make mistakes at first, maybe even burn your tongue and feel nauseous, but it is worth persevering to get it right in the end. There is no rule against inhaling pipe smoke but many do not and the nicotine is absorbed through the soft membranes of the mouth.

Cleaning pipes

Have a smoking knife that should combine at least a rounded, blunt blade for removing the dottle (dead ash), a tamping head and a little spike. All good tobacconists sell a reasonable range of these. Remember, when you remove the dottle, not to scrape away at the carbon building up on the inside of the bowl – you need this to protect the briar. Have also a good stock of pipe cleaners in various sizes for the different pipes that you have. Don't wash pipes or even the mouthpieces. If you need a new stem and mouthpiece get it made by the same pipe-maker or at least one who knows his craft. You need to run pipe cleaners through from the mouthpiece end to the shank-end and from the shank through into the bowl. Try to avoid pushing a pipe cleaner from the shank-end through to the mouthpiece as this can cause catching of residue and detritus just at the mouthpiece that disagreeably flies into your mouth on the first puff of the bowl after cleaning.

Resting pipes

The rule for resting pipes is very simple: never light an uncleaned or a warm pipe; in fact try to avoid smoking the same pipe more than once a day and, when you store them, place them in a pipe rack, mouthpiece uppermost, to avoid the drainage of residual tar and liquids down to foul up the mouthpiece.

Jars, pouches, lighters, stands (or racks)

Just about any airtight container can be used for storing tobacco, as long as it has not been tainted with any other substance. Ceramic and glass jars are the most readily available and the most suitable. There are, of course, antique tobacco jars, sometimes highly decorated in porcelain or metal and often bearing little epigrams on the delights of tobacco. In the early days these jars resembled tea caddies of a slightly later vintage and were made of precious substances. Recall that tonka beans, spread around in the mixture, will prevent it from drying out if it is to be kept for any period of time.

When choosing a tobacco pouch to carry your daily allowance, remember that the best are the folding leather pouches, often lined with plastic. Try to avoid the zip variety of pouch as the zips soon wear out.

As for lighters, there are several good specific pipe lighters on the market, with angled flames. Good examples are to be found at Davidoff and Dunhill. However, frankly, there is nothing wrong with good matches and, moreover, the matchbox can be used to coax the pipe alight by flapping it gently up and down over the top of the bowl.

Pipe racks need to be large enough to hold your entire collection and have rests that are far enough apart to enable each pipe of the various sizes to stand alone without rubbing and wearing against any of the others. There are also attractive circular stands for sale, which show off a collection to fine advantage.

'Estate' pipes

There is a steady market for 'estate pipes': old, second-hand pipes of excellent provenance, such as Comoy pipes, Charatan pipes, Astley pipes, Ashton pipes, Dunhill pipes and those made by H Simmons, formerly of 60–61 Burlington Arcade and makers of James Bond's toned-down cigarettes in novels by subsequent novelist John Gardner. (Of course, now, the screen Bond does not smoke at all; in fact no one smokes in Bond films anymore. These directors would take the smoke out of Bogart's *Casablanca*.)

Estate pipes can often be bought at auctions and in sales on internet marketing sites. Plainly, they need to be carefully examined and might need to be reconditioned to some extent, possibly by the substitution of a new stem, but do remember not to disturb the carbon blanket that encrusts the inside of the bowl. Of course, you do not want to buy one with too much encrustation as the pipe could well be burned out.

Types of presentation of pipe tobacco

Here there are, basically, **Aromatics** (also called **Cavendish** – such as Radford's Wild Cavendish, which may derive, in part, from the Middle Eastern *shisha*, smoked in hookahs or 'hubbly-bubblies'), and unflavoured **Straight** blends. These all come as **crimp cut** (short and curled); **curly cut** (dark and light corded together) and **navy cut** (thin slabs of pressed dark tobacco that has to be crumbled and rolled; a pleasure in itself). Other terms for preparation and presentation include: **rough cut**, **ribbon**, **flake** and **twist** (the last, though, is usually for chewing). A good internet site for a great range of pipe tobacco is 4noggins.com.

McClelland's Oriental Mixtures (especially the Grand Oriental Yenice Agonya Pipe Tobacco), Astley's Pipe Tobaccos and tobaccos from Gawith Hoggarth and Samuel Gawith (still made in the traditional way) are all very fine.

Vintage Blends and Mixtures

It is possible to buy vintage tobacco mixtures and blends, even of brands that have gone out of production. Examples are Amphora, Cesar Borgia, Four Monks, Danish Fruit Cake, Dunhill Standard (made by Murray's – now Dunhill pipe tobaccos are made by Orlik's in Denmark), Dunhill London Mixture, Charatan English Mixture and so on. This site is very much worth a visit: cubancigars4u.com. One danger to watch out for, in this connection, is that air might have got into the tobacco mixture and so dried and tainted it with age.

Famous pipe smokers

If you decide to take to a pipe, you will be in very fine (and varied) company indeed as, amongst very many other eminent people, the following have all much enjoyed (some still enjoy) a fine pipe of good tobacco – including one or two of the ladies:

Neil Armstrong (astronaut)
JS Bach (composer)
Tony Benn (politician)
Clive Brook (early British Hollywood matinée idol)
Lord Byron (poet and international rascal)
Thomas Carlyle (historian and writer)
Raymond Chandler (writer)
Lord Clarendon (statesman)
Samuel Taylor Coleridge (poet)

Sir Arthur Conan Doyle (writer)
William Cowper (poet)
Bing Crosby (singer)
Charles Darwin (natural scientist)
Madame de Pompadour (mistress of Louis XV)
Wyatt Earp (law man)
Albert Einstein (physicist)
Emperor Frederick III of Prussia
Clark Gable (actor)
Greta Garbo (actress)
Günter Grass (writer)
Ernest Hemingway (writer)
Oliver W Holmes (physician and writer)
Sherlock Holmes (fictional detective)
Thomas H Huxley (scientist)
King Hussein of Jordan
Rachel Jackson (wife of General Jackson)
Ben Jonson (playwright and poet)
Rudyard Kipling (writer)
Veronica Lake (actress)
Charles Lamb (writer and reluctant tobacco quitter)
Richard Le Gallienne (writer)
François Guizot (French statesman)
Jack Lemmon (actor)
Lord Lytton (statesman and poet)
Edouard Manet (painter)
Captain Frederick Marryat (writer)
AA Milne (writer)
Molière (actor and playwright)
Sir Isaac Newton (mathematician and physicist)
Sir Arthur Quiller-Couch (writer and educationalist)
Basil Rathbone (actor)
Sir Ralph Richardson (actor)
Samuel Rowlands (writer).
Bertrand (Lord) Russell (philosopher)
Anwar Sadat (former president of Egypt)
Arnold Schwarzenegger (actor)
Tom Selleck (actor)
Georges Simenon (writer)
Joseph Stalin (dictator)

Gertrude Stein (writer)
RL Stevenson (writer)
Jacques Tati (film producer and actor)
WM Thackeray (writer)
James Thomson (poet)
JRR Tolkien (writer)
Mark Twain (writer)
Vincent Van Gogh (painter)
HLM Queen Victoria
Robert Wagner (actor)
George Washington (American president)
Evelyn Waugh (writer)
Orson Welles (actor and director)
Harold Wilson (politician)
Lord Peter Wimsey (fictional detective)
HRH The Duke of Windsor
Sir Pelham G ('Plum') Wodehouse (writer)

Cigars

El Gallo, the famous bullfighter, was once asked what he did for exercise and, according to Ernest Hemingway, in *Death in the Afternoon*, he replied:

> I smoke Havana cigars.

Introduction

Havana cigars from Cuba are the top of the tree in the cigar world. All the tobacco plants used in Havana cigars are *Tabaco negro cubano* (of the genus *Nicotiana tabacum*) that Columbus found there in 1492. As a result of research, in 1907 an improved variety called *Habanensis* was created and, as a result of more research, from this, in 1941, *Criollo* was developed and this forms the essential basis for Havana tobacco research and cigar production. This in turn gave rise to *Corojo*, which has been used for wrapper leaves. Continuing research is still producing more varieties that are increasingly resistant to disease and climate change.

The names of great cigars (especially Cuban) are Spanish because the Spanish started the controlled cultivation of cigar tobacco in modern times. There are several growing regions on the island but the main one is Vuelta Abajo and even here not all the land is designated *Vegas Finas de Primera* and so allowed to produce tobacco for true Havana cigars. This is the only region that produces all types of leaf.

There is filler tobacco, central to the character of each cigar; different classifications making up the heart of the cigar (*tripa*, literally the gut), then the binder (*capote*) and then the wrapper (*capa*). The filler comprises mixtures of *volado* (lighter flavoured) tobacco from the base leaves and *seco* (stronger flavoured) from the middle of the plants and *ligero* (the strongest) from the top leaves. The wrapper leaf is grown under muslin covers, which are stretched across the fields, on poles, to shield the tobacco plants from the sun (*tapado*). The other leaves are sun-grown (*tabaco del sol*).

After growing and harvesting (in all a long and painstaking process), the tobacco leaves are air-cured in pairs, then they are tied in bunches (*gavillas*) and sent to be naturally fermented in the sorting house or *Escogida*. The wrapper leaves are subject to a separate process, involving one fermentation. Havana cigars are made of air-cured tobaccos and all filler and binder leaves are subject to at least two fermentations. Fermentation sweats out impurities in the leaf. The tobaccos in Cohibas (the Cuban international flagship brand first blended in 1966, originally for El Presidente Fidel Castro) are thrice fermented. The name Cohiba derives from the native Cubans' old name for tobacco. Cohiba have recently introduced the premium Behike range, named after the chief of Cuba's Taino tribe and containing in the filler a special, rare leaf called *medio tiempo*.

Next, the sun-grown leaves have a final sorting and are part-stripped of their stalks by *Despalilladores*, who also perform the grading of the leaves (*rezagado*). At each stage of sorting, leaves of each kind that do not meet the proper standards are set aside to be sold off for other uses, such as cigarette and pipe tobacco production, as well as for production of cheaper machine-made cigars. The wrapper leaves are stripped at a later stage. After this, the filler and binder leaves are given a second fermentation. Then the leaves are sent to be aged in warehouses, the longer the better. The filler and binder leaves are stored in hessian bales (each called a *paca*) and the wrapper is put into bales covered with Yagua (*tercios*). Yagua is the bark of the Royal Palm tree.

Selection of leaves to make the various brands of cigars is made according to the *tiempo*: *volado*, *seco* and *ligero*, as necessary. Up to three years after the first leaves were picked, they are selected by each brand's blender (*Ligador*) in the blending room, known as the *Barajita* (literally 'pack of cards', because the leaves are 'shuffled' there), and made up into hand-rolled cigars in Havana.

There are different lengths (in Cuba measured in millimetres), shapes and ring gauges (or diameters, each unit of gauge being 1/64th of an inch). The overall configuration of a cigar is known as the *Vitola*.

Hand-rolling

Proper Havana cigars are hand-rolled in the *Galera*, or workshop, by makers called *Torcedores* (literally 'twisters'). They serve long apprenticeships at this craft. Their main tools are the *tabla* – the board on which they roll the leaf – and a bladed tool (*chaveta*), a disc cutter (*casquillo*), a guillotine, presses and moulds, a template (*cepo*) to check the length and ring gauge, and *goma*, an odourless, tasteless gum, is used to finish the rolling process, which begins with leaf tips at the foot of the cigar (the end to be lit). The binder is prepared first and then the filler. The cigar is rolled, pressed, formed and then wrapped. Obviously choice, unblemished leaves are used to finish the product in the wrapper, with the leaf-veins facing inwards for a smooth finish.

The main colours of wrapper (from light to dark) are: *Claro*, *Colorado Claro*, *Colorado*, *Colorado Maduro* and *Maduro*. If there are slightly different shades of cigar to go into the same box, they are sorted dark to light, from left to right, in the box.

The *Torcedores* are graded into four levels of skill, all grades are overseen by supervisors and each grade is assigned different types of cigars to make so that the lower grades make the smaller cigars with less complex shapes. The *Torcedores* need to master all the blending characteristics as well as adjusting their filling, binding and wrapping techniques for each brand and each *type* within the brand.

By tradition, *Torcedores* are read to as they work (normally a newspaper in the morning and a book in the afternoon). This is done by a *Lector* (reader) but now a few factories use recordings. Montecristo cigars were named in 1935 after Alexandre Dumas' romantic novel *The Count of Montecristo* because the book was such a favourite with the *Torcedores* to whom it was read.

A sample of their cigars is regularly subjected to physical examination to determine consistency. Careful examination of the work is important as the *Torcedores* are paid by the pieces that they make. The quality control is such that even finished products not measuring up to the exacting standards applied to correct and regular colour, shape, blend, weight, gauge and draw (suction) are discarded. Nowadays there are devices used to test the draw of the cigars when the filler and binder have been rolled into the *bonche* (the combined filler and binder) and before they are finished with the wrapper leaf.

After making, they are rested for at least a week in carefully controlled conditions and then sampled by *Catadores*, who keep hold of smoking quality control. The *Catadores* must have one of the best jobs in the whole wide world and punctuate their tastings with cups of sugared mint tea to refresh the palate.

Cuban cigars are totally handmade, long-filler cigars (*totalemente a mano tripa larga*) and they are generally stored in a humidor to keep them moist. European (e.g. Dutch, Swiss, Italian and German) cigars are short-filler and dry and often machine-made of homogenized tobacco leaf. Small, dark Cheroots are especially associated with India and Burma (Myanmar).

Other Latin-American cigars that are made in a similar way to Cuban cigars include those from the Dominican Republic, Nicaragua and Honduras. Most factories in the Dominican Republic split the rolling into two jobs, one making the *bonche* and the other adding the wrapper. Also they often use a machine like a Rizla cigarette roller to make the *bonche*.

The *Parejo* is any straight-sided cigar and includes such types as *Coronas* and *Panetelas*. Shaped cigars are *Figurados* and include *Torpedo* (actually a double *Figurado*), *Piramide* and *Perfecto* and the rather odd *Culebras* (comprising a plaiting of three thin cigars together). Interestingly, cigars in the brand Cuaba come only as double *Figurados*).

Brands of Havana cigars and merchants

After Fulgencio Batista said 'Hasta la vista' to Cuba at New Year 1959 (taking about US $400 million of cash and goods with him in several airplanes), production of all tobacco and cigars in Cuba was expropriated by Fidel Castro and given over to the state organization Empresa Cubana del Tabaco. Now production of tobacco and cigars is in the hands of Tabacuba SA and marketing is in the hands of Habanos SA, a company jointly owned by Tabacuba SA and Altadis SA, a Spanish company (itself owned by Imperial Tobacco).

True Havana cigars are sold in boxes marked '*Habanos DOP*' denoting 'Protected Appellation of Origin'. However, following the Castro Revolution, some former plantation owners fled overseas and many brand-owners were foreign companies anyway. Some of these went to other places, such as the Dominican Republic, where they used seed originally from Cuba to plant, grow and produce tobacco in their traditional manner and some of them continued to use the old names of the brands of cigars that they had formerly manufactured, such as *Romeo y Julieta*, producing a duplication of some brand names. This duplication of names resulted from the fact that some countries, such as the USA, placed an embargo on the importation of actual Cuban cigars after the Castro revolution. Despite the use of the Cuban seed, the existence of different growing conditions means that the cigars produced in these other countries are not the same as those produced in Havana.

There are many brands of actual Havana cigars, from global brands (such as Cohiba, the flagship brand) to multi-local brands (such as Bolivar), niche brands (such as Cuaba) and local brands (such as La Gloria Cubana), all with their distinctive smoking characteristics and branding in the cigar band (*anilla* in Cuban Spanish) introduced in the 1860s and the fancy paper label-dressing (*habilitaciones)* of the famous cedar-wood boxes. The label-dressing was probably introduced by Ramon Allones in around 1845. The boxes also bear a mark *Hecho en Cuba* – 'Made in Cuba' – the date of manufacture, a factory code and a paper seal. Those sold in the UK are also marked with another coloured seal 'EMS', standing for 'English Market Selection'.

As with certain drinks, it is useless to try to describe the detailed characteristics of the different smokes that there are in this fascinating area; again the advice is to sample as you may. Generally speaking, the darker cigars render stronger tastes. The greatest part of the range is clear on the Habanos SA website.

The great cigar merchants and tobacconists in London used to include Robert Lewis (founded in 1787 in St James's Street; the shop is now owned by JJ Fox); they didn't stock humidors because they reckoned that the British prefer their cigars aged from five to seven years and dry. They must have been on to something because Edward VII, Churchill, Edward VIII (later the Duke of Windsor) and Groucho Marx were all customers. Some say that young cigars, up to a year old, are fine but that after that they go to sleep for a while and so need to be aged.

Min Ron Nee's book, mentioned at the end of this section, goes into the science of cigar ageing and he divides the potential periods as follows: first, the sick period (during which a cigar might still be smoked), then three consecutive, maturation periods, leading to what he describes as a near-ethereal smoking experience, provided that the cigar has the fortitude to age through each period, all measured in years. In summary, the maturation of cigars has a good deal to do with the continuing organic changes that occur in the materials used, resulting in a reduction in tannins, and a mellower smoke.

Many of the great cigar retailers in London allow customers to keep and age their purchases in their humidors, as 'customers' paid reserve'. At Dunhill each locker is called a 'Keep' while at Fribourg & Treyer the laconic phrase 'put by' was used.

Knight Brothers had been in the City of London for over 100 years and stocked just the full range of *Romeo y Julieta*, named by the manufacturer Rodriguez Fernandez Pepin in 1903. G Smith & Sons are in Charing Cross Road and Shervington's (formerly 'John Brumfit' – one of the first to popularize Havana cigars in England) is in Holborn Bars, near Staple Inn. Holborn Bars is one of the few rows of buildings left in central London to survive the Great Fire of London in 1666 and, if you have not been there, is well worth a visit on this account alone. Do not overlook too Staple Inn, behind it, formerly one of the several Inns of Court and now home to the Institute of Actuaries.

Dunhill also stocks comprehensive selections of Havana cigars as well as all the accessories. Then there are, amongst others, Sautter of Mayfair, Harrods and La Casa de Habano (now in Teddington). Hunters & Frankau (founded in 1790) have exclusive distribution rights to all Cuban-branded Havana cigars, marketed by Habanos SA, throughout the UK.

Humidors and cutters

Humidors are sealed boxes (or rooms) containing devices that keep the cigars inside at a constant humidity and prevent drying out. The ideal conditions are 16 to 18°C with a relative humidity of 65 to 70 per cent. Davidoff stocks a great range of Havanas as well as costly and ornate humidors, even made out of ebony and gold, amboyna burr (possibly the most expensive wood of all), mahogany and burr walnut, not forgetting all the famous names in lighters – Dunhill, Dupont and Cartier – cutters and leather and metal pocket cases.

There are five main types of cutters: first, there is the piercer, which pierces the sealed head of the cigar; secondly, there are the cigar scissors; thirdly, there is the simple guillotine, which slices the cap off; fourthly, there is the cigar punch, which extracts a small cylinder from the centre of the cap; and, finally, there is the 'V'-shaped cutter. JJ Fox (originally based in Burlington Gardens) has already been mentioned and carries a large stock of cigars and accessories.

Cases and holders

There are many types of cases from ordinary pigskin, calf and Morocco to exotic skins, such as crocodile, available at the shops mentioned in this section, and at shops such as Ducas. Of course, there are also antique cases available, even in silver and gold. The makers to look out for on this front include those mentioned under cigarette cases later. FE Smith's widow, Margaret, gave his gold cigar case to his greatest friend and political ally (as well as enthusiastic fellow cigar smoker) Winston Churchill. I have never felt that a cigar holder is justified and, to me, looks absurd with the larger-gauged cigars. Churchill used to fashion 'belly-bandos' out of paper to prevent the head of the cigar getting soggy, but he did often have an unlit cigar in his mouth. If you are just smoking cigars, there really is no need to worry about holders.

Lighting and smoking your cigar

Select your cigar and make sure that it is not too dry or too wet for your own taste: dryness is evident from the feel of the cigar and a crackling if you roll it in your fingers. Smartly pierce or cut the cap off *la perilla*, the head of the cigar (using one of the cutters described) and hold it to face your little finger and between the index, middle and ring fingers and thumb of your left hand. Most cigars have a cap, although some have a flag, twist or pig-tail, in which case be careful that you cut enough to draw but not so much that the wrapper unravels. Never use a petrol lighter to light a cigar or pipe (or even fine cigarettes). You might use a gas lighter or a strong match but, preferably, take and light a cedar wood spill with the right hand and gently apply the flame to the cigar, rolling it to and fro on *la boquilla* (the foot of the cigar) to enable the flame to take evenly. Once the cigar is fully and evenly alight, gently draw the smoke down and into your mouth and exhale it to get the cigar going. Don't go at it like a Trojan but don't be afraid of it either. The harder you smoke it the more it will burn and so overheat and become tarry to the taste and even hot to hold. Sit back and enjoy the smoke; luxuriate it in; let its rich vapours envelope you and free you of all care. You will find great satisfaction in the taste and the nicotine is absorbed through the soft membranes of the mouth. As with pipe smoke, there is no rule against inhaling cigar smoke, but, if you try it, you will cough the first couple of times and, probably, feel sick and giddy.

There is sometimes argument over whether it is correct to remove the name band from your cigar for smoking. This seems to derive from the difference between those who hold that it is tacky to display and advertise one's smoke and those who don't care. Most great cigar smokers, such as FE Smith, Earl of Birkenhead, Sir Winston Churchill and Groucho Marx, seem to have smoked their cigars without the band, but a word of detail: if you try to unpeel the band before you light up, you might easily tear the cigar wrapper leaf, so light up and start the smoke, let the heat loosen the glue and then unpeel it. Also remember that if you try to slide the band off at any stage you might easily drive the sharp paper edges of the tight band into the cigar.

You can hold a cigar like a cigarette but, for longer and larger types, it is a good idea to grip it as I suggest for lighting it in whichever hand is convenient to you. Don't keep tapping the ash off the end. You will find that the density of the ash will keep it in place for up to a couple of inches but, similarly, you do not need to risk burning clothing or furniture, so gently roll it off when approaching every inch or so. Some maintain that a spent good cigar should not be stubbed out but put into a safe receptacle (such as a small bucket) and allowed to expire with dignity. You will find that Havana cigars will plainly 'tell' you when they are spent. Far better to anticipate the burnt-out, acrid smoke of the last inch and a half and dismiss it at that point. Close observers of Sir Winston Churchill noticed that he seemed to discard his cigars half-smoked.

Anyone with a serious interest in pursuing further knowledge in the subject of Havana cigars should read Min Ron Nee's fine book *An Illustrated History of Post-*

Revolution Havana Cigars and join Hunters & Frankau's online Cigar Club, accessible through their internet site.

Cigarettes

The royal road to a cigar!

EW Hornung's gentleman thief Raffles on the merits of Sullivan Powell sub rosa Oriental Cigarettes

The background to, and something of, modern cigarettes

Cigarettes are possibly the earliest smokes, from 3,000 years ago, then often made in wrappers of corn and palm leaves. Modern cigarette tobacco is fine-cut shag in mixtures between any of Burley, Virginia (sun-cured and fire-cured) and Turkish and Balkan, maybe even a mixture of all of them.

As noted earlier, cigarettes have been factory-made from the mid-nineteenth century (machine-made since the mid-1880s) and the records of Fribourg & Treyer actually show that their first 1,000 cigarettes were sold by them, to order, in 1852. Rolling tobacco is also fine-cut shag but, maybe, has fewer additives, ranging from wood to saltpetre (a constituent of gunpowder), to make it burn evenly. Does one inhale Oriental tobacco? Yes, but it permeates one's soul, bringing calm in any crisis and wooing the nostrils of the gods. Turkish and other Oriental cigarettes often came in distinctive oval tubes but Sullivan Powell sub rosa Oriental Cigarettes came in big cylinders, tightly packed, swathed in thick tissue paper, in boxes of 25 or 100. There are again some Turkish cigarettes obtainable in the EU, but they have lessened strength and flavour.

There are, of course, those modern brands of cigarettes which are, like so many other cheap and cheerful things, available in just about all the bars in all the towns in all the world. You know the names of the brands and what they stand for – or, rather, don't stand for. Other than those, there are cigarettes still worth smoking, but they are, owing to legislation, mainly, shadows of the older brands, some of the old ones being: Sullivan Powell sub rosa Oriental Cigarettes (founded 1880); Benson & Hedges Cairo Cigarettes; Abdulla and Passing Clouds, not to mention Morland Specials, the James Bond cigarettes, formerly sold (at 600 a week to Ian Fleming) from a shop at 83 Grosvenor Street, Mayfair, in the dark blue and gold boxes. I cannot exactly say that I shall *not* see the like of such cigarettes again, since I left a light-blue box of oval Benson & Hedges Cairo Cigarettes in the house of a friend in Middlesex over twenty years ago and he recently told me that they are still there. Whether I shall ever have the heart to smoke them I cannot yet say. Unopened boxes and packets of vintage cigarettes are also sometimes found for sale as collectors' items.

There are, though, as I say, very good brands of Virginia cigarettes still available, such as instances produced by Imperial Tobacco – Davidoff Classic and Davidoff Lights – as well as Gauloises Blondes and Gitanes.

There was a time when Turkish, Balkan and Oriental tobacco blends and Turkish, Balkan, Oriental and Egyptian cigarettes definitely had the accepted edge in terms of cigarette consumption and the cheaper Virginia brands were known, disparagingly, as 'coffin nails', indicating (once again), incidentally, that people have been aware for a long time that excessive smoking can be bad for the health. The first time that Egyptian cigarettes were regularly stocked by Fribourg & Treyer (in two different sizes) was in 1880.

The irony is that many people who used to smoke the strong Turkish, Balkan and Oriental blends (all containing much more than the fifteen milligrams of tar currently permitted by the EU) might have had just two or three a day, which is hardly going to damage *anyone's* health much more than, say, walking down Baker Street. But there we are: the Nanny Superstate of the EU knows what's best for us as individuals in terms of purely personal action, and modern Britain tags along for the ride.

There is still Sobranie (Sobranie of London, established in 1879) Black Russian Cigarettes (in their black paper with gold tips), weighing in at nine milligrams of tar, which brings them within the EU limit, and Sobranie Cocktail Cigarettes, with their pastel-coloured papers, for the ladies. There is also a Turkish brand called Tor, which is available tipped or untipped, as well as blends such as Camel (introduced in 1913 by RJ Reynolds) and Lucky Strike (introduced, in 1916, by the American Tobacco Company to compete with them) amongst the best of the modern Turkish–Virginia blends in tipped and untipped varieties. The remaining Camel Turkish mixes (such as Camel Turkish Gold) combine Izmir and Samsun tobacco varieties with more robust Virginia tobacco and, in truth, the best cigarettes have often been blends of various different tobaccos but have not always included Virginia tobacco.

In 1917, Luckies started being advertised as 'Toasted' to indicate that the tobacco was fire-cured rather than sun- or air-cured. Originally, Luckies came in green packs but, from 1942, to aid the war effort (as green dye was needed for camouflage), they have come in the white packs, bearing the bulls-eye green, red and black motif. Hence the wartime slogan:

Lucky Strike Green has gone to war.

In Turkey itself, Tekel is the only Turkish cigarette manufacturer and, even then, it is foreign owned. They make Maltepe, Samsun, Tekel 2000 and Tekel 2001. Then there is also Birinci, cheap and strong.

Tobaccos have been cultivated in Turkey since the sixteenth century, when it was introduced from the west. By 1621 there was a ban on smoking (as in many other places, from time to time) with harsh penalties but, by 1683, the Ottoman Empire was content to tax tobacco. There has been Turkish cigarette production in Turkey since the nineteenth century, beginning in small artisan establishments called *atalye*. All Turkish tobaccos, from their cultivation and environment, have their own very distinctive characteristics that are in demand the world over for cigarette and pipe tobacco blends and mixtures and all, except one, are of the genus *Nicotiana tabacum*. The exception is Hasankeyf, which is of *Nicotiana rustica*.

Some specific Turkish tobaccos, with brief notes on the characteristics of the leaves, are as follows:

Adiyaman
This is yellow to light red in colour, close to Virginia tobacco; it is sweet and strong and used for cigarettes and pipe tobacco.

Balikesir
Again, yellow to light red in colour and another sweet and strong tobacco.

Basma
This light yellow to light red tobacco is mild, sweet and aromatic.

Bitlis
Bitlis is a light yellow to yellow, very sweet and aromatic tobacco.

Bursa
A light red to red and ranging from mild to strong, this has a pleasing 'apricot' aroma. The darker shades are (as is generally the case with tobacco) stronger.

Edirne
This is light to dark red in colour and is strong and sweet with a spicy aroma.

Izmir
Izmir is light yellow to yellow with dark brown dappling on the upper leaves and is mild and sweet.

Pazar
Light to greenish to dark brown in colour, Pazar and is a strong, cigar-type tobacco.

Samsun canik
A light to dark red in colour and sweet, spicy and strong.

Samsun maden
This is light red to red and is mild, sweet and aromatic and is extremely important in the production of high-grade Turkish tobacco blends.

Tasova
Tasova is light red in colour and mild and sweet.

Tombac
Light and dark shades of red, often dappled, Tombac is the sweet and aromatic tobacco favoured for the shisha (hubbly bubbly).

Trabzon
This is light to bright red in colour and is very strong, having the highest nicotine content of Turkish tobaccos.

Yayladag
Yellow to red in colour and sweet and strong with a spicy aroma. It is favoured both for cigarettes and also for pipe tobacco blends.

Some say that the best 'Turkish' tobacco is actually grown outside Turkey, in parts of the former Ottoman Empire, especially the prized **Yenice** variety, taken there and developed in Greece as well as in Macedonia and Bulgaria (hence the use of 'Balkan' to describe some tobaccos). Indeed, the Ian Fleming–James Bond Morland Specials were a Turkish and Balkan blend. Yenice is a fine-textured tobacco, reddish-yellow in colour, with a smooth, rich taste.

James Bond, when abroad, smoked local brands and this Turkish cigarette seems to have been his favourite cigarette (a Diplomate), given to him by Kerim Bey (head of Station T – Turkey – in *From Russia With Love*):

> Bond sat down and took a cigarette and lit it. It was the most wonderful cigarette he had ever tasted – the mildest and sweetest of Turkish tobacco in a slim long oval tube with an elegant gold crescent.

In the USA, Bond favoured Chesterfield cigarettes (introduced in the early twentieth century by Liggett & Myers). They are Virginia cigarettes, named after Chesterfield, County Virginia, and they are still going, along with another good Virginia cigarette, Winston (introduced in 1954 by RJ Reynolds). In the West Indies, Bond favoured Royal Blend. According to Sally Falk Moore, the (?late and ?lucky) Lord Lucan had been screen-tested to play James Bond and Lucan favoured the Peter Stuyvesant brand (named after the last Director General of New Netherland from 1647), also still going strong. There is also still the Dunhill brand, the more expensive ones omitting 'International' in the name. Sturdy, British Senior Service, untipped Virginia cigarettes are also still made; novelist and translator Dorothy L Sayers chain-smoked these as she worked.

Cigarette accessories

Lighters

There are several brands of cigarette lighters. For the young and trendy there are Zippos, and for James Bond wannabes there is still Ronson, but for those after the luxury end of the market there are vintage Dunhill Uniques, the first one-handed lighter, and then the modern ranges: Dunhill Mini Rollagas, Dupont Gatsby and the X-tend turbo, and the Colibri range (although the last is less of a luxury and more of a practical cigar lighter). Cartier also makes fine lighters.

Cases

The use of cigarette cases in this austere and utilitarian age is rare, especially since many people who smoke at all smoke the tobacco equivalent of a Ronald McDonald hamburger: smoking or eating cardboard, as you like, how you like, when you like and just about *wherever* you like from Buenos Aires to Vladivostok. However, cases used to be made in exotic skins (such as crocodile) or precious metals: gold, silver and even platinum and palisander, Brazilian rosewood (*Dalbergia nigra*). The fabled Fabergé cases made by Peter Carl Fabergé (1846–1920) and his work masters, such as those mentioned in the illustrations in plates 25, 26 and 32, in the firm of Imperial Russian jewellers founded by Fabergé are carried now as antiques by firms such as Wartski, London, Bentley & Skinner and Romanov Russia. The cases have a signature gem-set release catch and truly wonderful finishes, including, sometimes, softly undulating ridges in starburst designs or the samorodok (nugget-like) finish. There are also examples of cases with vividly coloured enamels applied over finely machined guilloché metalwork, often comprising a geometric, moiré wave pattern, illustrated in plates 25 and 32. The samorodok finish results in the pattern shown in plate 26 and derives from a difficult process of heating the metal to just below melting point and then plunging it in cold water. Much of the Fabergé output is distinguished by a restrained Louis XVI-style neo-classicism, although they also supplied some cases in the art nouveau style.

The firm of Wartski, London was founded by Morris Wartski in 1865 in north Wales and his son-in-law Emanuel Snowman opened a London branch in 1911. He started buying confiscated Fabergé items (including the iconic Easter Eggs) from the Soviet government and this was continued by his son, A Kenneth Snowman, who also wrote the book *The Art of Carl Fabergé*.

Bentley & Skinner derive from Skinner & Co (established in 1880) and Bentley & Co (established in 1934). Some other great makers are Boucheron (founded in Paris in 1858), Carl Blank and Carl Hahn, as well as English firms such as Asprey and Garrard.

Of course, and again for James Bond fans, there are plain gunmetal cases by other makers, such as Dunhill. Gunmetal is an alloy of copper, tin and zinc and, before tempered steel, it was used to make gun barrels.

Cigarette holders

There used to be a convention, outrageously defied by the writer Edgar Wallace with his telescopic holders, that a man's cigarette holder should be no more than four inches long. I have two which both satisfy this prescription: one is a Dunhill holder in shell-finished black briar and the other is in ebony (specially made to take the gauge of the late Sullivan Powell sub rosa Oriental Cigarettes). I also used to have an amber holder that could accommodate them, but I gave it away in a moment of madness. In my book *History of Men's Fashion* there is reproduced the famous photograph by Horst Tappe of Ian Fleming wreathed in smoke from a cigarette in a holder. I recently read a *Guardian* newspaper article by a female journalist who, while defending the right to smoke, observed that a man using a cigarette holder after 1960 looks either 'poofy' or 'sinister'. All that I can say is 'Come up and see me sometime' ... or see Peter O'Toole, for that matter.

Snuff

> Why, sir, where did you get your snuff? There is only one person I know who can mix snuff in this way.

This was said by George IV, as recorded in Captain Jesse's biography of George 'Beau' Brummell, on being presented with snuff by Sir Benjamin Bloomfield on a brief visit to Calais in September 1821. (The king's former friend Brummell was exiled there, for debt.) Although Brummell did not present himself, he obliged Bloomfield with some snuff when the king had run out of his own. Bloomfield replied to the king: 'It is some of Mr Brummell's, Sir' and there the conversation ended. One might speculate whether, if Brummell had swallowed his pride and taken his bow, he might have been forgiven for their breached friendship and considerably helped. Instead, he had before him nearly nineteen years of begging his remaining friends for sustenance. The king left Calais observing, maybe sadly, to Sir Arthur Paget in his party: 'I leave Calais and have not seen Brummell …' The fact is that the king had not expressly sent for Brummell, possibly fearing rebuff. Maybe he feared some repetition of Brummell excoriating him with another line such as 'Who is your fat friend?' Brummell, also fearing rebuff, had refused to present himself without command. But we do know, again from Captain Jesse's account, that the king had spotted Brummell, caught up in the press of the crowd, on his arrival in Calais and had exclaimed 'Good God – Brummell!' Brummell had gone deathly pale and had then gone inside.

Overall, the evidence (especially the fact that Brummell was asked to send snuff) points to the fact that the king's visit had presented Brummell with an opportunity to become at least partly rehabilitated, which pride ultimately denied him. He thought that he would see the king when he returned to Calais for the boat back to England but the king was pressed for time and went straight aboard.

Snuff is dried, ground tobacco, in a range of fineness and dryness, from coarse, moist, strong rappee to fine, light, 'dry toast' types usually flavoured with floral or fruit essences. The (high) dry toast types were, sometimes, referred to as 'Irish', 'Welsh' and 'Scotch'. 'SP' snuff is a fine, dry snuff slightly scented with citrus oils; mentholated snuff is flavoured with menthol crystals and eucalyptus oil (excellent for a blocked nose). Snuff is graded according to its fineness and the denominations are fine, demi-gros and gros (fine, medium and coarse); an additional denomination is '*carotte*' – extra coarse.

Snuff may regain favour with inveterate nicotine addicts who will still wish to visit pubs, restaurants and even private clubs after the Stalinist smoking ban took effect in Britain and other places.

There is evidence from the earliest European explorations of America that the American Indians took snuff. The Brazilian Indians were especially adept at making snuff and Brazilian tobacco was, early on, prized for making snuff in Europe. In Brazil it is called *rapé* – both rappee and *rapé* derive from the French verb rapper, 'to rasp', referring to the filing action involved, early on, in producing snuff. The first mill-factory to manufacture snuff was probably in Seville in the sixteenth century.

Nowadays African tobacco is mainly used and although the methods of manufacture have changed from ancient times the basic process remains the same. First there is the selecting of suitable tobacco leaf (sometimes stalk too), which is matured and dried and then ground to the required fineness for the type of snuff to be produced. After this it is sieved, any scents and flavourings are added and it is sealed up in wooden casks to mature. In ancient times, individuals sometimes made their own snuff by rasping the tobacco off a plug of tobacco, called a *carotte*.

Snuff became especially popular in England following a sea battle off the Spanish port of Vigo on 23 October 1702 between the victorious combined English and Dutch fleets and the combined French and Spanish fleets. A large quantity of snuff was among the prize (they had been hoping for silver) and Admiral Sir George Rooke distributed it amongst the crew. The same kind of Spanish snuff, labelled 'SP', is still available today. Moreover, during the battle, an English ship was seriously threatened by a French fire ship but it failed perilously to ignite owing to its cargo of snuff (which does not easily burn) and the English ship survived!

Fribourg & Treyer, snuff chandlers, were founded in 1720 at 34 Haymarket 'At the sign of the Rasp & Crown' (as suggested above, a rasp is a metal file once used for filing plugs, or *carottes*, of tobacco to make snuff). The records of Fribourg & Treyer demonstrate that, up until 1830, snuff comprised the greatest part of its business but that by 1850 the supply of snuff was equalled by the supply of cigars and tobacco and that by 1859 snuff was falling behind. One of the most enduring businesses in London, it was bought by Imperial Tobacco around 1982, but despite the fact that even in the twenty years to 1974 Fribourg & Treyer supplied more snuff than any other business in the world (and to all over the world) its lease was not renewed. After a brief move to Regent Street, the retail business was closed. 34 Haymarket is now a tourist shop but the façade is intact; one window pane bears the name Fribourg & Treyer and the old shelves are still visible, worn and grooved, from over 250 years of snuff jars being moved around to supply everyone from the actor David Garrick (1717–1779) to Queen Charlotte (1761–1818) to Princess Charlotte Augusta (1796–1817) to Beau Brummell (1778–1840) himself – even to Napoleon in exile on St Helena, and, in our own time, such people as cricket commentator John Arlott (1914–1991). Presumably, they all shared the motto:

> He that is not a friend at a pinch, is not worth a snuff.

So far as the windows are concerned: as John Arlott tells us in *The Snuff Shop*, from the earliest times the shop front was shuttered at night (with iron-bound wooden shutters) and because this continued throughout the Second World War when a big bomb blast at the top of Haymarket, outside the old Scott's restaurant, shattered nearly every other window in Haymarket the panes in the front of Fribourg & Treyer suffered not a crack.

The snuff recipes were taken over by Wilsons of Sharrow, another great snuff maker and chandler, founded in 1737, and they still make many Fribourg & Treyer snuffs as well as their own. They are all available from them direct, or (as are Smith's own excellent snuffs) from G Smith & Sons' cigar shop and, indeed, from all good tobacconists. There is also the excellent online supplier snuffstore.co.uk.

Bureau was a particularly sophisticated Fribourg & Treyer Regency favourite, blended from six different types of snuff. Spanish Sabillia was a very fine red snuff that enjoyed a popularity from the eighteenth century until 1890 as a tooth powder!

Besides Old Paris (strong and dark, made of Cuban tobacco), another of Brummell's favourites (both still made) was Fribourg & Treyer's Macouba snuff, which is scented with attar of roses (described as 'Otto of Roses' in the Fribourg & Treyer accounts): this was very probably used by him for mixing in with other snuffs.

Attar of roses is an essential oil, obtained by steam distillation of the petals of *Rosa damascena Mill.* (damask rose), largely grown in Bulgaria, Turkey, Russia, India, China and Iran. It takes many pounds of petals to make one tiny phial of this oil. Mrs Beeton calculated that 200,000 blooms are required to make a half ounce. John Arlott put it another way: five tons of roses, or fourteen million blooms, are needed to make one kilogram of attar. It was a rose of this type that was planted at the head of the grave of Edward FitzGerald (1809–1883) in Boulge Churchyard, Suffolk, in 1893, by the Omar Khayyam Society. The story of this bush is recounted in my *History of Men's Fashion*. In 2005 Peter Beales, of Peter Beales Roses, sent his head nurseryman to tend the original bush, which had become overshadowed by laurel bushes, and he probably saved it. This particular rose is not much to look at, being a pale pink and rather 'cabbagey', but it exudes the strong, wistful scent that we all know as 'rose'. Peter Beales Roses sell rose bushes, which derive from a cutting that Graham Stuart Thomas OBE, VMH took from the original grave-site bush. These flowers would not do as buttonholes – but a vase full of them, scenting the air, petals continually falling, certainly helps in what Dr Johnson would describe as the 'harmless drudgery' of writing a book.

Brummell seems to have become a customer of Fribourg & Treyer by around 1799 (at the age of twenty-one) and on 3 October 1799 he sent the Prince of

Wales a quantity of snuff, which brought the Prince to them as a big customer for the rest of his life.

Interestingly, the accounts show that Brummell actually moved around rather a lot and, although the house at 4 Chesterfield Street, Mayfair, bears the blue commemorative plaque and he was there in 1799, by 1800 he was at 95 Park Street; in 1801 he was in Upper Grosvenor Street and between 1803 and 1809 variously at Worthing (to be near to the Prince's Royal Pavilion at Brighton), 18 Bruton Street and 24 South Street. His modest snuff account had been regularly settled down to 30 June 1815 before he fled to France on 16 May 1816 and the balance (seemingly of £15-17s-6d) was written off on 17 December 1818.

Samuel Gawith & Co also make and market their own snuff, including a Black Rappee. Other snuff makers include Bernard Schnupftabak, founded in 1733 in Offenbach, Germany (but since 1812 they have been in Regensburg), Pöschl, founded in 1902 in Landshut, and some small producers still in Brazil, several of which make a snuff scented with essence from the Imburana tree (*Amburana cearensis*). The last two snuff windmills are in Holland.

According to House of Commons Fact Sheet G7, although smoking has been banned in the Chamber since 1693, snuff is provided, at public expense, to members and officials and is obtainable from the doorkeeper's box. A ban against smoking in White's club was the reason for the founding of the Marlborough club where (amongst others) the then Prince of Wales (later King Edward VII) could indulge in his cigars in appropriate company.

If you buy large amounts of snuff then, as with pipe tobacco, tonka beans are most useful in keeping it moist in storage.

Snuff boxes and horns old and new and snuff mulls

Before brought into use, snuff is undoubtedly best kept in airtight jars, which might be similar to the tobacco jars already mentioned. Fribourg & Treyer stocked highly glazed Wedgwood Jasperware jars that were sought after as ornaments. Once it is brought into use, there are various different containers that can be used. For personal use there is the pocket snuff box and this might be a modern pewter or rosewood box or an antique in amboyna (or other woods), porcelain (especially desirable are those painted by Richard Cosway), tortoiseshell, *papier-mâché* (look out for those made by the Martin Brothers or the Stobwasser factory in Berlin), silver, gold, Jasperware or enamel (most notably those made in porcelain enamel on hammered copper by the Battersea factory, and there are even porcelain boxes painted by Fragonard). The tobacconists mentioned as still selling snuff offer a range of the modern examples and the antiques can be found in many of the shops mentioned for jewellery in Chapter

3 and, notably, also the London Silver Vaults. Especially useful is a box with a 'Laurencekirk' airtight hinge, the invention of James Sandy in the late eighteenth century.

There are also larger table snuff boxes and horns (fashioned out of a ram's horn with a hinged metal lid). Inner Temple has a lovely silver table box, which was the gift of the great Edwardian advocate Sir Edward Marshall Hall, and Gray's Inn has a magnificent snuff horn.

Snuff mulls are small, capped, horn-shaped containers made out of many different materials, which are for carrying on the person and can be found in antique shops and auctions.

How to take snuff

According to an old prescription: take the box in the left hand and rap it briskly with the right hand. This loosens the snuff. Open the lid of the box with the left thumb: *on no account may a snuffer use both hands to open the box.* Tap the open box on the side, to gather the snuff up and present the box to the assembled company, and then take your own pinch, between the index finger and thumb of the right hand. Let your arm drop and pause for a moment before raising the snuff to each nostril in turn (without grimace), sharply sniffing it in. It is as well to close the nostril that is not sniffing with the index finger of the left hand. After this, close the box with a flourish and then wipe your nose on your sleeve or, failing that, with a brightly coloured snuff handkerchief. One variation on this method of taking snuff is to place the pinch in the 'natural snuff box', which is to be found by stretching out the left hand and raising the thumb: the indentation above the point that the thumb joins the wrist is the 'natural snuff box'.

CHAPTER 7

A Selection of Interesting Venues

Maybe it's because I'm a Londoner,
That I love London so,
Maybe it's because I'm a Londoner,
That I think of her, wherever I go.

From Hubert Gregg's song
'Maybe it's because I'm a Londoner'

I deal in this chapter with some unusual and interesting places that are not as obvious as the theatres, concert halls, opera houses, restaurants, shops and so on that are readily apparent to everyone.

Bookshops

No furniture is so charming as books.

Sydney Smith

There are many very good bookshops in London. Here is a handful of wonderful ones.

Dillon's Bookshop (Waterstone's), Torrington Place, WC1

Dillon's is situated in Bloomsbury and, besides being a general bookstore, carries a large selection of academic books to serve the students of the academic institutions for which the area is famed. It tends to attract more hurried, objective-led shoppers than Hatchards' sedate customers but it is still a wonderful shopping experience.

Foyles, 113–119 Charing Cross Road, WC2

Foyles was originally just in Charing Cross Road. However, now it has spread out across London and even has a branch in Manchester. One of the biggest general bookshops going (indeed until recently regarded as the biggest in the whole world), one slight criticism is that the organization and service may not be quite as good as some of the competition. It is also known for its booksignings and other literary events such as its luncheons. Ruled over for most of the last century by the autocratic Christina Foyle, it does now take telephone (and internet) orders.

Grant & Cutler, 55–57 Great Marlborough Street, W1

Grant & Cutler is a foreign-language bookshop near Oxford Circus, specializing in all living foreign languages (as they ironically put it 'From Afrikaans to Zulu'), but of course covering all the main European languages too.

Hatchards, 187 Piccadilly, W1

Hatchards has been a bookseller since 1797. Situated in Piccadilly, it probably offers the most knowledgeable and helpful service in relation to retail books and holds a large selection of signed copies and special editions. Entering the doors is rather like entering a country house library and there is total freedom to browse without being importuned by an assistant asking whether he or she can help you.

Heywood Hill, 10 Curzon Street, W1

Heywood Hill, in Curzon Street, Mayfair, has a commemorative blue plaque recording that novelist, diarist (and correspondent) Nancy (*Don't Tell Alfred*) Mitford once worked there. Famed the world over as antiquarian book dealers, to enter this shop is a necessary pilgrimage for all those who love books. Needless to say, the staff know their onions – and quite a lot about books too.

Second-hand

Skoob is a fantastic second-hand bookshop in Bloomsbury. It used to be in the Sicilian Arcade off Southampton Row but is now in the Brunswick Shopping Centre, WC1. They buy and sell all books but are especially strong on academic books for the student community. Knowledgeable, helpful staff and an online catalogue for their warehoused collection make for a good shopping experience. They offer discounts of up to ten per cent to certain groups, such as students. Other second-hand bookshops include those in the Charing Cross Road, such as **Any Amount of Books**, **Henry Pordes** and **Quinto**. There are also several such shops in Cecil Court, WC2, and in the streets around the British Museum. There are still, from time to time, stalls selling books on the South Bank.

However, on-line sales through seek-and-find portals, such as AbeBooks, have seriously knocked the second-hand bookshop trade.

Stanfords, 12–14 Longacre, WC2

This is a first-rate shop for maps, charts and travel guides. The flagship store is in Long Acre, Covent Garden.

Waterstone's (chain)

Waterstone's is a big countrywide chain but it is well organized and some stores even have comfortable sofas and refreshment counters to enhance the browsing experience. Unlike some bookshops, browsing is actively encouraged: just don't smear any chocolate brownies on any books that you are *not* going to buy. The Piccadilly branch (in the art deco former Simpsons of Piccadilly building) is now Europe's biggest bookshop.

Casini

> The scent and sweat and smoke of a casino are nauseating at three in the morning …
>
> Ian Fleming, opening of *Casino Royale*

... but even though the smoke has largely gone, people still go to play. Where are some of the best places in London? Here are several delightful venues, all 'members only', but there is no longer a cooling-off period between joining and actually playing.

Aspinalls, 27–28 Curzon Street, W1

This was founded by the playboy, tycoon and zoo-keeper John Aspinall and has been on its current site since 1992.

Clermont, 44 Berkeley Square, W1

This was the first club founded by Aspinall, in 1962 (in a splendid original house by architect William Kent), after a period of hosting surreptitious private gaming sessions during a period of prohibition. Later on, it was greatly favoured by the mysterious Lord Lucan as his base of operations, beginning his long day's night with his lamb cutlet luncheon. Annabel's nightclub is underneath.

Crockfords, 30 Curzon Street, W1

Crockfords is now in a wonderful town house in Curzon Street in the heart of Mayfair. The original Crockfords (or Crockies as it is known to regulars) was founded in 1828 in a purpose-built casino building (one of the first of its kind) at what is now 50 St James's Street (again another casino, dealt with below). The founder was William Crockford, who had been a fishmonger at Temple Bar, made a fortune out of horse racing and set himself up in rather a different kind of business that attracted the cream of Georgian society, including the Duke of Wellington himself. When Crockie died, he had just entered a horse in an important race: his death would have avoided the entry and there is a legend that members propped his corpse up in a window where he could be seen, apparently alive and well, to the members of White's club opposite. Nowadays they offer gaming on the open floor plus in two *salles privées* as well as a high stakes room: roulette, blackjack, punto banco and three-card poker are the games. The restaurant offers some of London's best food and wine, across a range of styles, including game in season. Some say that Crockies carries on the gourmet tradition established by Watier's Club, of which Brummell had been a founding father and original life president. They also permit private poker games (for a fee) and hold backgammon tournaments (for an entry fee).

Fifty, 50 St James's Street, SW1

Fifty is, as mentioned above, in the original home of Crockfords. This is once again a casino, having in the meantime (during a period of prohibition) been home to the Devonshire Club and even the Jamaican High Commission. Also distinguished by fine cuisine and bar facilities, both in different rooms, there is a club lounge and a nightclub (membership of which may be had separately). The games again take place on a spectacular gaming floor and include roulette, blackjack, punto banco and stud poker. The maximum and minimum stakes here vary, as in the other two mentioned, and there are again *salles privées* for high-rollers. According to news reports in November 2009 the administrators have been called in and gaming at this club has been suspended until the business is sold.

Les Ambassadeurs, 5 Hamilton Place, W1

Les Ambassadeurs is off Old Park Lane, in a town house once owned by the Rothschild banking family. It is known to members as 'Les A'. They also have sumptuous dining facilities, including a private dining room annexed to one of their two *salles privées*. The views from the first floor and balconies, over Hyde

Park, are truly spectacular and the gaming includes roulette, blackjack, stud poker and punto banco. In fact, the punto banco becomes quite an event here; the players take turns to deal the cards and the table is frequently crowded, producing the seductive atmosphere of a Bond novel. Indeed, the casino scene at the beginning of the film of *Dr No* is in a casino called Les Ambassadeurs.

Palm Beach, 30 Berkeley Street, W1

Inside it is done out around a palm tree theme and even the chandeliers suggest them. There is just one big, packed floor for roulette, blackjack, poker and punto banco. There is a restaurant area and a bar and plenty of seating, together with table service.

Ritz Club, Piccadilly, W1

Situated underneath the Ritz Hotel in Piccadilly, is this comfortable club with its intimate bar and splendid dining facilities.

Pubs

> Before the Roman came to Rye or out to Severn strode,
> The rolling English drunkard made the rolling English road.
>
> GK Chesterton

I have confined my attentions here to central London and even then to a very few, largely to those that are known mainly to Londoners but not so much to visitors.

The Dolphin, 44 Red Lion Street, WC1

This is a delightful pub on the street corner in a Victorian building. Look out for the still hands of a clock that commemorate the time of a wartime bomb blast that stopped it and several lives.

The George, 77 Borough High Street, SE1

Rebuilt in 1676 after a fire, this is situated just off Borough High Street, down a cobbled courtyard, and is the only remnant of a galleried coaching inn left in London; even so a good part of it was lost to development by a railway company. The Philistines fumbling in their greasy tills are not an entirely new phenomenon. The remains of the place are safely preserved by the National

Trust. It is very close to the site of the former Tabard Inn, which was the starting place for the pilgrims in Chaucer's *Canterbury Tales*. The atmospheric bars all connect and the middle bar was a favourite haunt of Charles Dickens. In the galleried upper reaches, there is a restaurant. I remember having some good mulled wine here one winter's night.

The Lamb, 92 Lamb's Conduit Street, WC1

The Lamb is a perfect example of a Victorian pub and still has the etched glass 'snob screens' around the bar, designed to shield the customers from the bar staff. The walls are full of framed pictures of old stars of the stage and it serves a good range of Young's beers.

The Lamb & Flag, 33 Rose Street, Covent Garden, WC2

This is in Rose Street and is at least 300 years old. Its old name had been the Bucket of Blood from the fact that bare-knuckle fights had used to take place here. One room is called the Dryden Room, after the poet John Dryden. This pub offers a simple range of pub grub.

The Nell Gwynne, 2 Bull Inn Court, WC2

Named after Charles II's favourite mistress and in a little court, which itself is named after an older inn on the site, the Nell Gwynne dates from 1897 and is a real hideaway. Mind the stairs to the lavatories. I wonder whether the landlords have ever been sued.

The Olde Cheshire Cheese, 145 Fleet Street, EC4

The current building is largely seventeenth century and rebuilt after the Great Fire of London in 1666. It is situated in Wine Office Court, which leads up to Dr Johnson's House in Gough Square as well as the statue of Hodge, his 'very fine cat'. The Chop Room holds Dr Johnson's chair from the Mitre Tavern that used to stand on part of the site (marked with a plaque) of what is now Hoare's Bank (near Temple Bar), and there are portraits of Johnson and Boswell. Also in the Chop Room is Polly, a stuffed African grey parrot, which was so famous for its entertaining mimicry that when it died it received many newspaper obituaries. Amongst others who drank here are Alexander Pope, Voltaire, William Thackeray, Charles Dickens, Sir Arthur Conan Doyle, Mark Twain and WB Yeats. There is a very atmospheric bar to the right as you enter, with an open fire in the winter. There is a legend that Dickens used to perform 'the first cut of the Ye Puddings' in the Cheshire Cheese on the first Monday in October.

These old English puddings could be up to eighty pounds in weight and were crammed full with steak, kidneys, oysters, larks and mushrooms.

The Old Mitre, Ely Court, between 8 and 9 Hatton Garden, EC1

In between numbers 8 and 9 Hatton Garden there is an alley with an arched entrance bearing the sign 'Ye Olde Mitre 1546'. It was originally built for the servants of the Bishops of Ely, whose palace was nearby. Queen Elizabeth I forced the bishops to lease land to Sir Christopher Hatton, hence the name Hatton Garden, the modern-day centre of the British jewellery trade. The palace and the original pub were demolished in 1772 but the pub was rebuilt and a stone mitre from the palace gatehouse is built into the structure. The trunk of an ancient cherry tree is also preserved inside; it originally marked the boundary between the let land and the diocesan lands. Legend has it that Good Queen Bess danced the maypole around it. Behind the pub, in Ely Place, is St Etheldreda's Roman Catholic chapel, named after a queen of East Anglia, and England's oldest surviving Catholic church.

The Only Running Footman, 5 Charles Street, W1

The original role of servants called 'footmen' was to run before the master's carriage, brandishing a stick, to clear the route. When roads improved this function became otiose and footmen just became house servants. However, the last of them to have exercised the function of running before a carriage bought a pub in the early nineteenth century and renamed it after his former occupation. There has actually been a pub on this site since 1749. It is cosy and, depending on the day and time, can be surprisingly tranquil, in the heart of Mayfair.

The Punch, 99 Fleet Street, EC4

This late-Victorian building houses an award-winning and splendid gastro-pub with a truly traditional Fleet Street atmosphere. Previously called The Crown and Sugarloaf, it was renamed The Punch after a rebuild in 1894 to 1895, in honour of the *Punch* magazine journalists and artists who frequented it.

The Red Lion, 2 Duke of York Street, SW1

There has been a public house on this site since at least 1788. Today, it stands in a building that dates from 1821, although the pub interior is a near-perfect example of a late Victorian Gin Palace, with a patina-encrusted Lincrusta ceiling and walls and partitions comprising ornamented glass and mirrors in mahogany frames. This is a busy place and often the customers spill out on to the pavement.

The Seven Stars, 53–54 Carey Street, WC2

This pub dates from 1602 and is one of the few remaining buildings that survived the Great Fire of London in 1666. Justifiably often described 'quaint', it is where (as described under that cocktail on page 64) I learned a useful embellishment to the Bloody Mary cocktail. I also usefully learned that pouring beer or lager into wet glasses makes the drinks go flat. The stairs up to the lavatory are as might be expected from a building of this age and the ascent should not be attempted after more than four pints of bitter.

The Tipperary, 66 Fleet Street, EC4

This is London's first Irish pub, dating from 1606, and, therefore, another of the few buildings to have survived the Great Fire. 'Mooneys' is inscribed in a flagstone at the entrance and inside there are ground-floor and first-floor bars. Look out for the pair of looking glasses advertising Jameson Whisky from the time before the Irish (and the Americans) started spelling it 'whiskey'. The wooden panelling is decorated with holes and, in olden days, wagers used to be set according to the hole from which would next appear a live rat's head. Unfortunately, the original bar was stolen during a restoration. The landlords have been known to arrange slap-up *Beaujolais Nouveau* breakfasts to greet the first arrival of each year's wine.

The Two Chairmen, 39 Dartmouth Street, SW1

A delightful, small, wood-panelled pub in a backwater hard by St James's Park, The Two Chairmen is named after the men who used to carry sedan chairs.

Ye Old White Horse, 2 St Clement's Lane, WC2

A very traditional and cosy pub, in the heart of Dickensian London (*The Old Curiosity Shop* is just around the corner) and close to the London School of Economics, Ye Old White Horse has been on this site for around 200 years and the cellars go back much further. They serve a range of cask ales and excellent door-stop sandwiches.

Some Top Wine and Spirit Bars

Ah, fill the Cup! What boots it to repeat
How time is slipping underneath our Feet.
Unborn To-morrow and dead yesterday,
Why fret about them if TODAY be sweet?

Edward FitzGerald, from the
translation the *Rubaiyat of Omar Khayyam*

American Bar, Savoy Hotel

The bar itself opened in 1898 and received its name 'The American Bar' in the 1930s. Famous barmen here have included Harry Craddock (author of the *Savoy Cocktail Book*), Joe Gilmore, Peter Dorelli and the current head barman Salim Khoury. The whole hotel is in a state of renovation until summer 2010.

Balls Brothers, 20 St James's Street, SW1

A bar with some real buzz in the evenings and a great selection of wines.

The Boot & Flogger, 10–20 Redcross Way, SE1

Tucked away, small and nearly Dickensian in atmosphere, the food and wines are Davy's standard fare.

Daly's Wine Bar, 210 Strand, WC2

In fact situated on the corner of Essex Street, this bar is greatly beloved of the legal profession, as it is right opposite the Royal Courts of Justice and by the Temple, serving food and a range of wines, including champagne.

Dukes Hotel Bar, 35 St James's Place, SW1

This can become a busy place, attracting a seriously cosmopolitan crowd. As already mentioned, bar manager Alessandro Palazzi prides himself on his superlative Martinis and he even gives master classes in how to make them. Favoured by Ian Fleming, the bar in Dukes Hotel is where he is supposed first to have encountered the phrase 'shaken, not stirred' for a Martini cocktail: the phrase was used by the head barman there in the 1950s. The expression went on to become immortalized as one of James Bond's catchphrases when ordering his favourite cocktail. At Dukes they make Martinis at the table and with frozen ingredients and so avoid dilution with ice. They also use lemons from Amalfi for the oils that they contain but they finish the Vesper Martini with a twist of orange peel.

El Vino, 47 Fleet Street, EC4

This is the trading name of Bower & Co, founded by Alfred Louis Bower, Lord Mayor of London between 1924 and 1925, in Mark Lane in 1879 as wine merchants. He developed a tasting room that became a wine bar and soon there were three more, including this, the flagship bar. Famed for the rich mix of Fleet Street characters and lawyers, there is even a brass plate to one of them who used to hold forth at the high front desk near the doors ('Here stood Reg Wood OBE. Banker, raconteur, wit. 1945–1982') as well as the chair favoured by press baron Lord Harmsworth. The long bar at the front and the sitting area beyond are backed up by a good lunchtime restaurant. Maintaining the long Fleet Street tradition of the liquid lunch, there is also a big range of sandwiches to soak up the substantive part of the meal. This bar is undoubtedly the template for John Mortimer's 'Pommeroy's' bar in his *Rumpole* books. Some say the fictional bar's name derives from the old advertisement for Pommery Champagne on the wall of El Vino. The proprietors used to insist that ladies should not stand (and be jostled) at the bar but this was successfully challenged on the basis that it represented unfavourable discrimination on grounds of sex, and now … ladies are free to stand and be jostled at the bar.

Gordon's, 47 Villiers Street, WC2

With its old cellar areas now used for seating and famed for its dusty state and ancient site, this is one of the oldest licensed drinking places in London. They have a good selection of wines and are especially famed for the fortified wines. They also serve very reasonable food.

Mulligans of Mayfair, 13–14 Cork Street, W1

Famed for its oysters and Guinness, it is right in the centre of the area of the great tailors.

Hotels

> Not an 'otel but an 'ome away from 'ome for my friends.
>
> Rosa Lewis, on her Cavendish Hotel

Everybody has heard of the Ritz, the Savoy, the Dorchester, Claridge's, the Connaught, the Hilton, the Sanderson and the Berkeley hotels. They are luxurious, world famous and very expensive. There is even a story of an English courtier once having telephoned Claridge's, asking to speak with 'the king'. The unruffled reply was: 'Which one?' There are some other, lesser-known, discreet and luxurious London hotels that I suggest deserve a trial.

Brown's Hotel, 33 Albemarle Street, W1

Set in Albemarle Street, in the heart of Mayfair, Brown's Hotel is famed for its great British breakfasts (greatly appreciated by James Bond creator Ian Fleming) and afternoon tea in a comfortable English-style setting. It opened in 1837, the first year of Queen Victoria's reign, and is still going strong under the guiding hand of famed hotelier Rocco Forte. It formed the setting for Agatha Christies's fictional *Bertram's Hotel.*

The Cavendish Hotel, 81 Jermyn Street SW1

Built on the site of the notorious old Cavendish Hotel, the creation, from 1902, of legendary cook and hotelier Rosa Lewis (dramatized as the 'Duchess of Duke Street'), the Cavendish offers every modern convenience and is situated right in the middle of the world-famous shopping areas of Jermyn Street and Bond Street. From the top of the tower, where there are pleasant suites (one even with a balcony), there is a magnificent view of the London skyline. It is a shame that one of the recent owners of the place sold off the magnificent portrait of Rosa Lewis that used to hang on the stairs. These days, nothing is sacred. Still, she has a Westminster City Council commemorative plaque outside, just where she used to stand, goblet of champagne in hand, 'watching the trot'.

Dukes Hotel, 35 St James's Place, SW1

Dukes has already been mentioned as a bar. The whole place has also recently been subject to a grand refurbishment. It is tucked away in a side street just off St James's Street in the heart of the area famed for London's gentlemen's clubs and shops.

Flemings Hotel and Apartments, Half Moon Street, W1

Yet another hotel that has been subject to recent and ambitious refurbishment, resulting in comfort and luxury, Flemings Hotel comprises part hotel (in the traditional sense) and part serviced apartments (maybe for those intending a longer stay), situated in Mayfair's Half Moon Street.

The Goring Hotel, 15 Beeston Place, SW1

Within a stone's throw of Buckingham Palace in Belgravia and overlooking splendid gardens is the Goring Hotel, which was founded by the Goring family nearly a century ago and is still in their ownership and run according to their guiding principle of top-rate customer service, in a setting that subtly blends the traditional with the contemporary.

The Hotel Russell, Russell Square, WC1

The Victorian Hotel Russell is immortalized in TS Eliot's poem 'The Journey to the Heaviside Layer':

> Up, up, up past the Russell Hotel,
> Up, up, up to the Heaviside Layer ...

He also sometimes went here for drinks (courting his second wife, Valerie) after work at Faber & Faber in the north-west corner of the square (where a blue plaque commemorates him). This hotel occupies the whole of the eastern side of Russell Square and is situated just around the corner from the British Museum. Having been the subject of a massive and impressive renovation programme, it has lovely views out across the square and also has enormous conference facilities.

The Stafford, 17 St James's Place, SW1

In a building that dates back to the late seventeenth century is this small but luxurious hotel. Since 1995 it has been owned by Daniel Thwaites plc, a brewing company that sympathetically refurbished it. It has its own American Bar and still fosters strong transatlantic links.

Restaurants

> When you have lost your inns, drown your empty selves, for you will have lost the last of England.
>
> Hilaire Belloc

Bertorelli, 44a Floral Street, WC2 (and branches)

This branch in Covent Garden provides an ideal setting for an elderly relative's milestone birthday as they are prepared to make a long table for a big family gathering and, being Italian, enter into the spirit of the occasion, with British–Italian food and a decent range of wine.

Bleeding Heart Yard, off Greville Street, EC1

A well-established and fine French food restaurant in an historic yard, which takes its name from an alleged seventeenth-century murder, possibly of an Elizabeth Hatton. The urban legend suggests that she gave a ball in her house, off the yard, on the night of 26 January 1626 and a disaffected suitor appeared and took her hand, danced her once around and disappeared into the night with her. In the morning, she was found, savagely and mortally wounded, in the yard; her heart still beating. This place has a strong, and strangely romantic, atmosphere.

Chor Bizarre, 16 Albemarle Street, W1

If you are after a fine north Indian cuisine, why not try the Chor Bizarre restaurant in London's Mayfair. The name is a pun on the Urdu/Punjabi words for 'thieves' market'. Warm and inviting, expect the very best in Indian food and drinks from around the world, including some fine Indian beers. The service is friendly and helpful, with ready explanations of more recondite dishes. Suitable for either business lunches or dinner dating.

Corrigan's, 28 Upper Grosvenor Street, W1

A recent arrival, this restaurant prides itself on Irish-influenced British cuisine and good wines at very fair prices all suggesting the reason for its speedy accumulation of awards and acclaim, for all of which it is included here.

Gay Hussar, 2 Greek Street, W1

Dating from the days when Hussars could be harmlessly gay, this is a tremendously cosy and amusing Hungarian restaurant and my abiding memory of it is the chilled wild cherry soup.

Green's (of St James's), 36 Duke Street, SW1

Green's in Duke Street, St James's, is just opposite the Cavendish Hotel and has been a virtual institution for some time, offering a panelled space with upholstered leather banquettes as well as an oyster bar. It specializes in seafood and even the cod and chips with minted mushy peas is superb, especially when accompanied by the house champagne. Also worth trying is Haddock Parker

Bowles (named after the founder and owner Simon Parker Bowles, the former husband of HRH Camilla, Duchess of Cornwall). It is a noted watering hole for the rich and famous, although the prices are remarkably reasonable. It is a suitable place for either a business lunch or, especially on the stalled banquettes, an intimate dinner for two.

The Ivy, Cambridge Circus, WC2

The Ivy is a famed showbusiness haunt in the very middle of theatre-land and offers a superb menu with an equivalent wine list. Founded in 1917, the name derives from a popular song of the day, when actress Alice Delysia replied to the owner's apologies for building works going on: 'Don't worry we will stick together like the ivy!' It is difficult to get a table and so book very well in advance. Because of all the rubber-necking that goes on, it is maybe not the ideal place for a dinner date.

Joe Allen, 13 Exeter Street, London WC2

Joe Allen is an American restaurant in Covent Garden, right in the middle of theatre land, so whether it is a pre-theatre snack or a post-theatre supper that you are after this warm, cosy restaurant can serve up just what you need, together with a wine from its extensive wine list. Its entrance is marked only by a small plaque.

Le Caprice, Arlington House, Arlington Street, SW1

This is a famous French restaurant in Arlington Street, just down the way from the Ritz, and can double as a lunchtime venue or as a setting for a dinner date. Maybe, though, the food is not always quite all that it is cracked up to be.

L'Escargot, 48 Greek Street, W1

Founded by George Gaudin in 1927, this was the first restaurant to offer fresh snails, farmed on the premises (in the basement kitchen). As well as the 'public' restaurants, they also offer private dining facilities.

Le Gavroche, 43 Upper Brook Street, W1

Another kind of institution, Le Gavroche, founded by the redoubtable Albert and Michel Roux, doubles as a luncheon restaurant and a place for a dinner date. It was the first English restaurant to win three Michelin stars and the tradition of excellence continues.

Livebait (London, Leeds and Manchester)

A chain of fish restaurants, Live Bait has established a reputation for excellent seafood – especially shellfish – ranging from Dorset crab to lobster and oysters, but it also prides itself on its version of cod and chips with mushy peas. These places are casual, tiled, utilitarian and not terribly intimate. My favourite branch is in The Cut, SE1.

Mayflower, 68-70 Shaftesbury Avenue, W1

The fact that this Chinese restaurant is so favoured by Chinese people (for whom there is, as so often, a separate menu) is a recommendation in itself.

Mirabelle, 56 Curzon Street, W1

This is a renowned French restaurant set in intimate surroundings with an outside terrace for summertime.

Mon Plaisir, 19-21 Monmouth Street, WC2

Founded by the Viala brothers in the 1940s, this is billed as London's oldest French restaurant and has four dining rooms, an excellent menu and wine list, all at remarkably reasonable prices. And it has a pewter bar from a Lyonnais brothel …

New Diamond, 23 Lisle Street, WC2

This is on the site of a restaurant in which a fight occurred many years ago, when a member of the then staff emerged from the kitchen with a cleaver and severed an offending customer's ear. How they then served it is not recorded. The current restaurant threatens nothing of the sort and the thought of their oysters in ginger with spring onions makes my mouth water even now.

New World, 1 Gerrard Place, W1

If you fancy a Chinese meal, *especially* their dim sum at lunchtime, in fact available until the early evening, where better to head than Soho's New World restaurant in Gerrard Place, off Gerrard Street? It is an enormous restaurant but so popular that you might have to wait a little to get a table. The only other slight downside is that the service can be brusque and, sometimes, even verging on the rude. However, generally, it is best to put this down to the swift pace at which everything is done.

Rules, 35 Maiden Lane, WC2

Not far from Joe Allen, over in Maiden Lane, is a great British institution as much as a restaurant. Rules was founded in 1798 and is one of London's oldest surviving restaurants, still favouring game in season (from venison and hare, through grouse, partridge, teal, pheasant and on to woodcock), estate-reared Scotch beef, together with its famous pies, oysters and its traditional English puddings, all complemented by a large wine list. There are also private dining rooms available, where Edwardian bucks entertained their current favourites. These rooms today are, more prosaically, the choice of businessmen courting clients and holding company celebrations.

St John, 26 St John Street, EC1

This is the Smithfield address of the original restaurant, serving innovative combinations of food. Its Spitalfields sister restaurant, **St John Bread and Wine**, is at 94–96 Commercial Street, E1.

Scott's 20 Mount Street, W1

This used to be on Coventry Street off Leicester Square and is a fish and shellfish restaurant. The old place had been a favourite of Ian Fleming's.

J Sheekey, 28-32 St Martin's Court, WC2

This is yet another theatre-land fish and shellfish restaurant and is ideally situated for pre- and post-theatre suppers in agreeable surroundings.

Simpson's-in-the-Strand, 100 Strand WC2

Simpson's-in-the-Strand began life in 1828 as the Grand Cigar Divan and as a chess club and coffee house but soon spread out its wings to fine dining. Here nearly everything comes on big silver trolleys: joints of meat and game in season. The plush downstairs restaurant is the place to be seen and it serves up about the best 'power breakfast' (as I have heard it called) or business lunch that you could possibly find. It is not cheap but everyone should try out the fare, which it promotes as the Best of British.

Sofra, 36 Tavistock Street, WC2

Sofra is a Turkish chain with several branches serving well-made Turkish food (subtly influenced by international cuisine) and Turkish as well as New and Old World wines across the spectrum. At lunchtimes they also lay on a buffet at a set price, to which you just add the cost of drinks. The lentil soup and the houmus are wonderful, as is the authentic Turkish coffee and Turkish baklava afterwards. There are other menus too and they also provide an outside catering service. I especially like the window tables in the branch in Tavistock Street, Covent Garden, in the house in which Thomas de Quincey wrote his tragic *Confessions of an English Opium-Eater*; the manuscript of which was stained with pink rings from his laudanum glass ...

Sweetings, 39 Queen Victoria Street, EC4

Another virtual institution and situated in the City of London, Sweetings is the last word for oysters and gulls' eggs (in season), maybe accompanied by its own version of Black Velvet. It is an ancient and venerable seafood place but open only for lunch (ideal for a business lunch) and there are no table reservations.

Temple Bar Tandoori, Crane Court, London, EC4

Hidden down one of those ancient alleys off Fleet Street (just east of Fetter Lane), you have to know that it is there. Asians tend to rate this, for the food, as one of the best Indian restaurants in London. The atmosphere is hardly intimate but it is agreeable enough.

Wiltons, 55 Jermyn Street, SW1

This old restaurant, established in 1742, was rather messed up as the result of renovations (as places often are) but the pampering service and the traditional English food are much the same as they ever were. The alcoves could provide a setting for an intimate dinner but, generally, this is another place for an ideal business lunch.

Wong Kei, 41–43 Wardour Street, W1

Normally this enormous place, over several floors, is packed with people enjoying plates piled high with excellent Chinese food. If I ever think that the service at New World can be brusque, I just recall the occasion in here when I was warned 'No bang chopstick!' There used to be a curious rule relating to the lowest restaurant area: only single diners were allowed in, so you had to aim to arrive separately and sit next to each other, then *pretend* to strike up conversation, risking the instruction 'No talk!'

A Few Interesting Tea Shops (Ignoring All the Big Hotels), London's Top Coffee Shop and its Number-One Ice Cream Parlour and Tips on Some Early Morning Breakfast Cafés

Picture you upon my knee
Just tea for two
And two for tea
Just me for you
And you for me … alone

From the lyrics to 'No, No, Nanette' (1925)
by Irving Caesar

Bar Italia, 22 Frith Street, Soho, W1

Bar Italia in Soho is, probably, the best coffee shop in London.

Fortnum & Mason, St James's Restaurant, Jermyn Street, SW1

Enter here through the corner door at the junction of Jermyn and Duke streets. This is a solid, comfortable, reasonably priced place – and just what you'd expect, really, with its ranges of teas, sandwiches and cakes.

Lisboa Patisserie, 57 Golborne Road, W10

This is a delightful and consistent Portuguese patisserie that combines nicely with a visit to the market at Portobello Road.

Louis Patisserie, Harben Parade, Swiss Cottage, NW3

This Hungarian patisserie is just the place to warm up after a winter's day walk on Primrose Hill. The sausage rolls (I prefer mine cold) and the dark chocolate triangles are a must.

Maids of Honour, 288 Kew Road, Richmond, Surrey

A century and a half after Robert Newens brought his bakery and tea shop to its current location in Kew Road, the business is still going strong. Some say that the actual cakes made here and called 'Maids of Honour' derive their name from Henry VIII discovering his maids of honour eating them. No visit to the spectacular Kew gardens is truly complete without a tea in this establishment.

There is also more substantial fare on offer as well as cakes, excellent pies and the sausage rolls that they claim are the best in London.

Maison Bertaux, 28 Greek Street, Soho, W1

Slap bang in the middle of Soho, this place serves amazingly good French cakes and savouries, which are baked daily on site.

Marine Ices, 8 Haverstock Hill, NW3

On Haverstock Hill, on the way to Hampstead Village, is Marine Ices, founded in 1931 by the Italian Gaetano Mansi, and widely considered to be the best ice cream parlour in London.

Raj Tea Rooms, 67 Highgate High Street, N6

These tea rooms are, beyond any doubt, run by the biggest 'character' in the business: David d'Arcy Brewster, both of whose parents were in the Indian Service. Excellent, traditional tiffin and teatime fare, such as buttered crumpets and big unfussy pots of tea, are available. At closing time, anyone left will probably be taken to the nearby Flask opposite The Grove or the Rose & Crown in the High Street – or, maybe, even the Wrestlers on the Great North Road. Any of these further excursions rewards the effort.

Richoux, 172 Piccadilly, W1

This occupies the site of the old grocery shop Jacksons of Piccadilly and is done out in a kind of swirling Edwardian style, but it is a relaxing enough place for a pot of tea and sandwiches and cakes, conveniently located opposite the Royal Academy and the Burlington Arcade.

Smithfield Meat Market cafés

If you happen to be out on the tiles all night and need a breakfast, maybe with a pint of lager beer, you will find little open in the West End of London – it is very far from a twenty-four-hour city. You need to go to the area of the eight-hundred-year-old Smithfield Meat Market and ask your cab driver to find you a breakfast café or a 'gastro-pub'. Don't worry: the meat porters (for whom these places are open) are quite used to people tripping in for a plate of bacon and eggs at 5.00am in evening dress and you will not raise eyebrows. You should aim to get home before 8.00am as, after that, being out and about in evening dress looks very strange indeed.

The Wolseley, 160 Piccadilly, W1

Formerly a car showroom, this has been turned into a smart, trendy place for morning coffee and afternoon tea.

Fish and Chips Shops

Egon Ronay said that these were 'England's most distinctive contribution to world cuisine.' The first production of deep-fried fish and chips was around the fish docks of northern England in about 1860, when beef dripping was used. Nowadays, of course, it is vegetable oil. It is interesting, perhaps, to note that curry houses pre-date fish and chips in England by fifty years. The first in London was the Hindostanee Coffee House in George Street, in 1810, serving Indian dishes, coffee and hookah and spreading the word about Indian cuisine. England's curry houses must also represent another significant contribution to world cuisine. We should not forget that the popular dish of chicken tikka masala is a British twist on Indian gastronomy and a contradiction in terms, since *tikka* is a tandoori preparation of marinated meat but lacking any accompanying sauce (*masala*). There is a legend that chicken tikka masala was devised, on the hoof, by a versatile Indian chef when a British customer asked for 'gravy' to go with his chicken tikka.

Geales Fish and Chips, 2 Farmer Street, W8

Established in 1939 and recently renovated, here you may have anything from cod and chips to Duchy of Cornwall oysters, followed by traditional English puddings such as treacle tart and custard or Eton Mess. It is good grub but the presentation is a little 'twee'.

The Fryer's Delight, 19 Theobald's Road, WC1

If East Enders know their fish and chips then you know that you are on to a good thing here as there are often serried ranks of black cabs parked up nearby. Their cabbies are in here.

The Laughing Halibut, 38 Strutton Ground, SW1

Far too much on your plate can be something to complain about because it is wasteful, and when it is as wasteful of fish and chips as good as these, complain away! Better still, explain how much you actually want.

The Sea Shell, 49–51 Lisson Grove, NW1

Famous for most of its forty years, here you can get much more than just fish and chips, such as crab cakes, Scotch smoked salmon, goujons of lemon sole, whole Dover sole, sea bass, followed by apple cake and hot chocolate cake – and all with a thoughtful wine list.

Toff's, 38 Muswell Hill Broadway, N10

The winner of very many awards, year after year, it is worth the trek up the hill just for a plate.

Locations and Titbits on Major West End London Clubs

My female friends they all agree
They hardly know their hubs;
And heart and voice unite with me,
'We hate the name of Clubs!'

Thomas Hood

It is worth mentioning something of London clubland. Here is a little bit about the main West End London clubs, including a few that are a little different from the traditional clubs. To join most of them you need to be proposed and seconded by existing members and then subject to election, which often means securing no vote to exclude you, originally by the dropping of a black ball into the election box (hence 'black-balling' as an expression to denote exclusion). Maybe these days some clubs are taking black balls by e-mail. Most have wonderful facilities, including bars, smoking rooms, dining rooms, libraries and overnight accommodation for members at very favourable rates. Many also have reciprocal arrangements with other clubs for members to use the facilities of some other clubs when their own clubs are closed and there are reciprocal arrangements between London clubs and out-of-town clubs and overseas' clubs too. I do not deal with the City clubs such as the Livery Companies or, except the MCC, those clubs outside the West End of London. For any who wish to know more about clubs generally, after this little taster, there is the book mentioned under the heading 'Cavalry and Guards' below. I do not even attempt to list famous members as the lists would be legion. The year of foundation is given after each name.

Army and Navy (1837), 36 Pall Mall, SW1

This is still nicknamed 'The Rag' long after a former member complained that his dinner had been a 'Rag and Famish affair', after a gambling 'hell' of that name off Cranbourne Alley where broken-down gamblers played for small change. Membership is open primarily to officers and former officers of the armed services of any Commonwealth country. Amongst its treasures is Nell Gwynne's fruit knife: 'Who would like to squeeze my lovely juicy oranges? Sixpence each!' (the true price back then).

Arts Club (1863), 40 Dover Street, W1

Founded as a haven for bohemian artists, this charming, friendly club recently opened its facilities to the newly revived Eccentric Club.

Athenaeum (1824), 107 Pall Mall, SW1

Behind its classical edifice there lies one of the most intellectual of London clubs. It was at the foot of the stairs here that Thackeray and Dickens patched up their feud, which began with some unpleasantness at the Garrick Club, and at desks here that many famous writers have worked: Sir Richard Burton translated the *Arabian Nights*. Possibly the other members did not know what he was up to. There is a special rule provision for the election, without ballot, of certain eminent men.

Beefsteak (1735), 9 Irving Street, WC2

Basically this is an eating club that encourages an eclectic mix of eminent men of the age and comprises mainly a long table in a long room. Originally, the membership was restricted to twenty-four, and even the Prince Regent had to wait his turn. The steward and the waiters are by tradition all called 'Charles'.

Black's (1982), 67 Dean Street, W1

Situated in the building that, between 1764 and 1767, housed 'The Club' founded by Dr Samuel Johnson and Sir Joshua Reynolds, this place is welcoming, cosy, tranquil and young but very civilized – and the food is simple but superb.

Boodle's (1762), 28 St James's Street, SW1

Edwin Boodle had been the head waiter in the original Almack's in Pall Mall. The famous bow window is where the Duke of Wellington had liked to sit, 'watching the damned people get wet'. Ian Fleming was a devoted member, often lunching there, and based the club 'Blades' on it in the Bond novel *Moonraker*.

Brooks's (1764), 60 St James's Street, SW1

Charles James Fox gambled away a fortune here, in its country house-style splendour – even, sometimes, borrowing off the waiters at desperate end-game. So liked was he that his friends saved him from utter ruin. Among club curios is Napoleon's death mask.

Buck's (1919), 18 Clifford Street, W1

Founded at the end of the First World War by Captain Herbert Buckmaster and a group of Household Cavalry colleagues, it was originally a young man's club for members of the Household Cavalry and their friends and promoted sporting interests. PG Wodehouse said that, but for the absence of a swimming pool, it was the model for the Drones Club in his stories. 'Buck' was an autocratic and pugnacious character who ruled the club from his room until his death in 1966. The state of its affairs was dire. But such was the members' affection for the place that they had a massive whip round and saved it.

Caledonian (1891), 9 Halkin Street, W1

To become a member it is necessary to have at least one Scottish grandparent, to have served Scotland in some capacity or 'to have the closest association with Scotland'. There is a portrait of Bonnie Prince Charlie in the splendid building, which was originally built as a family town house. Somehow they lost the historic passport that the Earl of Mar gave to Rob Roy MacGregor during the Jacobite Rebellions following the deposing of James VII of Scotland (James II of England) in favour of William and Mary.

Canning (1911), 4 St James's Square, SW1

This is now accommodated within the Naval and Military. Originally founded as the Argentine Club, it fostered strong links with Argentina. Since 1948 it has been renamed the Canning in honour of George Canning, who famously declaimed that he had 'brought the New World into existence to redress the balance of the Old' and it exists to foster relations with all of South America.

Carlton (1832), 69 St James's Street, SW1

Formed as a rallying point for opposition to the 1832 Reform Bill (and the Reform Club), Stanley Baldwin, as Prime Minister, was once moved to apologize to diners in the annexe for dining in day clothes as his evening clothes were out of reach. It was, for a long time, *the* club for Tory party grandees but is no longer quite so favoured. Its original premises were bombed out in the War and it now occupies tranquil accommodation in the former premises of Arthur's Club. In 1967 Edward Heath outraged members by lunching in the Red Room with the Soviet premier Alexei Kosygin. The Junior Carlton has been subsumed in the senior club.

Cavalry (1890) and Guards' (1810) – merged 1976, 127 Piccadilly, W1

Membership of this club speaks for itself. In 1974, before the merger and when 127 was still just the Cavalry Club, IRA gunmen fired on the club from a passing car. As Anthony Lejeune points out in his fine book *The Gentlemen's Clubs of London*: 'A foolish gesture. It would be difficult to think of an institution less likely to be intimidated.'

The Colony Room Club (1948), 41 Dean Street, W1

Founded by the rough diamond 'character' Muriel Belcher and much favoured by the zanier artists, this is a real boozer's club – but you just have to know that it's there.

East India (1849), 16 St James's Square, SW1

Beautifully situated, this now incorporates the Devonshire, the Sports Club and the Public Schools Club. It was founded to provide a London base for members of the Indian Service. Having long outlived its original purpose, the splendid library and portraits speak of its history. On 21 June 1815, despatches from Wellington arrived in the square for members of the cabinet who were dining at number 16. Consequently, the first news in London of the victory at Waterloo was read to the crowd beneath from the balcony of what is now part of the club.

Eccentric (2008)

Although its original roots go back to 1781, the penultimate incarnation (1890) ended in dissolution in 1988, but the club has been again revived under the patronage of HRH The Duke of Edinburgh, and has been given a temporary home with the Arts Club. The owl is its symbol and it used to have a clock with a reverse dial as well as a picture of a lissom-looking naked lady above the sign:

TIES MUST BE WORN AT ALL TIMES

I am member number nineteen of the revived club but – maybe in the best spirit of the club – I have never yet attended it.

Garrick (1831), 15 Garrick Street, WC2

Behind its gloomy façade, it is famous for adhering to the principle that 'it is clear that that it would be better that ten unobjectionable men should be excluded than one terrible bore should be admitted'. Actors, lawyers, men of letters represent the bulk of the membership here. Sir Henry Irving was, at first, black-balled but then brought in by a flurry of protest, but the journalist Bernard Levin was black-balled and never admitted after he made some remarks about the administration of justice that offended some over-sensitive legal boys.

The Groucho (1985), 45 Dean Street, W1

Inspired by the famous Groucho Marx joke 'I don't want to join any club that will have me as a member' it started off as a club for those in publishing but its membership has broadened out to include those in the media and arts. This one is trendy and hip – but, again, you have got to know that it is there.

Lansdowne (1935), 9 Fitzmaurice Place, Berkeley Square, W1

This is a club that has always had men and women as full members and so it has been frequently dismissed as a 'cock-and-hen club', but then others are following suit as a result of some intrusive legislation even into the rights of individuals to form private clubs! The peace treaty ending the American War of Independence was signed in the glorious Round Room (when the house had belonged to Prime Minister Lord Shelburne). The club has a swimming pool and other fine sports facilities.

Marylebone Cricket Club (MCC, 1786), St John's Wood Road, NW8

The first cricket club connected with this club was founded by Thomas Lord on what is now Dorset Square and the first match took place in 1787 between Middlesex and Essex. After one move it finally settled at Lord's Cricket Ground in St John's Wood London NW8 (with its famous Long Room), from where the MCC still plays its part in governing the sport of cricket, as it is part of the Cricket Council.

National Liberal (1884), 1 Whitehall Place, SW1

This is nicely positioned near the river, but the atmosphere is (to my mind) rather dour and dull. The best feature is probably its sweeping staircase and the presence of cheerful Savages. Recently, a high percentage of Liberal party supporters reckoned that they did not know much about the party's political policies: but someone of their number (before the general election in May 2010) added that it did not matter very much as they will never get the chance to implement them anyway!

Naval & Military 1862, 4 St James's Square, SW1

It was founded by a group comprising mainly officers in the Buffs and moved in 1866 to the magnificent Cambridge House at 94 Piccadilly. Because the gate posts indicated the driving directions 'In' and 'Out' this became its nickname. From 1999 it has been in the former house of the Astors at number 4 St James's Square (the front columns ingeniously painted 'In' and 'Out'). This is one of the few of the remaining original houses in the square, dating from Henry Jermyn's development (from 1662) of the only garden square in the parish of St James's. It is next to the former Libyan Embassy, opposite the monument to WPC Yvonne Fletcher, shot dead on duty, near her fiancé, during a protest outside the Libyan Embassy in 1984. This event marked the eleven-day police siege of the building, the longest police siege in London's history, during which WPC Fletcher's police hat was left to lie where she had fallen.

Oriental (1824), Stratford House, 11 Stratford Place, W1

Originally founded to provide a home from home for returning officers of the British East India Company and others in the Indian Service, it suffered a severe setback in 1842 when its secretary absconded with several thousand pounds. Although it had suffered perennial financial problems, around 1957 the club granted a lease of its freehold site in Hanover Square and, thus sustained, moved to its present site, where it continues to flourish. A member of staff called Ellen Elizabeth Moore (known to members as 'Alice') served the club for sixty-five years, from 1916 until 1981.

Oxford & Cambridge (1833), 71–77 Pall Mall, SW1

This club has limited general interest because, as its name suggests, it is for alumni of Oxford and Cambridge universities. It is housed in a purpose-built building and there was an early dispute about whether smoking should be permitted in any part and a special meeting was called to settle the matter. The smokers won. But not for ever.

Pratt's (1857), 14 Park Place, SW1

This is a jolly and scruffy little club, which came into being when, in 1841, the then Duke of Beaufort took some company around to his steward's house in Park Place where they ate and drank and gamed in the basement kitchen. His steward's name was Nathaniel Pratt and he had formerly been a croupier at the nearby Crockfords gaming house. His house, originally a lodging house, gradually just *became* a club and the main entertainment remained and remains in the basement, which is reminiscent of an ancient tavern. The club steward and the waiters are, by a tradition similar to that at the Beefsteak, all called 'George'. It was one of Churchill's favourite boltholes in the 1920s and 1930s.

Reform (1836), 104 Pall Mall, SW1

The club in this grand building – as much a temple as a club – was founded in support of the electoral reforms of the Reform Act 1832 and even now members must subscribe to these principles. Of course, it is immortalized in the Jules Verne novel *Around the World in Eighty Days* as the club to which his hero Phileas Fogg habitually went each day before undertaking his romantic adventure, over a wager that he made there.

RAC (1897), 89–91 Pall Mall, SW1

This is one of the biggest clubs and has magnificent accommodation and even gardens, as well as a large swimming pool and other sporting facilities, together with all the usual facilities of a club and even some unusual ones, such as its own sub-post office, Turkish baths and a barber. Its purpose is the furthering of motoring. The Long Bar in the basement is a great place for an informal lunch, such as bangers and mash and onion gravy.

RAF (1917), 128 Piccadilly, SW1

Originally opened in Bruton Street as a club for then RFC officers on sick leave in London, after the end of the First World War the RFC became the RAF and the current premises were acquired.

Royal Thames Yacht Club (1775), 60 Knightsbridge, SW1

This is the oldest yacht club in England.

St Stephen's (1870), 34 Queen Anne's Gate, SW1

This club comprises a surprising blend of conservative politicians and consulting engineers. Founded at the suggestion of Benjamin Disraeli it was formerly in premises closer to the Houses of Parliament and convenient for the division bell. But the accommodation was taken over for actual parliamentary purposes and the club moved to very agreeable premises in Queen Anne's Gate.

Savage (1857), 1 Whitehall Place, SW1

Always somewhat informally arranged and peripatetic, this club now occupies one of the brighter corners of the National Liberal Club. I am told by a friendly Savage that there are two accounts as to how this club got its name. The first is that it was named, in mischief, after Richard Savage, a disreputable eighteenth-century playwright, in the Crown Tavern in Drury Lane. The second is that a waitress at one of the early gatherings of the prospective club refused to serve the members, describing them as 'savages'.

The club maintains, maybe against the 'politically correct' spirit of the age, the emblem of a North American Indian in full headdress. Qualifications for membership included a requirement that one be a writer, artist, musician, actor, scientist or lawyer, and it has always enjoyed a reputation for bohemianism and wonderful, member-led entertainments. An old actor from Sir Henry Irving's troupe, Edwin Odell, was an early member and virtually lived at the club (on a sofa, permitted him by the club servants), although he seldom paid for anything. Eventually the committee expelled him but his supporters hired a carriage and parked it outside the club and there plied him with food and drink to keep him going. The committee relented and he was reinstated. One night, nearing 100 years old, he found the Duke of York (later King George VI) sitting in his accustomed chair and yelled at him, 'Out of my chair, sir! Get out! At once!' which, gracious man that he was, apologetically, he did. This chair is marked with a plaque: 'Here Odell sat'. The club has a bust of Odell by famous sculptor Albert Toft. Members address each other as 'Brother Savage' and are well known for their generosity and charity.

Savile (1868), 69 Brook Street, W1

At first called the 'New Club' it was named after its second premises in Savile Row. It used to be said that to become a member here it was necessary to be an atheist or to have written a book! But, in truth, it has always encouraged a mixture of different types and especially writers – Robert Louis Stevenson even used to pester the staff to open up early so that he could begin his day's writing.

Professor George Saintsbury resigned to join the Athenaeum but still dreamed of the luncheons at the Savile.

Travellers (1819), 106 Pall Mall, SW1

Its original foundation required that prospective members must have travelled at least 500 miles in a radius from London. Its splendid architecture is based on the Palazzo Pandolfino in Florence. Although Prince Talleyrand was accepted for honorary membership (and enjoyed the benefit of a specially adapted hand rail on the stairs, which is still there) it is as much remarkable for those that were refused, including Thackeray, Cecil Rhodes and Lord Lytton. It also enjoys the unique distinction that two of its members (on separate occasions) shot themselves in the Billiards Room.

Turf (1861), 5 Carlton House Terrace, SW1

This is often regarded as a kind of junior White's and has strong links with the Jockey Club in Paris, although owing to an 'incident' the number of *rosbifs* visiting the Paris club together was, at least for a time, *limited*. It began as the 'Arlington' in Bennett Street and members wished to call it just 'The Club' but realized that they had been beaten to it a long time before by Dr Johnson and Sir Joshua Reynolds. In 1965 they moved to the current splendid accommodation in Carlton House Terrace.

White's (1693), 37–38 St James's Street, SW1

First and last, but hardly least, White's is often thought of as the top club, or at least as *primus inter pares*, especially by its own members. By that I mean not just the top club in London or Britain, but everywhere. White's Chocolate House was founded one year before the Bank of England by Italian Francesco Bianco on the site of the current Boodle's. This makes it the earliest surviving establishment of its kind, although there had been others, such as the St James's and the Cocoa Tree, which all began as houses of public resort, but the 'public' that came to frequent them, on close inspection, was found to include some infamous highwaymen and so (partly to exclude them) the concept of the club was born.

After one move across the road and a terrible fire (on the site of what became Arthur's Club and is the current Carlton Club) eventually White's settled at the top of St James's Street in 1753. By this time there was the emergence of the 'Old Club' and the 'Young Club'. In 1781 the two clubs merged and White's as we know it was born. In 1811 the famous bow window on the ground floor was built out over the old entrance steps (which are still visible) and from here Brummell and his *coterie* passed judgment on the fashionable world. The Betting Book contains many curious wagers, including a wager of £1,000 that a man could survive for twelve hours under water. Some broken-down fellow was found and paid to prove the truth of this and his life and the bet were lost.

Despite all, in the words of its historian, Percy Colson, White's remains 'an oasis of civilization in a desert of democracy'.

CHAPTER 8

Some Interesting Points of Conduct and Some Reflections

Manners maketh man.

William of Wykeham

I am not too keen on over-use of the word 'etiquette' as it suggests that someone's knowledge has come from a dedicated manual rather than from more natural training, learning, observing and experience, so I say 'conduct' instead. As I mention in the Introduction, this book is not a primer and the following includes a few small (but important) detailed points of conduct and observations of customs that are sometimes lost in the hurry of the modern world.

One or Two Little Things at the Table

If you are nearest to a female who needs to leave the table early (for any reason), and even if there are staff present, don't just get up when she leaves but take her to the door and open and close it for her.

On drinking soup: if you watch carefully you will notice that the working class and the upper class sweep the spoon towards them to scoop up the soup whereas the middle classes universally sweep it delicately away from them. This is not the only point on which the working class and the upper class have more in common than they have with the pretentious middle classes.

Yes, asparagus is eaten with the fingers, which need to be cleansed in a finger bowl and dried on a small towel or napkin. It is impossible to eat shellfish, such as crab or lobster claws (the best part), without grappling with them and oysters should be loosened in the shell on which they sit (this doesn't always happen when they are *shucked* or opened), dressed with a little Tabasco and black pepper and lemon juice – keeping the natural juices on board too – and just tipped into the mouth. Meat on the bone and fowl bones should be worked with your eating irons and not, despite modern tendencies, picked up and chewed.

It is not just holding the knife as a pen that is regarded as not quite *comme il faut* as frequently wiping the fork against the knife is also bad form. These habits exhibited by SMERSH agent 'Captain Nash' – aka 'Red' Grant – were plainly noted by James Bond when he, Tatiana Romanova and 'Nash' eat in the dining car in the novel *From Russia With Love*, but Bond didn't read enough into the signs, even though Tatiana had also told him that 'nash' in Russian means 'ours'. In the film, Nash's *faux pas* is turned into choosing red Chianti to accompany fish – but red wine with fish is not *necessarily* a blunder, as mentioned in Chapter 7 of this book.

Unless you simply cannot avoid it, try to avoid using your handkerchief at the table – certainly don't blow your nose – but if you have to smother a sneeze 'crush it like a vice of blood upon the thresh-hold of the mind'.

Toothpicks might even be provided at the table, but again, try to avoid using them there and it is far better to attend to the teeth privately in the lavatory.

Everyone knows to pass the Port in accordance with the old naval custom of passing it *from port to port* – to the left – but, if the Port starts its round with you as the host, really you should fill the glass of your right-hand neighbour before passing the Port to the left and then it makes its way back to you to fill your own glass. To get the Port moving, never ask for the decanter direct, but the host should ask the guest nearest to it: 'Do you happen to know the Bishop of Norwich?' If the hint isn't taken, this is followed up with: 'The Bishop is a good fellow – but he never passes the Port!' After the Port has done its round once, the host asks the guests to name the vintage and the shipper. The expression 'No heel taps!' is a traditional exhortation to finish the bottle so that another may be brought. It used to be usual to give the Port a chance and not to smoke before at least the first glass had been drunk. It should also be noted that, in some institutions, where members dine on very long tables, there are traditions for circulating, or dispensing, the Port in messes of four (comprising each two pairs of diners facing each other across the table), and one should inquire of the office of the institution concerned as to its particular traditions.

Making Excuses

I once made the mistake of declining a heavily pressed social invitation from some of my oldest friends by ultimately telling them the truth – 'I can't be bothered today.' They didn't speak to me for three months. We may deduce from this that, in social situations, one needs to be a good liar to survive. For example, if asked 'How do I look in this?' never reply 'Very pleased!', and if you want to decline an invitation, always plead having accepted another invitation or some other sufficient reason, such as being away. It really is astonishing how well these, often transparent, lies go down. Also on the subject of invitations and travelling, there is a modern tendency to speak of going 'up' to Manchester or Scotland from London but really one goes 'up' to Town and 'down' to everywhere else.

Knowing When to Arrive and When to Leave

Ideally one should be neither the first to arrive nor the first to leave any gathering (and certainly *never* the last to leave). Aiming to be twenty minutes late used to be 'fashionable'; as for leaving, it is best to go after the first to leave but before the party hits the top of the arc. This both makes one's company rarer and the more sought after and one also avoids the unseemliness that, sometimes, follows high revelry.

Stationery

Traditionally, one would have writing paper in plain vellum, engraved from a copper plate, with the address and telephone number. The flap of the envelope would bear one's coat of arms (if any); this should never be 'borrowed' or faked. Visiting cards should be made of good thick card (also engraved from a copper plate), bearing one's name and address and, maybe, club, but traditionally no telephone number. A man's card normally measured around three inches by one and a half inches and a woman's card would have been around three and a half inches by two inches. Nowadays, one could expect to find telephone numbers galore (home, business and mobile numbers), e-mail addresses and even website addresses and, I have to say, why not indeed, as we all use these fast forms of communication in the modern age. Moreover, since domestic servants were central to the use of social visiting cards, hardly anyone uses cards any more, except for their profession or business. Excellent suppliers of stationery are Smythson.

How to Stop a Fight

> A plague on both your houses!
>
> William Shakespeare

It sometimes happens that high spirits and alcohol produce, even amongst the best company, situations in which the *tired and emotional* might begin to appear inclined to throw a punch and end up in the cells.

The cells are not very pleasant places to spend a night: the bunk is hard, the blanket is rough and of dubious provenance (not to mention the previous users); there is no privacy with the lavatory; you will have to ask for the copious amounts of water that you will, inevitably, need and there is a rigid no-smoking policy. This is not even to mention all the paperwork on the way in and out and the interminable wait the next morning before you are hauled up, creased, unshaven, tousled and ashamed, before the Beak for his scrutiny and admonishment, followed by your stammering apology and the signing of the register that you agree to be bound over in some notional sum to keep Her Majesty's Peace for twelve months …

The situation is often preceded by animated conversation (usually over something anodyne, such as who was the best BBC programme *Blue Peter* presenter when we children or, of course, some sporting event), raised voices and posturing. Often this happens because there is a festering and deep-seated rivalry, dislike or resentment between those concerned – maybe at work or in a social or sporting club. Normally, it is shielded from close inspection by the normal rules of nice conduct but, bring a *leeetle* bit too much alcohol into play – or, maybe, a pretty face into view – and there might be an explosion threatening to take the gilt off the gingerbread for *everyone* present. The main thing to do is to divert the adversaries' attention in a dramatic or amusing manner, unless it is possible to get one away from it all without his feet touching the ground, so to speak. When I say the 'best company' you might be amazed at just how badly even thinking men, such as professionals, can behave: I have known, in their company, the threat of flying chairs and I even know of an instance when someone had his lights punched out in the cloakroom of one of the better London clubs, ultimately resulting in a substantial settlement of a claim for compensation. It has to be said that the claim for compensation was pretty *infra dig*, but, at least, the fellow who made it was not a member of the club in question. Suggested diversionary tactics are as follows. Mentioning some recent tragedy in the news can have the effect of shaming those who are not too drunk to notice. Making some humorous quip has been known to save the situation – indeed there is even an example from the great Brummell himself. As a schoolboy at Eton he was once in a group that threatened to put the bargee off the bridge into the river when Brummell interceded: 'My good fellows, don't. The man is in a high state of perspiration and would be sure to catch cold.'

If none of this works one can have recourse to saying something like: 'I'm feeling the worse for wear and I really must be off – and Jim [here take a firm grip of an arm], I can easily drop you as it is late and time for carriages. Do you happen to have seen my case/coat/hat?' If performed with resolution and firmness, this does often work.

And a final rouse is suddenly to say – loudly – 'Good heavens! Isn't that [someone that one or other or they both respect] over there?' (However, this really works only in somewhere crowded, which means that you will not be rumbled immediately.)

All these rouses unavailing, a full Nelson arm-lock is the ultimate preventative measure – *but just make sure that there is someone to perform the same restraint on the second man.*

Some Reflections

Feminine wiles

Go, and catch a falling star …

John Donne

One or two of the gentler sex have let parts of their methodology slip and fifty years of living fills in the blanks. First, they look into our eyes, then at our hands and then at our shoes. They discover whether we are humorous and kind and whether they might feel safe with us in dangerous places and what we do and what we have and where we live; whence we came and whither we might go – and then they might just look at us some more, from a little further back, and sketch out a future in which shadow-shapes of children figure and play in the sun. They add all this up and make some calculation, in which a passion-tempered logic prevails, and then they consider whether we might be in with a chance. But it has got very little to do with our spinning any lines. Generally, our clothes don't matter, because they can change all that – all except the shoes. Shoes last and are moulded to our forms most of all and, of all our clothes, tell most about us and they know that they are stuck with those, so their friends need to admire our shoes. If we get to the stage of shoe inspection then we know that *it's time to find the lines at last* – job offer in Caracas, mad Uncle Harry, decided to take up smoking a pipe again ... If all else fails, a warning that she might well become a golf-widow.

Buying your own furniture and London penthouses

Who could forget Michael Jopling's feline dismissal of a senior Tory politician as 'someone who buys his own furniture'? However, many people have to top up from time to time and both provincial and London auctions provide excellent opportunities to avoid the pitfalls of buying tell-tale, spongy new sofas and armchairs and polished, cherry-wood or bleached-lime dining tables and chairs from a department store. The aptly named Lots Road Auctions is a good starting point in London, as are local auctions in the country. The alternative, of course, is to buy ultra-modern, marble-pillared, glass-topped tables and similar furniture for a modernized St James's Square penthouse. On its south side, there are some great examples inside an externally unprepossessing 1960s' block. A few of them overlook both the square itself, with views up Duke of York Street to St James's church on the north side, and Pall Mall and the RAC on the south, with Buckingham Palace off to the west and the statue of the Grand Old Duke of York and the London Eye off to the east. Not only is this the very first London garden square (begun, in 1662, by Henry Jermyn, Earl of St Albans) but it is plum in the centre of the magic quadrangle, described in my *History of Men's Fashion* as the '*gods' quad*', and within easy walking distance of all that central London has to offer. This square is, arguably, one of the most sophisticated addresses in the metropolis; certainly for a bachelor or a couple – and the flats are so spacious that there have even been couples with small children living there.

Religious tolerance

It is curious to reflect that this humankind can cure, contain and control so many diseases and travel in space but, when it comes to the Supreme Being and the Creator of all things, some men and women are prepared to kill others of this humankind to drive home the point that *their* method of worship is best. Often religious fervour and extremism is just a front (and an unconvincing one) for the activities of psychotic murderers. Generally speaking, religious leaders should more encourage all believers in God to see the various religions and denominations as boats travelling on different rivers, but which all lead down to the same sea – and that God does not name the different streams or count the colours of the boats.

Social mobility

British society has always allowed social mobility as much as any other. However, it used to take a couple of generations to make the transformation complete. Think of Old Jolyon Forsyte in John Galsworthy's *The Forsyte Saga*. He was the son of builder 'Superior Dosset' Forsyte, sprung from yeoman stock and according to Swithin's researches 'small beer'. Old Jolyon had become a partner in tea merchants Forsyte & Treffry but was unacceptable for membership of a club, which, nevertheless, admitted his public-school-educated artist son, Young Jolyon.

Beau Brummell's family had variously kept a sweet shop and lodging house in Bury Street, St James's. Owing to his father's good fortune in securing the post of Secretary to Prime Minister Lord North, the Beau's Eton education, an early inheritance and exceptional personal qualities, Brummell swiftly rose to the pinnacle of the British establishment and became the Leader of Fashion.

Now 'trade' does not attract the stigma that it did once: for example, the great nineteenth-century shoe-making family of Joseph Box could not have their daughters presented at court until they had sold the business. Moreover, now movements from the working class into the lower-middle class and, from there, on into the professional upper-middle class mainly result from a combination of education and ambition and, still, service to the state in the armed forces and the civil and foreign service.

CHAPTER 9

Gifts for Her

I never hated a man enough to give him his diamonds back.

Zsa Zsa Gabor

Before you shell out, just bear Zsa Zsa's words in mind, as her position, although well-put, is hardly unique!

I have dealt, to some extent, with jewels, pearls and chocolates on pages 53–56 and 94–95 in chapters 3 and 4 and the places to shop for them and I set some of the background to scents on pages 20–29 in Chapter 2.

Jewels and Pearls

Apart from what has already been said about types and selection of gems and pearls (on pages 53–56 in Chapter 3), bear in mind that there are old cuts of stones (rose-cut diamonds, for example) and settings and new cuts (brilliant-cut diamonds, for example) and settings. Moreover, don't just confine yourself to the front of the settings – look behind and consider the workmanship there. Bear in mind too that auctions often produce a very realistic market price for stones as the next bidder down from the sale price is seldom that far below.

Certain stones suit some women and others do not: green eyes often suit emeralds or imperial topaz and diamonds; brown eyes suit rubies and diamonds and blue eyes suit sapphires – or Tanzanite – and diamonds. Tanzanite (Zoisite) is a stone that was first found in north Tanzania and is always heat treated to obtain the trichroism for which it is noted – blue, violet and deep red. Good examples are becoming difficult to obtain and it is very rare; most of it comes from Mount Kilimanjaro. It is also very soft and so is not set in pieces that are likely to be rubbed or knocked.

Some superb jewellers and jewel traders have already been mentioned in this book (on page 59). However, there are a couple more to include in this connection: Tessier (by appointment only) and Graff. Do not forget that it is often worth looking around reputable shops on holiday, especially in countries that are (as described earlier) famous for particular stones, but avoid the 'gem museums' to which your obliging taxi driver will take you in parts of Asia. His game is to secure a commission on over-priced sales.

Semi-precious Stones

Besides precious stones (diamonds, rubies, emeralds, sapphires and Imperial topaz [varying from amber, yellow to pink] and pearls), there are some splendid semi-precious stones to be had, such as amber (not actually a mineral as it is fossilized tree resin, in many colours from yellow to red); amethyst (purple quartz); aquamarine (a pale blue form of beryl); bixbite (a red form of beryl); cymophane (a type of chrysoberyl, with inclusions that make it opalescent and give rise to the usual name of 'cat's eye'); green sapphire; garnet (various chemical compositions, in red, green orange and yellow); heliodor (yellow beryl); morganite (a pink form of beryl, named after banker and collector JP Morgan); petrol-blue Paraiba tourmaline; precious opal (a mineraloid – that is, not having a crystalline structure); peridot (olivine); and spinel (red magnesium aluminium). Do not forget that the workmanship in the cutting and the settings, if very well executed, might sometimes far out-value the raw materials used.

Chocolates

I have covered some great chocolate makers on pages 94–95 in Chapter 4. A combination of a Sense of the Occasion and Common Sense should do the rest.

Scents

Unless the lady in question has an expressed favourite scent, you need to decide what she might like. For dark, sultry women, you can hardly go wrong with Jean Patou and Joy or, if you can find it, Guerlain's Ode. For a redhead, maybe try their Milles Fleurs, and for a blonde Chanel No 5 often goes down a treat. Lighter scents include those by Floris, such as White Rose, Edwardian Bouquet and Night Scented Jasmine. There is also a new Floris scent that is actually EDP called Madonna of the Almonds.

Furs

Furs seem to be back to some extent and, if you are really pushing the boat out, you cannot really beat an Imperial Russian blue sable coat (*martes zibellina* from the Barguzin Valley). After that, you come down to stranded wild stone martin (*martes foina*); stranded wild mink (in the family *Mustelidae*); astrakhan (also called karakul and Persian lamb); blue fox (*vulpes lagopus*) and silver fox (*urocyon cinereoargenteus*). If you are after rabbit (coney), you might as well say goodbye to a good night out before you head to the shops. London furriers include Buchler Lisbeth, Paul & Deanfield and R Danzig & Sons.

Flowers

Our ancestors meant and read all sorts of coded meanings into the types of flowers given but no one much does this anymore. If you are seriously interested, you can seldom beat cut, fragrant, coloured roses and David Austin Roses are one of the best suppliers around. Orchids, gardenias, camellias and even little scented violets also meet with favour. Great London florists include Moyses Stevens and Harrods. For plants, there are, as already mentioned, Clifton Nurseries and Mc Bean's Orchids. Peter Beales Roses supply rose bushes of many varieties, both old and new. Groves Garden Centre has a fabulous selection of violet plants. Try to avoid giving her carnations, as they are hardly romantic flowers.

Hats, Shoes, Handbags and Gloves

Not many women wear titfers anymore ('titfer' is Cockney rhyming slang – 'tit-for-tat = hat') but there are noted designers and suppliers for those special occasions, such as David Shilling, Sylvia Fletcher at James Lock & Co, and there is also Herbert Johnson.

For shoes, Manolo Blahnik and Jimmy Choo seem to be favoured, and if you have her foot size you are, probably, 'in' already.

For handbags, Birkin (made by Hermès originally for actress Jane Birkin), Chanel and Louis Vuitton are some of the leaders in this field, but don't forget that there seem to be rituals of matching bags and shoes, so it is undoubtedly best to ask her exactly what she wants. Moreover, if you demonstrate this consideration, you are less likely to end up with *impromptu* presents of ties and socks that are going to frighten the horses.

Gloves, as hats, are not in general favour, except for the practical purpose of keeping warm and dry, but good new gloves may be found at Pickett and Chester Jefferies and vintage types can be found in antique shops and auctions.

Watches

The makers mentioned under the watches section of Chapter 3 also make ladies' watches and, of course, the sources for vintage pieces are the same.

A Penultimate Thought

If the lady in your life happens to smoke, what about a vintage Fabergé case, such as the splendid example in plate 32? If she does not smoke, there is always a vintage Fabergé vanity case, such as that in plate 33.

A Final Thought

If you are really stuck and need a 'holding' present, no woman has ever complained about receiving a Hermès scarf.

CHAPTER 10

Anglo-American Dictionary of Sartorial Terms

England and America are two countries separated by a common language.

George Bernard Shaw

British English	**American English**
bespoke	custom
bowler or coke hat	derby
braces	suspenders
buttonhole (flower)	boutonnière
cane (i.e. malacca, partridge, whangee)	walking stick
cloakroom	hat check
coat	jacket
co-respondent shoe	spectator shoe
cravat	ascot
crup	cordovan (horse leather)
derby shoes	blüchers
dinner jacket	tuxedo or dinner suit or Cowes coat
double-breasted lapels	peaked lapels
evening pumps	opera pumps
frock coat	Prince Albert frock
full brogues	wing tips
galoshes	rubbers
gumboots (wellington boots, wellies)	rubber boots
jumper	sweater
lounge suit	sack suit
lounge suit coat	jacket
mac	raincoat
marcella shirt-front	piqué shirt-front
morning coat	cutaway coat
over-boots	galoshes

overcoat	coat
oxford shoes/boots	balmorals (sometimes)
pants/boxer shorts	under-shorts
pick-and-pick weave	sharkskin
plus twos/fours	breeches, breeks knickerbockers (also, sometimes, used in British English)
reefer jacket	blazer or (sometimes) pea coat
short black morning coat	stroller
slip-on shoe	loafer
sock suspenders	garters
sports' coat	sport coat or odd jacket
step lapel	notched lapel
training shoes or trainers	sneakers
trews (Highland)	pants
trousers	pants
turn-ups (on trousers)	cuffs
under-vest	singlet
waistcoat	vest (in fact, an old English term, also used by London bespoke tailors)

CHAPTER 11

Thoughts of Home from Rio De Janeiro

I travelled among unknown men
In lands beyond the sea;
Nor, England! did I know till then
What love I bore to thee.

William Wordsworth

I began this book with reflections on True Britannia, but I have made a break for the border – indeed a border very far away. Do I miss England? Yes, of course I do, for exiles always mourn. I miss my home, but as I remember it from long ago. As Proust said: '*Les vrais paradis sont les paradis qu'on a perdus.*' Also, maybe I love the memory of many of its physical features so much that I can hardly bear to see what has become of some of them.

I miss the very obvious things, such as family and friends, red post boxes and the spring rain and flowers – snowdrops, daffodils, tulips, May blossom, and keep all the orchids of the east and south for violets. I miss cherry blossom and the gathering summer sun, and then the autumnal crispness; reddening leaves; blackberries and sloes suddenly in the hedges; the lengthening *and* the shortening of the days; distinct seasons; driving on the proper side of the road; the sight of classic cars; the joyful sound of hearty English laughter and the comforting, the familiar, such as the music introducing *Match of the Day* and Big Ben on the *News at Ten*, but I also miss more personal things too: walks by a certain tidal river (the curlews' plaintive calls), ending with fresh crab claws and hot, buttered crumpets and a pot of Darjeeling tea *à point*, in a pre-warmed pot, left to brew; the eye-watering smoke of bonfires of dead leaves and the crunch of ice on the ground at Christmas time; my heart skipping a beat halfway across the Albert Bridge that spans the Tamar; the rattle and creak of the heavy, slow – too slow – procession of train on tracks echoing my thoughts: 'Homeward bound, homeward bound'; my parents' calls of 'Good night and God bless you!'; lunch in a City pub (maybe The Punch in Fleet Street) or a club with a friend; a consoling dinner and diverting argument with another after some self-made upset; a solitary – sometimes winning – game of blackjack head-to-head at Crockford's, under the barrelled, Wedgwood ceiling (that and the Adam dining room there, a pair of nearly hidden glories of London); the sound of gulls crying, wings flashing, in the harbours at Fowey or Mevagissey or over the sands and crashing surf at Perranporth; the surprised squeal of the brakes on a great, big, red London 'bus on the sudden declivity at the traffic lights at Aldwych; particular peals of bells, from the world famous 'oranges-and-lemons' of St Clement Danes to the less famous, but more cheerful, St Clement's on the Tresillian river; the comforting tranquillity of musty, country churches, hallowed by 700 years of prayer, buoying up hopefulness, sometimes, against loss and near despair; rows of the headstones of people that I knew, together in death as they were in life; monuments to whole communities of concordant feelings, common experience, rivalries and loves and hates and striving; touchstones of unsung honour and the redemption of all shame.

I miss the magic of the London museums, the theatres and the cinemas; the majesty of the Royal Opera House; the grim defiance of the façade of Buckingham Palace; the opulence of St James's Square; the grunt and rumble of a London cab or the whine and swish and roar of an underground train; the late George Melly thundering out some jazz in a low-ceilinged, smoke-layered Ronnie Scott's. I miss the face of the man-in-the-moon.

I miss the spirit of commemoration; the statues and the plaques; the stoical faces in the rushing crowds; tall, kindly, old men, in battered, brown felt hats, which they doff with unselfconscious, pre-War form, sometimes to chaste spinsters in tweeds and woolly hats, their soft, speckled hands trembling (even in repose) as if to reach out for the children that they never had; well-wielded irony – as well as 'a piece of my mind'; the proper appreciation of the merits of warm smalls, half hose, gloves, mufflers and Shanks's mare; the sight of the Post Office Tower and Centre Point; the grime and filth of Tottenham Court Road; a solitary City walk and lunchtime communion in a City church; Hodge's statue in Gough Square, incorporating representations of shells of oysters that Dr Johnson walked and bought for his 'very fine cat' to soften his decline; Sofra restaurant's lentil soup on a cold day; illegally feeding the pelicans in the park; a leisurely, self-indulgent visit to the tailor's or the shirt-maker's; sound London shoes; Sheffield steel scissors – click, click, click – with all the economy of skill; the scent of after-haircut mist.

I miss blackbird song and the cooing of wood pigeons, the pheasant's startled shout and the cawing of rooks; the silhouette of twisted oaks against a setting sun; real Cornish pasties; the smell of apples on the ground and trapped sea air in mossy valleys. I miss splits and jam and clotted cream; prickly picnic rugs; the buzz of really persistent and intrepid flies around sticky, crusty cherry tart on the Ledrah at Trenarren, on the beach at Treyarnon Bay or at Caerhays on picnics long ago; the sizzle of fried hog's pudding; the scent of freshly baked saffron cake, yeast buns and a proper cup of tea; nutty, warm, amber, hoppy, frothy English beer – and decent gin and greasy fish and chips, heavy with salt and Sarson's malt vinegar; juicy bangers and mash and onion gravy and hot, hot, hot Colman's mustard and proper roast beef and Yorkshire pudding and horseradish sauce; Marmite soldiers; lamb cutlets and mint sauce and rice pudding and junket covered in grated nutmeg – and Kelly's Cornish ice cream; treacle pudding and custard. I miss slightly gritty, membrane-curling farmhouse Cheddar cheese; a glass of sherry; big, solid, dew-laden scented roses' nodding heads – Great Maiden's Blush and Josephine Bruce; 'mend-and-make-do' and 'keep-your-own counsel' – 'pride cometh before a fall' – 'there, but for the Grace of God, go I' and 'don't make a fuss'; a sun-burnt copy of *The Observer*'s unique mid-week edition, celebrating Churchill's life; my mother in gentle tears over that and her, always pacing up and down the house, last thing at night – locking-up, making sure; my father enjoining her to 'Come on, Joyce!'

I miss first films in the St Austell Odeon with its great big single silver screen, now all smashed down; a film later on in the Odeon Muswell Hill; a bulldog's friendly – but stubborn – face; the gentle endurance of spaniels; the sharp, sweet, stabbing fragrance of English garden jasmine.

I miss shyer girls with auburn hair and sea-green eyes, smelling of Chanel and the earth of which they are made, and clean hair and summertime, dreaming their dreams in their books, on the train or the 'bus. I miss the irreplaceable, individual scents of the houses of those I have loved and the smell of a room where I succeeded in something against the odds; even the unforgettable smells associated with apprehension, fear and sadness. I miss shops where I am instantly understood; jars of proper sweets – succulent liquorice and butterscotch gums and crunchy sherbet lemons (bless you, Maynards, for taking in Lion sweets, and Dad too for sending them to me!) and melting milk chocolate and fudge and big, hard, painful chunks of toffee and Veuve Clicquot without a mortgage form; Louis Patisserie sausage rolls and chilled, chocolate triangles at Swiss Cottage after a Sunday walk on Primrose Hill; blackish-crimson carnation, camellia and gardenia buttonholes; a really well-made Bloody Mary – a meal in itself; dripping umbrellas; the smell of bristly, tweed, country caps and big, warm, wet, rubbery, beige riding macs; the smack of a golf ball against the beating wind; the scent and smudge of English mud and rain and the dew of moorland mist; a high, hard right-and-left; the tremendous sight of a tiny middle-aged woman, mastering, as a matter of hard-earned course, a great, snorting Arabian stallion and, eventually, letting me ride her *second-*

favourite horse; my sister on ponies called 'Twinkle' and 'Stardust' and old 'Silver', who remembered circus tricks. I miss my sister's grave.

I miss the curling-up of fine pipe tobacco smoke and the twisting bluish fumes of well-kept Havana cigars; crystal brandy balloons and the trapped sunbeams in pre-1914 Armagnac; long-lived Port wine and the sulphurous glow of 'England's Glory' matches; the smells of lit cedar spills and apple-wood fires – with orange peel thrown on; horses and hounds across the coals; the smell of the damp and mustiness of attics, hiding pointless secrets of old clothes in long-forgotten, dirty trunks and broken picture frames; Floris scents; the first ripe peach; sun-warmed, garden raspberries; the comforting, comfortable, well-worn leather of a club chair, when no one knows where you are; the solid satisfaction of a seat in a train or a 'plane, when you are travelling alone to somewhere that you really want to be; the views of London from Muswell Hill, 'Ally Pally', Highgate (half close your eyes and think of a twisting road at home), Hampstead, Parliament Hill, Primrose Hill and Greenwich Park; springy, tended English lawns; bowling greens and men in summer whites and dogs on leads and cats that don't caterwaul all night; a noisy shambles of a summer carnival that takes a week to arrange, lasts a sensible three quarters of an hour and ends in the village pub: the dilettante attitude and the devil-may-care.

I nearly even miss the smoke of the Euston Road.

Finis

Bibliography

Amis, Kingsley, *The James Bond Dossier* (Jonathan Cape, 1965).
Arlott, John, *The Snuff Shop* (Michael Joseph, 1974).
Campbell, John, *F E Smith, 1st Earl of Birkenhead* (Jonathan Cape, 1983).
Carleton Hacker, Richard, *The Ultimate Pipe Book* (Autumngold, 1989, vol. 2).
Colson, Percy, *White's 1693–1950: The Story of White's Club* (William Heinemann, 1951).
Conan Doyle, Sir Arthur, *The Complete Sherlock Holmes* (Penguin, 1988).
Coombes, David, *A Careless Rage for Life: Dorothy L Sayers* (Lion, 1992).
Cooper, Artemis, *Diana Cooper's Scrap Book* (Hamish Hamilton, 1987).
Craddock, Harry, *The Savoy Cocktail Book* (Pavilion, 2007 [new edition of 1930 original]).
Culpepper, Richard, *The Complete Herbal and English Physician* (Richard Evans, 1816).
Cunnington, CW and P, *A Handbook of English Costume in the Nineteenth Century* (Faber & Faber, 1970).
Dahl, Roald, *My Uncle Oswald* (Michael Joseph, 1979, together with short stories in 1964 and 1974).
Dunhill, Alfred, *The Pipe Book* (Barker, 1969, vol. 2).
Embury, David A, *The Fine Art of Mixing Drinks* (Doubleday, 1948).
Encyclopaedia Britannica (1985, vol. 15).
Epstein, David S, *The Gem Merchant* (Gem Merchant Publications, 2003).
Evans, George, *The Old Snuff House of Fribourg & Treyer at the Sign of the Rasp & Crown 1720–1920* (Donald Macbeth, 1920).
Everett, Susanne, *London: The Glamour Years 1919–1939* (Popular Culture Ink, 1985).
Fielding, Daphne, *The Duchess of Jermyn Street* (Eyre & Spottiswoode, 1967).
Fleming, Ian, *Casino Royale* (Jonathan Cape, 1953).
——, *Moonraker* (Jonathan Cape, 1955).
——, *From Russia With Love* (Jonathan Cape, 1957).
——, *Dr No* (Jonathan Cape, 1958).
——, *For Your Eyes Only* (Jonathan Cape, 1960).
——, *Thunderball* (Jonathan Cape, 1961).
——, *On Her Majesty's Secret Service* (Jonathan Cape, 1963).
Foulkes, Nick and March, Charles, *Dunhill by Design* (Flammarion, 2006).
Galsworthy, John, *The Forsyte Saga: A Modern Comedy* (Heinemann/Octopus, 1976).
Gately, Ian, *Tobacco: A Cultural History of how an Exotic Plant Seduced Civilization* (Grove Press, 2003).
Griswold, John, *Ian Fleming's James Bond* (Author House, 2005).
Hemingway, Ernest, *Death in the Afternoon* (Jonathan Cape, 1932).

Hillyard, Paul, *The Book of the Spider: From Arachnophobia to the Love of Spiders* (Hutchinson, 1994).
Jackson, EB, *Sugar Confectionery Manufacture* (Springer, 1995, vol. 2).
Jesse, Captain William, *The Life of George Brummell, Esq.* (Saunders & Otley, 1844).
Lejeune, Anthony and Lewis, Malcolm, *The Gentleman's Clubs of London* (Macdonald & Jane's, 1979).
Lees, R, *Sugar Confectionery and Chocolate Manufacture* (Blackie Academic and Professional, 1996).
Lycett, Andrew, *Ian Fleming* (Weidenfield & Nicolson, 1995).
Marshall, Michael, *Top Hat and Tails: The Story of Jack Buchanan* (Elm Tree, 1978).
Mercer, Vaudrey, *The Frodshams: The Story of a Family of Clockmakers* (The Antiquarian Horological Society, 1981).
Mill, John Stuart, *On Liberty* (Cosimo Classics, 2005).
Moore, Sally Falk, *Lucan: Not Guilty* (Sidgwick & Jackson, 1987).
Morley, Sheridan, *Gladys Cooper: A Biography* (Heinemann, 1979).
Nee, Min Ron, *The Illustrated History of Post-Revolution Havana Cigars* (Hong Kong, 2003).
Ouseley, Sir William, *Travels in Various Countries of the East* (Rodwell & Martin, 1819).
Oxford Dictionary of National Biography (Oxford University Press, 2004).
Rowse, AL, *A Portrait of Q* (Methuen, 1988).
Royal Society of Chemistry, Charles Sell (ed), *The Chemistry of Fragrances* (RSC, 2006, vol. 2).
Russell, W, *Eccentric Personages* (Ward, Lock & Tyler [London], 1865).
Skinner, Cornelia Otis, *Elegant Wits and Grand Horizontals* (Michael Joseph, 1964).
Snowden, Christopher J, *Velvet Glove, Iron Fist: A History of Anti-Smoking* (Little Dice, June 2009).
Snowman, A Kenneth, *The Art of Carl Fabergé* (Faber & Faber, 1962).
Storey, Nicholas, *History of Men's Fashion* (Pen & Sword, 2008).
Thomas, Jerry, *The Bartender's Guide* (Dick & Fitzgerald, 1862, reprint 2008).
Thornton, JP, *The International System of Garment Cutting* (Minster & Co, circa 1911–1913 editions).
Tidswell, Herbert H, MD, *The History and Antiquity of the Tobacco Habit* (J & A Churchill, 1912).
Titman, GA, *Dress and Insignia Worn at His Majesty's Court, issued with the authority of the Lord Chamberlain* (Harrison & Sons, 1937).
Turin, Luca, *Perfumes: The A–Z Guide* (Profile, 2008).
——, *The Secret of Scent* (Faber & Faber, 2007).
Voges, Ernst, *Tobacco Encyclopaedia* (Tobacco Journal International, 1984).
Waddy, HT, *The Devonshire Club and Crockford's* (Eveleigh Nash, 1919).
Woodcock, Thomas and Robinson, John Martin, *The Oxford Guide to Heraldry* (Oxford, 1990).
Wright, David, *A Pipe Companion: A Connoisseur's Guide* (Running Press, 2000).

Newspapers and Periodicals

British Medical Journal, 15 January 1910.
The Economist, 20 December 2001 (special Christmas edition).
New York Times, 5 June 1900, 3 January 1909, 16 April 1950.
New Yorker, July 1964.
Tailor & Cutter, 1897–1898.
The Times, 30 December 2007.
Travel Magazine, December 1922.
Town Topics, October 1886.

Other Sources

Decision of the Lord Lyon King of Arms, on the Petition of Hamilton (decision received on 15 May 2006).
Fribourg & Treyer Accounts.
Guidance note of the Lord Lyon on Baronial Additaments and Territorial Designation.
Henry Poole's Records relating to the origin of the dinner jacket/tuxedo.
House of Commons Fact Sheet G7.
National Archives (various).
Note attached to a Warrant, dated 1 December 2009, granted by the Lord Lyon, in relation to the Barony of Cartsburn.
Policy statements of the Lord Lyon concerning Scottish Feudal Baronies.
Stevens, J Earle Jr, 'The Prince and Mrs Potter: Why the Dinner Jacket is called 'Tuxedo': Grenville Kane's Account as Told to J Earle Stevens Jr' (The Tuxedo Park Library, 1979).
Undated company pamphlet on the history of Joseph Rodgers & Sons Ltd.

Useful Internet Resources

www.askandyaboutclothes.com
www.asuitablewardrobe.dynend.com
www.cigars.co.uk
www.cutterandtailor.com
www.easyandelegantlife.com
www.filmnoirbuff.com
www.gentlemansgazette.com
www.styleforum.net
www.thelondonlounge.net
www.thenakedapegetsdressed.blogspot.com

Index